"A breezy glide through Philly history, Murphy's new book should give every lover of this historic place new insight into the characters, places, and events that shaped it through four centuries."

—**Sam Katz,** Executive Producer,
History Making Productions

"Even the most knowledgeable expert on Philadelphia history is likely to learn some new and interesting facts from *Real Philly History, Real Fast.* Jim Murphy has a way of bringing Philadelphia's obscure and offbeat history to light in a wonderfully readable fashion."

—**Paul Steinke,** Executive Director,
Preservation Alliance for Greater Philadelphia

"Jim Murphy has probably forgotten more Philly history than most historians know. *Real Philly History, Real Fast* makes readers want to discover the iconic places, and the men and women from all races and walks of life who made this city great. Each page of his excellent book contains a fact that will elicit anything from a smile to a 'wow!' Billy Penn would be proud!"

—**Tim McGrath,** author of *James Monroe: A Life*

Real Philly History,

REAL FAST

Real Philly History, REAL FAST

Fascinating Facts and

Interesting Oddities about the City's

Heroes and Historic Sites

 JIM MURPHY

TEMPLE UNIVERSITY PRESS
Philadelphia • Rome • Tokyo

TEMPLE UNIVERSITY PRESS
Philadelphia, Pennsylvania 19122
tupress.temple.edu

Library of Congress Cataloging-in-Publication Data

Names: Murphy, Jim (James F.), 1944– author.
Title: Real Philly history, real fast : fascinating facts and interesting
   oddities about the city's heroes and historic sites / Jim Murphy.
Description: Philadelphia : Temple University Press, 2021. | Includes
   updated articles originally published in the Society Hill Reporter and
   the Queen Village Neighbors Association Magazine. | Includes
   bibliographical references and index. | Summary: "An alternative,
   history-focused guidebook to a selection of Philadelphia's heroes and
   notable places"—Provided by publisher.
Identifiers: LCCN 2020043393 (print) | LCCN 2020043394 (ebook) |
   ISBN 9781439919248 (paperback) | ISBN 9781439919255 (pdf)
Subjects: LCSH: Historic sites—Pennsylvania—Philadelphia—Guidebooks.
   | Philadelphia (Pa.)—History—Anecdotes. | Philadelphia
   (Pa.)—Biography—Anecdotes. | LCGFT: Guidebooks.
Classification: LCC F158.36 .M87 2021 (print) | LCC F158.36 (ebook)
   | DDC 974.8/11—dc23
LC record available at https://lccn.loc.gov/2020043393
LC ebook record available at https://lccn.loc.gov/2020043394

Printed in the United States of America

9 8 7 6 5 4 3

To Penn & Ben:

William Penn and Ben Franklin—

Philadelphia's two superstars—for jump-starting

this marvelous city.

And to all those who have helped me learn

so much about it.

Contents

Part IV Heroes, Sung and Unsung

Part V Mob Rule

Part VI In the Neighborhoods

Part VII Hidden in Plain Sight

Part VIII Marvelous Museums

Part IX Historic Architecture

Part X Where History Comes Alive

Part XI Beyond Center City

Acknowledgments

With Thanks . . .

To all the people I interviewed for this book . . . and to anyone who helped me along the way. Key among them are Bernice Hamel, who first asked me to write for the *Society Hill Reporter*; *Reporter* editor Sandy Rothman, graphic designer Judy Lamirand, and Society Hill Civic Association communications expert Matt DeJulio; Amy Grant, creative guru and idea-generator-in-chief during *QVNA Magazine*'s five-year run; Philly author and historian Tim McGrath, for his help on several of my naval stories; and Ed Mauger, Bob Skiba, Nick Cvetkovic, and Harry Kyriakodis, plus other members of the Association of Philadelphia Tour Guides who taught me so much about Philadelphia. And to fellow guide and longtime friend Tom DiRenzo, a Temple grad who suggested I pitch this book idea to Temple University Press. To its great team members, Aaron Javsicas, Ashley Petrucci, Ryan Mulligan, Kate Nichols, Ann-Marie Anderson, Gary Kramer, and Heather Wilcox, for all their help in making this book a reality. To Wikipedia and Wikimedia, for making it easy to start researching things I knew nothing about and to quickly locate nomination forms for the *National Register of Historic Places*, a huge time-saver. And to my best friend and wife, Rosemary, for her patience and support (and marvelous Italian cooking) during this ten-year writing project. I appreciate everyone's help.

How to Use This Book

Dear Reader,

This book is just what it says: *Real Philly History, Real Fast*.

It's a quick and easy way to learn about Philadelphia's heroes and historic sites. At your own pace, wherever you like. On the subway. While waiting for someone. Even in the bathroom.

It's Unlike Any Book I Have Ever Seen about Philadelphia.

Fast facts and bullet copy tell you quickly about each notable subject. And you'll find interesting oddities in every one of the fifty or so stories here. I wish I had owned this book when I was growing up . . . and when I started studying to become a certified tour guide.

Of course, *Real Philly History* is not a complete guide to every site in Philadelphia. That would require a far longer book and still be impossible to write. And this book is geared mostly to Center City. Read through it and I believe you'll have a much greater appreciation for the marvelous and often-overlooked history and heroes we have in Philadelphia. And you'll learn things most longtime residents still don't know.

A Bonanza of Philly Secrets Lies Within.

Turn the pages and you'll find the answers to numerous questions. What is the Philadelphia Eagles' connection to the U.S. Custom House? Which famous artist may have been Philadelphia's first nude model? Where is the country's first quarantine station still located? Who was the Philadelphia Revolutionary War naval captain who terrorized the English in their backyard? Which city clock face is larger than Big Ben in London? Where was the Liberty Bell secretly damaged? (It wasn't here in Philly.) And which Philadelphian has more than forty communities named after him?

You'll Find Hidden Gems Like These on Every Page.

I hope these stories whet your appetite to learn more about Philadelphia's fabulous and often unknown history. This book is like a Philadelphia survey course—quick, fun, and entertaining. And you'll see "Nearby Attractions" at the end of every story that offer you more places to visit.

What Got Me Started on This Book?

At the request of Bernice Hamel, founder and then–managing editor of the *Society Hill Reporter*, I began writing these articles about Philadelphia in 2011. Six years later, I moved over to the *Queen Village Neighbors Association Magazine*. To me, each topic was a detective story I had to investigate to get the facts. I'd see a historical marker or site I knew nothing about and start digging. My thinking was that if it interested me, it would interest my readers. And that approach seems to have worked. I hope you agree.

Here's a Bonus, to Help Make Exploring Philly Easier.

When I was a teenager, I learned an easy way to remember streets south of Market Street from my mother. This memory aid continues to help me find my way around the city today. So I'm including it here. I've never seen it in print before.

How to Remember Philly Streets
(Going South from Market)

I went to the **Market** *to buy some* **Chestnuts**. *Changed my mind and bought some* **Walnuts**.
Chased by a **Locust**, *I ran from* **Spruce** *to* **Pine** *into a lumber* (**Lombard**) *yard.*

South *of it, I saw a girl standing on a bridge* (**Bainbridge**)
   over the water (**Fitzwater**).
Her name was **Catharine**, *she was a* **Christian**, *and her father*
   was a **Carpenter** *in the* **Washington** *and* **Federal** *army.*

So, now you have a simple way of knowing the names of Philly's major streets going south from Market Street for about fourteen blocks.

I hope you find it helpful.

More Great Ways to Learn about Philly

Want to know more about Philadelphia history? Try three superb online sources: *The Encyclopedia of Greater Philadelphia*; *Hidden City Philadelphia*; and *History Making Productions*, where films by Sam Katz's marvelous company are free. And to find out what's happening in Philly now—and every weekend—go to *VisitPhilly.com*.

My Recommendations

Go out and about, use this book, and visit the great sites included. Have fun and enjoy yourself. See the city that William Penn built in a formidable forest and that Ben Franklin improved in so many ways.

Then, let me know what you think of my book. Just e-mail me at murfman1@comcast.net or visit my website at realphillyhistory .com. I hope to put some unusual and interesting tours up there. And, of course, I'll add new tidbits and facts about Philadelphia. My goal: To have you say, "I never knew Philadelphia was so interesting."

If you really like the book, please recommend it to your friends, neighbors, and colleagues. Give copies away. And buy them for every occasion: Christmas, Easter, graduations, and more.

Thank you.

I hope to see you sometime on the wonderful streets of Philadelphia.

Jim Murphy

Philly history researcher. Story-teller. Certified member of the Association of Philadelphia Tour Guides.

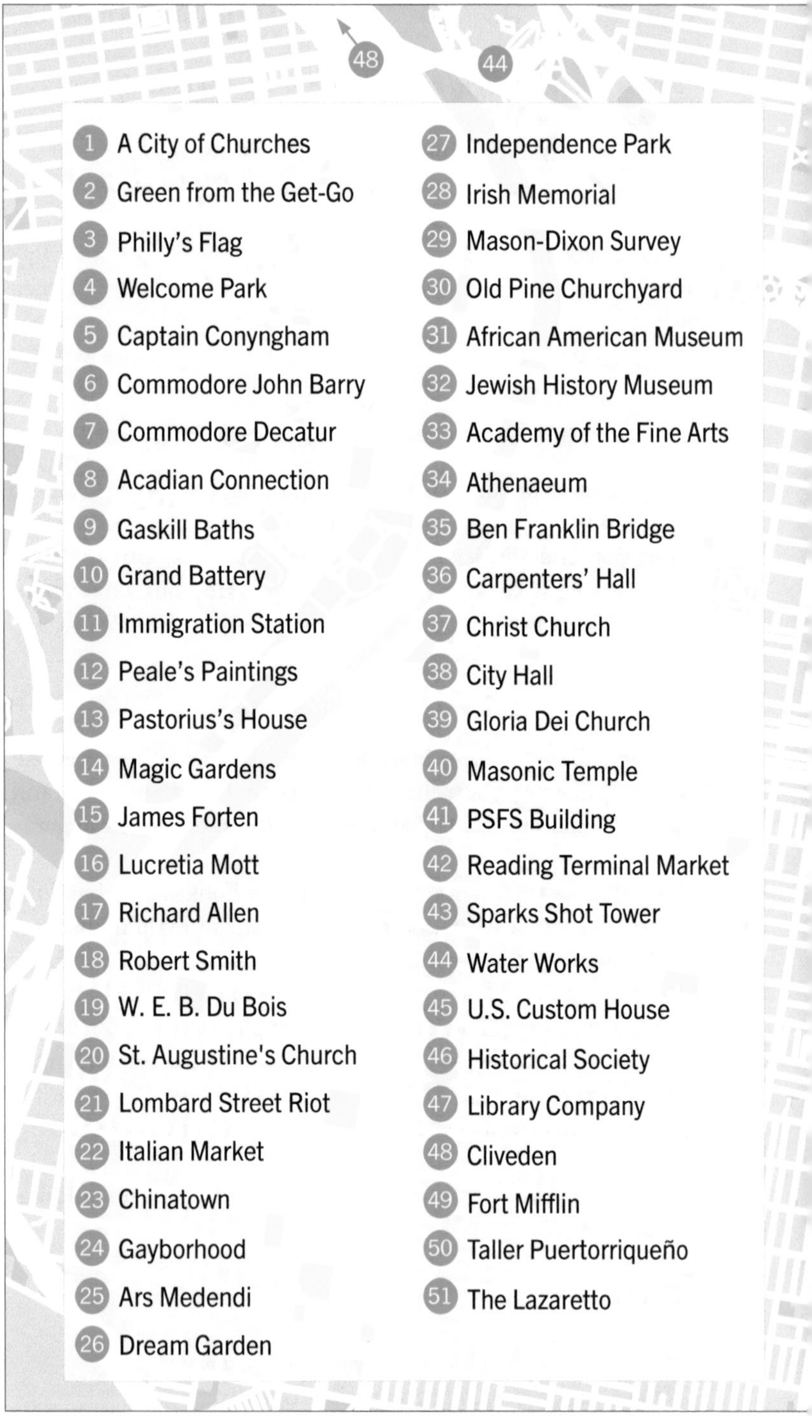
㊽
㊹
① A City of Churches
② Green from the Get-Go
③ Philly's Flag
④ Welcome Park
⑤ Captain Conyngham
⑥ Commodore John Barry
⑦ Commodore Decatur
⑧ Acadian Connection
⑨ Gaskill Baths
⑩ Grand Battery
⑪ Immigration Station
⑫ Peale's Paintings
⑬ Pastorius's House
⑭ Magic Gardens
⑮ James Forten
⑯ Lucretia Mott
⑰ Richard Allen
⑱ Robert Smith
⑲ W. E. B. Du Bois
⑳ St. Augustine's Church
㉑ Lombard Street Riot
㉒ Italian Market
㉓ Chinatown
㉔ Gayborhood
㉕ Ars Medendi
㉖ Dream Garden
㉗ Independence Park
㉘ Irish Memorial
㉙ Mason-Dixon Survey
㉚ Old Pine Churchyard
㉛ African American Museum
㉜ Jewish History Museum
㉝ Academy of the Fine Arts
㉞ Athenaeum
㉟ Ben Franklin Bridge
㊱ Carpenters' Hall
㊲ Christ Church
㊳ City Hall
㊴ Gloria Dei Church
㊵ Masonic Temple
㊶ PSFS Building
㊷ Reading Terminal Market
㊸ Sparks Shot Tower
㊹ Water Works
㊺ U.S. Custom House
㊻ Historical Society
㊼ Library Company
㊽ Cliveden
㊾ Fort Mifflin
㊿ Taller Puertorriqueño
(51) The Lazaretto

Map numbers correspond to chapters. (Map courtesy of Lucid Digital Designs.)

Real Philly History,
REAL FAST

~ Part I ~

William Penn's Huge Impact on Philadelphia

---

1 A City of Churches

Philadelphia attracted people from many different religions.
While escorting fifteen Chinese high-school students on a tour from South Street to Welcome Park in June 2015, I suddenly heard them excitedly talking to their translator. Their question: "Why does Philadelphia have so many churches?"

My answer to them: Because of William Penn and his "Holy Experiment." Both dramatically impacted our city.

You can easily see that for yourself. Just walk a few blocks . . . and look with fresh eyes at the numerous historic churches or synagogues all around you. They are Philadelphia's unique treasures.

And unlike other cities and colonies that had just one official church, our structures have long represented many different religious denominations. Among them: Jewish, Catholic, Quaker, Episcopal, African Methodist Episcopal, German Reformed, Muslim, and Presbyterian.

Near a number of these marvelous churches, you'll see distinctive signs headlined in red that say: "Old Philadelphia Congregations."

One side of each large marker proudly proclaims: "Philadelphia is a city that not only tolerated but welcomed diverse modes of religious practice from the beginning." The other side tells the story of the individual institution.

Among the churches are:

- St. Augustine's Church (Catholic)
- Old First Reformed (United Church of Christ)
- Old St. George's (United Methodist)
- Congregation Mikveh Israel (Jewish)
- Seamen's Church Institute (Ecumenical)
- Christ Church (Episcopal)
- Arch Street Meetinghouse (Quaker)
- Old St. Joseph's (Catholic)
- Old St. Mary's (Catholic)
- Holy Trinity (Catholic)
- Society Hill Synagogue (Jewish)

- Mother Bethel (African Methodist Episcopal)
- Old Pine Street (Presbyterian)
- St. Peter's Church (Episcopal)
- Old Swedes' Church—or Gloria Dei (Episcopal)

(A website called *Beyond the Liberty Bell* lists fourteen historic houses of worship in our area. For addresses, visiting hours, and more, see beyondthelibertybell.org/churches.html.)

The man responsible for promoting this diversity was William Penn, founder of Pennsylvania and our city. Imprisoned numerous times in England for his Quaker religious beliefs, he was given more than forty-five thousand square miles of land by King Charles II to settle a debt owed to his father.

Penn used that grant for his Holy Experiment in the New World. Not only did he espouse religious tolerance and freedom of religion for all; he treated the Lenape natives with respect and paid them and the Europeans who were here for their land.

Full disclosure: Penn was not entirely above the evils of his time, and new reports in 2020 say he kept up to twelve slaves at Pennsbury Manor, his country estate in Bucks County. What's more, no Jews or women were permitted to vote or hold office in Pennsylvania.

But the freedoms he offered were unprecedented.

And people who had been persecuted for their beliefs, especially in Europe, flocked to Pennsylvania.

From its founding in 1682, Philadelphia quickly became America's largest and most important city. Despite starting fifty-two and fifty-eight years after Boston and New York respectively, Philadelphia zoomed past both in population and importance by the Revolutionary War.

People of various religions, races, skills, and classes lived and worked here together, as demonstrated by records of Elfreth's Alley—often referred to as "our nation's oldest residential street." Ed Mauger, a founding member of the Association of Philadelphia Tour Guides and former associate dean at Rutgers–Camden, who is now deceased, called Elfreth's Alley "America's first melting pot."

A Scottish physician visiting a Philadelphia dining establishment on June 8, 1744, described his fellow customers this way: "I dined at a tavern with a very mixed company of different nations and religions. There were Scots, English, Dutch, Germans, and

Many historic Philadelphia churches and synagogues still work together to broaden interfaith understanding. You'll see these *Old Philadelphia Congregations* signs throughout the Center City area. (Map design courtesy of Joel Katz Design Associates. Photo by Jim Murphy.)

Irish; there were Roman Catholicks [*sic*], Churchmen, Presbyterians, Quakers, Newlightmen, Methodists, Seventhdaymen, Moravians, Anabaptists, and one Jew."

That was the ecumenical society that William Penn—whom Thomas Jefferson called "the greatest law-giver the world has produced"—left as a legacy.

William Penn gave us the precious gifts of religious freedom and tolerance. Now we just have to preserve and protect them in today's modern world.

Fast Facts

Name: Philadelphia, aka the City of Brotherly Love

Number of Churches in Philadelphia by the 1790s: More than thirty-three

Distinctive New Muslim Building in Philly: Bait-ul-Aafiyat Mosque, built by the Ahmadiyya Muslim Community near Broad Street and Glenwood Avenue and topped by a white minaret

Biggest Attractions of Penn's "Holy Experiment": People of all faiths were welcome to practice their religions here, and, unlike many colonies, Pennsylvania had no religious tax.

Fast Growth: By 1770, Philadelphia was both the largest city in the colonies and the largest one George Washington ever saw.

Related Attractions: Elfreth's Alley, City Tavern, and Chief Tamanend Statue

This updated story first ran in the January 2017 issue of *QVNA Magazine* and is reprinted with permission.

Green from the Get-Go

Penn's plan for his city included five public squares.

From the very start, William Penn wanted his city of Philadelphia to be a "greene Country Towne, which will never be burnt and always be wholesome."

With good reason. In 1665, Penn saw bubonic plague kill some one hundred thousand people—about a quarter of London's population. A year later, a devastating fire destroyed up to four-fifths of the walled city of London.

So, when Penn decided to build his City of Brotherly Love, he wanted wide streets and large one-half-acre and one-acre lots—with room on the sides for gardens, orchards, or fields.

Penn's famous 1682 City Plan of Philadelphia also included something unprecedented: a gridiron street pattern featuring four eight-acre public squares for the enjoyment of the community and one ten-acre center square. Today, those are Washington Square, Franklin Square, Rittenhouse Square, Logan Square, and Penn Square.

Penn's design was also the first city plan in the United States to provide for long-term urban growth.

So important was Penn's thinking that the American Society of Civil Engineers added Penn's plan to its List of Historic Civil Engineering Landmarks in 1994. Penn's plan joined such other American icons as the Golden Gate Bridge, Hoover Dam, and Panama Canal on the prestigious list.

Penn was also praised for designing street widths appropriate to their usage. High (now Market) Street and Broad Street were one hundred feet wide, much broader than any street in London at the time. Streets fronting the river were sixty feet wide, with the rest fifty feet wide.

Interesting Oddities

- With the grant of forty-five thousand square miles that Penn received from King Charles II of England, he hoped to develop a city that was ten thousand acres in size. When he couldn't purchase the land he originally wanted at Upland (now Chester), he moved his sights farther north. Eventually, Penn purchased a little more than 1,200 acres, much of it "an undeveloped riverfront tract from three Swedes of Wicaco, the Svensson or Swanson brothers," says *Philadelphia: A 300-Year History*. (While he was not obligated to buy land already occupied, Penn did. He tried to set a Christian example and maintain good relations with those who came before him, including the Native Americans.)
- First named after nearby prominent landowners by surveyor Thomas Holme, the city's east-west streets were renamed in 1684 after trees that Penn said "spontaneously grow in the country." Today's differences: Sassafras became Race Street, Mulberry became Arch, and Cedar was renamed South Street.
- Penn heavily promoted his new land through a series of pamphlets designed to attract landowners. As benefits, he noted that Philadelphia "lies 600 miles nearer the Sun than England" and "[is] about the Latitude of Naples in Italy."
- While Penn never developed the squares on his city plan, he placed them in the four quadrants of the city and in the center. Each one took on a unique identity, and these popular neighborhood squares now provide refreshing green space in the heart of the city.

Trees still are an important part of William Penn's "greene Country Towne." This pretty view is from Panama Street near Thirteenth Street. (Photo by Jim Murphy.)

• By 1831, Washington Square served as an arboretum to help educate the public about horticulture. It contained more than fifty varieties of trees, including seven that were European. Two of the North American varieties were introduced by explorers Meriwether Lewis and William Clark from the Rocky Mountains.

While Penn wanted people to spread out across his city, Philly residents stayed close to the Delaware River. They also developed their own system of alleys or cartways. By 1698, nine lanes ran from Front to Second Street, thwarting Penn's plan and violating his dream of a green country town.

However, Pennsylvania, which means "Penn's Woods," is aptly named. Rebounding from the early 1900s, when forest cover amounted to only 30 percent of the state's land area, that figure in early 2016 was 59 percent.

Fast Facts

Debt King Charles II Owed Sir William Penn: £16,000
Size of William Penn's Grant from King Charles: Forty-five thousand square miles
Pennsylvania Was Named For: Penn's father, Sir William Penn, at the king's direction
Size of Penn's City of Brotherly Love: Two square miles
Amount William Penn Paid the Lenni Lenape Tribe for Their Land: £1,200
Years William Penn Lived in Philadelphia: Fewer than four years
Name of the Ship That First Brought William Penn to Philadelphia: The *Welcome*
Related Attractions: Christ Church, U.S. Custom House, and Independence Seaport Museum

This updated story first ran in the May 2016 issue of *QVNA Magazine* and is reprinted with permission.

③ Philly's Flag

Are the city's colors modeled after Sweden's?

Looking back, I made a mistake.

I volunteered to write a story about Philadelphia's city flag and its connection to early Swedish settlers.

Why not? It sounded easy, if not all that interesting. I was wrong on both counts.

I spent days doing research online, visited the Swedish American Historical Museum on Pattison Avenue, went to City Hall, and even spoke with the exuberant Brenda Exon, also known as "the Philly Pride Lady" or "the Philly Flag Lady."

The City of Philadelphia's flag. (Artwork: David B. Martucci. Credit: North American Vexillological Association.)

Now, I'm much better informed about the people who settled New Sweden, fights between the Dutch and Swedes, and why Sweden was so important to Philadelphia and our founder William Penn.

And yes, our city flag, which most of us know very little about, is believed by some (but not yet proven) to commemorate Sweden's colonization of Philadelphia.

Our Flag's Details

Colors: Azure (sky blue) and golden yellow

Seal: Two female allegorical figures flank the shield. The left figure symbolizes peace, with an olive wreath on her head, plus hope, with the anchor in her hand. The right figure symbolizes plenty or prosperity.

Above the Seal: Scales of justice

Inside the Seal: A plough (or plow) represents agriculture, and a sailing ship symbolizes the city's port and maritime commercial trade.

Below the Seal: *Philadelphia Maneto*, which translates to "Let Brotherly Love Continue"

The Swedes played a big role in the development of William Penn's Philadelphia. When he was unable to buy the land he wanted where Chester is today, Penn built a 1,280-acre city between two rivers. He bought much of that land from the Swedish Swanson brothers of Wicaco.

For many years in the 1600s, the Swedes and the Dutch jockeyed for position along the Delaware River—without breaking into too many outright hostilities. But like two young boys who enjoyed sparring, they were always aware the big bully—England—could come along at any time and eat their lunch. Eventually, England did.

New Sweden Attracted These Unusual Personalities

John (Johan) Printz, the new Swedish governor in 1643, was described as weighing four hundred pounds and drinking three horns at every meal, furious and passionate, "difficult of access, and sending home messengers, who brought him intelligence, 'bloody and bruised.'"

Peter Stuyvesant, the director of New Amsterdam, "stumped about on a silver leg," boldly destroyed a Swedish fort, blockaded the river, and forced the Swedes to withdraw.

John Claude Rysingh, told to use only the mildest measures against the Dutch, disregarded those instructions and took possession of the Dutch's Fort Casimir, near today's New Castle, Delaware. Outraged, Stuyvesant retaliated with seven armed ships and seven hundred men, forced the Swedish commander to surrender, and then besieged Fort Christina near Wilmington.

"Thus fell New Sweden," says a 1908 paper titled "Dutch and Swedish Settlements on the Delaware."

Interesting Oddities

* A magazine article titled "Two Swedish Pastors Describe Philadelphia 1700 and 1702" says, "Here there are fanatics almost without number. Because there is freedom of conscience, here they have gathered together, of every opinion and belief."
* The Swedes' most important legacy may be the log cabin. No, it's not American. When the Swedes came to New Sweden, Finland was part of the kingdom of Sweden. And Finnish Swedes here built log cabins, similar to those they lived in at home. Practically all the buildings in New Sweden were made of logs. Local

residents who moved west took the log cabin idea with them. The rest is history.

- Philly sports teams have worn Swedish colors—or "Philly Colors"—several times. The Eagles wore blue and yellow in 1933, their first NFL season, and again in 2007 at a home game against the Detroit Lions to celebrate the club's seventy-fifth anniversary. The 1938 Phillies took the field in Swedish blue and yellow versions of their uniforms in honor of New Sweden's three-hundredth anniversary.

Now, back to the key question: Does the city flag carry the colors of the Swedish flag? Brenda Exon, an energetic proponent of Philadelphia's flag, thinks it does and is trying to prove it. So far, though, she hasn't found a definitive connection. However, when she heard that some people wanted to redo and redesign the flag, she was aghast. "This is an historic flag—the FIRST city flag in the nation."

Brenda, who helped start a nonprofit corporation called Partners for Civic Pride, enthusiastically promotes the flag wherever and whenever she can. The flag talks about peace, hope, justice, and prosperity, she says. "It's like a road map, showing how to make Philly the best it can be, and it is a flag of unity for everyone in Philadelphia. When people learn that, they embrace it totally."

Fast Facts

Name of Colony: New Sweden
Dates Existed: 1638–55
First Ships to Arrive: *Fogel Grip* and *Kalmar Nyckel*
Leading the Expedition: Peter Minuit, former governor of New Amsterdam
Claim to Fame: Finnish Swedes built America's first log cabins in the Philadelphia area. The structures eventually spread across the country.
Related Attractions: American Swedish Historical Museum, Gloria Dei Church, and Fort Mifflin

This updated story first ran in the March 2018 issue of *QVNA Magazine* and is reprinted with permission.

Welcome Park

**It's one of the only places in Philly's historic area to honor
city founder William Penn.**
Considering all that William Penn did for Philadelphia and our
nation—while living here fewer than four years—he is seriously
unappreciated by the very city he founded.

In part, that's because the remarkable Benjamin Franklin over-
shadows just about everybody else in local history.

But when we start looking closely at what Penn really accomplished, we should be celebrating his birthday every October 14 at
Welcome Park, just across from the City Tavern at Second Street
above Walnut.

And we should be honoring him during Welcome America
festivities each summer. Why? Because Penn promoted tolerance
and religious freedom in Pennsylvania, while other colonies put
people to death for their beliefs.
He set up a framework of government that allowed for trial
by jury and other rights, plus
peaceful change by amending
the legislative process. And, in
the words of Thomas Jefferson,
"he was the greatest law-giver
the world has produced."

What's more, he attempted to
treat Native Americans he met
fairly and paid them for their
land. He helped plan Philadelphia, one of America's most important cities. And he even established a Friends Public School in
1689 for all Philadelphia chil-

This statue of William Penn is a
mini-version of the thirty-seven-foot
figure on top of City Hall. (Photo by
Jim Murphy.)

dren. (Penn was a part of the Religious Society of Friends. Some derisively called the group "Quakers," because their members reportedly quaked or trembled when the spirit of God visited them.)

A product of his time, Penn was far from a perfect human being. He kept up to twelve slaves at Pennsbury Manor, his country estate. And only males who believed in "Jesus Christ, the Saviour of the World" were permitted to vote and hold public office in Pennsylvania. That ruled out Jews and Muslims.

Yet people of all religions were free to worship and practice their faith here. And members of many different sects, who had previously been persecuted for their beliefs, flocked to Pennsylvania.

Interesting Oddities

- Pennsylvania was named not for William Penn but for his father—Sir William Penn, an admiral—by King Charles II.
- Penn's first choice for his city was the present city of Chester (then called Upland). When that land was too expensive to buy, he set his sights on a rectangular space of about 1,280 acres between the Schuylkill and Delaware Rivers that became Philadelphia.
- To promote Philadelphia, Penn said it offered "Seven Ordinaries [or taverns] for the Intertainment of Strangers" and "a good Meal to be had for sixpence." Plus, the town had quickly grown by some 357 homes, "large, well built, with good Cellars, three stories, and some with Belconies."
- While Quaker Oats still denies that William Penn is the person pictured on its cereal, an ad from *Fra Magazine* in 1909 disproves this claim. The ad says, "Here you see the picture of William Penn, standard bearer of the Quakers, and of QUAKER OATS," and it includes two illustrations of him.
- Lord Baltimore claimed that Philadelphia was actually located in Maryland. So, Penn hurriedly returned to England in 1684 to try to resolve the boundary dispute in front of the king. The matter was not completely settled until 1760, when the Pennsylvania–Maryland border was defined as "the line of latitude fifteen miles south of the southernmost house in Philadelphia."

Despite Penn's many accomplishments, he is rarely remembered in his own city. Even though his thirty-seven-foot statue sits atop City Hall, many Philadelphians, tourists, and national sports broadcasters think it's Ben Franklin. Moreover, many Philadelphia visitors' guides I've seen don't mention Welcome Park, the site devoted to Penn's life and contributions, at all. Some don't even note it on maps.

And during about twenty minutes of looking, I couldn't find any books, T-shirts, photos, or other items about William Penn at one of our city's major tourist bookstores. However, in 2021, that's finally changed. Now a biography of William Penn stands there prominently among our American heroes.

It's about time.

Fast Facts

Place: Welcome Park

Named For: William Penn's ship, the *Welcome*

Location: Second Street at Sansom Street Alley

Open: Twenty-four hours a day

Built By: Friends of Independence National Historical Park in 1982

Occasion: Three-hundredth anniversary of the founding of Pennsylvania

Designers: Venturi, Scott Brown and Associates

What to Look For: A marble map of the original city; a replica of the William Penn statue atop City Hall; a replica of the Slate Roof House, where Penn lived (and wrote his Charter of Privileges) and where his wife Hannah delivered John, Penn's only child born in the New World; and a timeline of his many accomplishments and roles

Nearby Attractions: City Tavern, Merchants' Exchange, and Christ Church

This updated story first ran in the May/June 2013 issue of the *Society Hill Reporter* and is reprinted with permission.

Part II

Military Leaders

5 Captain Gustavus Conyngham

This daring Errol Flynn–type character (as author Tim McGrath calls him) captured more vessels than Commodore John Barry and Captain John Paul Jones combined.

As a youth, when my family drove to upstate Pennsylvania on summer vacations, I remember noticing the name "Conyngham" on road signs along Route 80 near Luzerne County.

I always wondered about the origin of this strange name. Little did I know it belonged to one of the most important—and now least-known—heroes of the Revolutionary War.

Gustavus Conyngham (or Cunningham, as some spell it) started the war as a privateer, bringing back needed supplies to the colonies. On March 1, 1777, he received a commission as captain in the Continental navy from Benjamin Franklin in Paris. It was signed by John Hancock.

In short order, as commander of the *Surprise*, Conyngham captured two British ships, was reluctantly arrested by French officials at Dunkirk after England demanded that he be held as a pirate, and had his commission papers taken by the French.

Freed with the help of Franklin, Conyngham took command of a new ship—the aptly named cutter *Revenge*—after it left port and then took the fight right to England's front door, the English Channel.

That's when the terrorized British named him "the Dunkirk Pirate."

Some Amazing Feats

- In all, Conyngham and his crew captured or sank sixty vessels, says Tim McGrath, author of *Give Me a Fast Ship*. In one very lucrative day in the West Indies, he seized four ships.
- In part because of Conyngham, Britain's shipping insurance rates jumped an average of 28 percent during its war with the colonies and spiked as much as 40 percent. This was higher than rate hikes experienced during the global Seven Years' War.

Captain Gustavus Conyngham, Continental Navy. Eighteenth-century print, after a miniature portrait by Louis Marie Sicardi, reproduced in *Letters and Papers relating to the Cruises of Gustavus Conyngham*, edited by Robert Wilden Neeser, 1915, and credited to the collections of James Barnes. (U.S. Naval History and Heritage Command Photograph.)

- Twice imprisoned, Conyngham frequently attempted escape. What's more, he and his crew twice fought off British marines who were taking his captured ship back to port. He also tunneled out of prison one time, escaping a second time by bribing a guard.
- King George III considered Conyngham the most terrifying Continental navy captain of them all. He reportedly told his minister that it would give him pleasure to be at the hanging of Conyngham, if he could only catch him.
- To stop Conyngham, British admiralty ordered at least five warships to cruise the English Channel. Yet many English ship owners, afraid to put to sea, placed their wares in French and Dutch vessels instead.
- When the English caught and threatened to hang Conyngham, General Washington's reply was succinct: If they did, he would hang six British officers then in his custody. Before any hangings took place, the resourceful Conyngham escaped and went back to harassing British shipping.

Did a grateful nation thank Captain Conyngham when he returned to Philadelphia and asked the Continental Congress to pay him for his time served and property seized? Not at all.

Because Conyngham could not produce proof of his commission from Franklin—which the French took in 1777—he was shabbily treated by Congress and never paid for his services. The U.S. Navy knew better, though, eventually naming three different destroyers after him.

The Rest of the Story

On November 8, 1902, the *New York Times* reported on "the accidental discovery of a time-worn document in a small printseller's shop in Paris." The winning $2 bidder on a John Hancock signature discovered that he had actually bought the missing commission papers issued by Ben Franklin to Gustavus Conyngham. The discovery proved Conyngham's claim, just 125 years too late.

What can you do? Visit Gustavus Conyngham's grave at St. Peter's Churchyard, 313 Pine Street, Philadelphia, and thank him for helping us win the Revolutionary War. **He's an extraordinary real-life action hero who deserves our recognition for his courage, boldness, and fighting skill.** Pay tribute to Philadelphia's own "Dunkirk Pirate." It's the least we can do.

Fast Facts

Name: Gustavus Conyngham
Born: About 1744 in County Donegal, Ireland
Died: November 27, 1819, in Philadelphia
Rank: Captain, U.S. Navy
Date Commissioned: March 1, 1777
Date Missing Commission Was Found: About 1902
Ships Captured: Sixty
Nickname: "The Dunkirk Pirate"
Town Named in Honor: The borough of Conyngham, Pennsylvania
Nearby Attractions: Old Pine Street Church, Mother Bethel Church, and Washington Square

This updated story first ran in the March/April 2015 issue of the *Society Hill Reporter* and is reprinted with permission.

6 Commodore John Barry

**This American hero is often photographed . . .
and often overlooked.**

One of my warm-weather delights is to pick up a bagel and coffee at about 8 A.M., sit on a bench at the south side of Independence Hall, and read the morning papers. As a side benefit, I hope to absorb a bit of the genius and creativity our Founding Fathers displayed here during our country's earliest and darkest days.

While sipping my coffee one fall day, I suddenly noticed a large bronze statue of a military man with just the word BARRY on the front of it. I don't know how I had missed this impressive statue before. I also wondered why a military man was honored here in a place known for political decisions. What was his contribution?

Little did I know that Commodore John Barry played an extraordinary role in our country's history. Without his heroism and leadership, we might well be swearing allegiance today to the queen of England.

Yet, as local author Tim McGrath says in his interesting 2010 book, *John Barry: An American Hero in the Age of Sail*, Barry is less well known today than some of his contemporaries, such as John Paul Jones, possibly because he was not a braggart. His nickname among naval historians? "Silent John."

Some of John Barry's Remarkable Accomplishments

- He won the first and last successful battles the Continental navy fought with the British (plus many in between).
- He served on land with his sailors at the Battle of Princeton in January 1777, when Philadelphia was threatened by the British and his next ship was still under construction.
- He captured two British transports and the schooner *Alert* in the Delaware River in March 1778, with just a small band of men and several barges. The move infuriated the British, who had recently taken Philadelphia.
- He helped physically drag and carry two unwilling members of the Pennsylvania State Assembly from their lodgings to the

Commodore Barry's statue points at the Delaware River, where he won many key victories against the British. (Photo by Jim Murphy.)

nearby state house to ensure a quorum was present so that Pennsylvania could set a date to ratify the U.S. Constitution. Physically imposing at 6 feet, 4 inches tall, Barry was well suited for this unique mission.

- He traveled 237 miles in a twenty-four-hour period while piloting the *Black Prince*, the fastest-known day of sailing in the eighteenth century.
- He was the first flag officer of the United States and is often considered the father of the U.S. Navy.

His statue, which dominates the center of Independence Square, portrays Barry in uniform, defiant and aggressive.

In one arm, he carries a naval spyglass, a sheathed sword by his side. With his right hand, he points strongly, possibly directing his men to fire another broadside . . . or gesturing south toward the Delaware River and Bay, where so many of his important victories took place (and where a bridge in his honor was opened in 1974; the Commodore Barry Bridge spans the Delaware River from Chester, Pennsylvania, to Bridgeport, New Jersey). He also seems to be saying, "I'm over there," pointing to his grave behind St. Mary's Church at 252 South Fourth Street.

How Did Others View Barry?

James Fenimore Cooper, a popular American nineteenth-century writer and a navy veteran himself, wrote, "Perhaps of all the [Revolutionary-period] naval Captains . . . he was the one who possessed the greatest reputation for experience, conduct, and skill."

President John F. Kennedy was so awed by his skills that he kept Barry's sword in his office as a source of inspiration. And Gilbert Stuart's portrait of Barry hung in President George H. W. Bush's White House.

My advice is to walk over to Independence Square, look at the statue of John Barry, and think about the things this man did to help ensure our nation's success. He is a genuine American hero.

While today's visitors to Independence Square may not know exactly who Commodore Barry was, the innate power of his statue still attracts hordes of photographers every day.

One friend, who lives nearby, says he can't recall ever walking through Independence Square without seeing someone taking photos of the Barry statue. "It's amazing," he says.

While Barry's statue may not be as popular as the *Rocky* statue near the Art Museum, almost 240 years after he helped defeat the British, he's still noticed.

Perhaps that's another major victory for him after all.

Fast Facts

Location: Independence Square, Fifth and Walnut Streets
Statue Dedication Date: March 16, 1907
Donated By: Friendly Sons of Saint Patrick, of which he was a member
Cost: $10,300

Sculptor: Samuel Murray

Dimensions: Granite base, 12' square; pedestal, 11' high; statue, 9'6" high

Nearby Attractions: Barry's grave, Independence Hall, and the President's House

This updated story first ran in the March/April 2012 issue of the *Society Hill Reporter* and is reprinted with permission.

7 Commodore Stephen Decatur Jr.

This American naval hero was killed in a senseless duel.

Walk through St. Peter's Churchyard at Third and Pine Streets and look for the tallest monument. You'll see a large gray fluted column some twenty feet high, topped by an eagle. The name Stephen Decatur appears below.

Who was this, you wonder? It turns out that he was an extraordinary man who captivated the country with his courageous naval feats.

He was a hero. Admiral Horatio Lord Nelson praised Decatur for "the most bold and daring act of his age" after his crew destroyed the grounded frigate USS *Philadelphia* in Tripoli. His untimely death attracted more than ten thousand people to his funeral, including President James Monroe, former President James Madison, and most members of Congress and the Supreme Court.

And he was a man who rashly died in a duel defending his honor, an act that was all-too-common among his fellow naval officers.

How prevalent was the practice? In *Smithsonian Magazine*, Ross Drake says, "Between 1798 and the Civil War, the Navy lost two-thirds as many officers to dueling as it did to more than sixty years of combat at sea."

With Decatur's untimely death in a duel against a fellow officer, the country may well have lost a future president of the United States, says Vice Admiral Walter E. "Ted" Carter Jr., superintendent of the U.S. Naval Academy from 2014 to 2019.

Stephen Decatur's monument is the tallest one at St. Peter's Churchyard. (Photo by Jim Murphy.)

The country also lost one of its most heroic warriors. In 1804, during the First Barbary War, Decatur earned the admiration of the country after completing a daring, highly publicized mission. He and a crew of about seventy volunteers boarded the damaged frigate USS *Philadelphia* in Tripoli Harbor several months after it ran aground there. The Americans killed the Barbary pirates aboard and set the ship ablaze so that it could never be used again.

Soon after, Decatur and his men chased down a Barbary pirate captain who had killed Stephen's younger brother James after pretending to surrender. Although his crew was reportedly outnumbered five to one, Decatur boarded the ship, fought the captain hand-to-hand, and eventually shot him dead to avenge his brother.

In May 1815, during the Second Barbary War, Decatur was ordered by President Madison to attack Algeria and stop the practice of paying tribute to pirates once and for all. Why? Ships of countries who didn't pay were attacked. The pirates then took the goods and enslaved or killed the crew members. This threat was not empty.

Over two hundred years, estimates the Historical Society of Pennsylvania, about one million Europeans and U.S. citizens endured "abuse, incarceration, enslavement and even death, within North Africa."

In quick order, Decatur and his men captured several ships, including the flagship of the Algerian fleet, killing its leader. Using gunboat diplomacy—or a conspicuous display of power—Decatur quickly got peace agreements with Algeria and then Tunis and Tripoli, earning him the name "the Conqueror of the Barbary Pirates."

Interesting Oddities

- Decatur is often cited incorrectly for the quote, "My country, right or wrong!" What he actually said during an after-dinner toast in 1816 was "Our country—in her intercourse with foreign nations may she always be in the right; and always successful, right or wrong."
- During the War of 1812, Decatur captured the HMS *Macedonian* and had it taken to Newport, Rhode Island. It was the first British warship ever brought into an American port as a prize of war.
- Decatur wisely invested reward money from the capture of the *Macedonian* in real estate and a home near the White House designed to be "fit for entertaining." The Federal-style town house, by Benjamin Henry Latrobe, one of the first formally trained architects in the United States, is now a U.S. National Historic Landmark.

At age forty-one, with the promise of great years ahead, Decatur lost his life in a senseless duel with a fellow naval officer.

Commodore James Barron, who surrendered the unprepared USS *Chesapeake* to the British in 1807 and was suspended from his command for five years, had been stewing over critical comments Decatur made after the event, first at Barron's court-martial and then many years later. Both men were shot in the duel. Decatur died. What a waste!

Fast Facts

Name: Stephen Decatur Jr.
Born: January 5, 1779
Died: March 22, 1820, in a duel
Buried: St. Peter's Churchyard, 313 Pine Street
Claim to Fame: Extraordinary military career and youngest man ever promoted to the rank of captain in the U.S. Navy, at age twenty-five
Number of Towns Named after Him: At least forty-eight, plus seven counties and five naval ships
Historical Marker Location: 600 block of South Front Street (east side, about one-half block below South Street)
Nearby Attractions: Mason-Dixon Survey historical marker, USS *Olympia*, and Seaport Museum

This updated story first ran in the September 2017 issue of *QVNA Magazine* and is reprinted with permission.

⚍ Part III ⚎

Gone—But Not Forgotten

---

8 Acadian Connection

Longfellow's popular poem *Evangeline* still has people searching for the tombs of the Acadian heroine and her lost lover, Gabriel, in Philadelphia.

Until recently, I knew few details about the Acadians or "Cajuns" who came from the Nova Scotia region of Canada and ended up in Louisiana.

Since then, I've learned that about 11,500 Acadians were brutally displaced by the British in 1755. And about 450 of these unfortunates ended up living in Philadelphia on the north side of Pine Street between Fifth and Sixth Streets, some for many years.

When the Acadians arrived here on three sloops on November 18, 1755, they were not welcomed with open arms.

Why? They were French-speaking in a British colony. They were "Papists," so government officials feared they would collude with Irish Catholics to betray Pennsylvania to the French. And it was a time when Philadelphians greatly feared French and Native American attacks from the west. At first, the Acadians were confined under guard to their ships.

Fearing that such close quarters would quicken the spread of disease (which eventually did kill about half of them), Governor Robert Hunter Morris ordered that the Acadians be moved to Province Island, near where Philadelphia International Airport is today.

Aided by Anthony Benezet, a Philadelphia Quaker who was born in France, the Acadians received desperately needed clothing and food from him and other members of the Society of Friends. Benezet also helped the deportees get lodging in one-story wooden houses on Pine Street.

Despite the British province's best efforts to indenture the children as apprentices or send the families out to the surrounding areas, the deportees remained in Philadelphia.

And these proud Acadians, who considered themselves prisoners of war, steadfastly refused to work for any support they received from Pennsylvania.

In all, Pennsylvania paid out some £10,000 over twenty years to support the Acadians. But their living conditions were often miserable.

This area is very prosperous today. But the north side of Pine Street between Fifth and Sixth Streets is where many Acadians began living in one-story wooden houses about 1755. (Photo by Jim Murphy.)

Evangeline Resurrects a Culture

The Acadians' expulsion was largely forgotten history, until Henry Wadsworth Longfellow published *Evangeline* in 1847. This remarkably popular, 1,400-plus-line epic poem catapulted the Acadians into the public eye some ninety-two years after their expulsion from Canada.

The full poem is available online at www.bartleby.com/42/791 .html.

Interesting Oddities

- Many of the Philadelphia Acadians who died are buried in Washington Square.
- A Canadian Royal Proclamation in 2003 acknowledged the expulsion of the Acadians but did not apologize for it.
- Even though Evangeline is a fictional character, a statue of her stands in the courtyard of a French church in Grand-Pré, Nova Scotia. Another one was donated to the town of St. Martinville, Louisiana, by the cast and crew of the 1913 film *Evangeline*.

Where in the world is Evangeline? Believe it or not, people still are searching for her and Gabriel.

Longfellow himself said, "In my rambles through Philadelphia, I passed the almshouse of the Friends [then at 312 Walnut Street], and was deeply impressed by its quiet and seclusion.

"When I wrote the poem the image of this place came back to me, and I selected it for the closing scene. The story was not connected with it by any tradition."

But people believe what they want. And many think that the churchyard that inspired Longfellow's final scene—where the lovers are side-by-side in their nameless graves—is at Holy Trinity Church, 615 Spruce Street.

Who knows? After all, the site is right down the block from where many of the Acadians lived—on the north side of Pine between Fifth and Sixth Streets. But then, the story is really just fiction.

Fast Facts

Evangeline: Published in 1847

Longfellow's Immense Popularity: National parades with marching children were held on his birthday, a fireside copy of *Evangeline* was a fixture in many homes, and he is the only American poet commemorated with a bust in Britain's renowned Poet's Corner.

Claim to Fame: *Evangeline* went through six printings in six months and within ten years had been translated into a dozen languages.

Song: "Acadian Driftwood" by The Band (a YouTube video with visuals is available at www.youtube.com/watch?v=te7KW4K-00E)

Nearby Attractions: Pennsylvania Hospital, Mikveh Israel Cemetery, and Old St. Mary's Church

This updated story first ran in the July/August 2015 issue of the *Society Hill Reporter* and is reprinted with permission.

⑨ The Gaskill Street Baths

Two separate bathhouses served residents of this 1890s "slum."
From 1860 to 1900—just forty years—Philadelphia's population doubled in size. The immigration mix changed dramatically too. By the turn of the twentieth century, the city's newcomers were no longer mostly Irish, German, English, or Scottish.

Now people from Eastern Europe—Jews and Slavs (Poles, Slovaks, Ukrainians) from the Russian and Austro-Hungarian Empires—plus Italians and Greeks from Southern Europe flocked to the city.

By 1900, a total of 1,293,697 residents lived here, many in squalid conditions. Long-standing problems of overcrowding, lack of ventilation, and poor sanitary conditions became even worse.

Among the areas affected was South Philadelphia's densely populated district of Southwark. (Today, that area mostly includes the neighborhoods of Queen Village and Pennsport.)

Philly's new foreign-looking and -speaking immigrants were considered unclean, unhealthy, and uncivilized. New proof in the 1880s that specific microorganisms could cause disease (including typhoid, cholera, tuberculosis, diphtheria, and more) compounded the problem. Public baths and cleanliness became the solution.

Until then, haughty movers and shakers of the time had believed that a moral defect among immigrants kept them from bathing. They overlooked one simple fact: the lower classes simply didn't have ready access to baths. In her book *Washing 'the Great Unwashed': Public Baths in Urban America, 1840–1920*, Marilyn Thornton Williams notes that in 1899, not one in twenty families in Philadelphia had access to a bath.

The *Philadelphia Ledger* proclaimed, "Every dirty man or woman is a menace to the health of the community," says David Glassberg in the article "The Design of Reform: The Public Bath Movement in America." A Chicago bath advocate went even further: "The greatest civilizing power that can be brought to bear on these uncivilized Europeans crowding into our cities lies in the public bath."

About 1894, Sarah Dickson Lowrie, a prominent upper-class Philadelphian, was the first to recognize the problem locally, says Melissa M. Mandell in her article "The Public Baths Association of Philadelphia and the 'Great Unwashed.'"

The city's first public baths were opened at 410–12 Gaskill Street on April 20, 1898. The Gaskill Baths: Exterior view at Gaskill and Leithgow Streets, undated. (Public Baths Association of Philadelphia, Historical Society of Pennsylvania.)

While teaching a Saturday sewing class in the mission building in the densest, most wretched of the city's slums—presumably Southwark—Lowrie "was informed by her students that there was no way for them to take a bath in the winter."

Finally understanding the issue and becoming an advocate, at a private dinner party hosted by retail mogul John Wanamaker, Lowrie proposed the idea of establishing public baths.

One attendee, Barclay H. Warburton, editor and publisher of the *Philadelphia Daily Evening Telegraph*, assigned a reporter to investigate the lack of bathing facilities in the poorer areas of the city. Later, he helped raise money for the effort and urged the formation of a group to carry it out.

The result was the establishment of the Public Baths Association (PBA) of Philadelphia, which was incorporated in March 1895. **The PBA formally opened its first baths on April 20, 1898,** at 410–12 Gaskill Street in "one of the oldest and most thickly populated sections of the city." By the PBA's own count, says Williams, in a typical slum block near the new baths, there was "but one bathtub for 155 people."

The PBA considered the Gaskill Street Baths an immediate success, noting that it was "patronized by all nationalities, Hebrews, Italians, Germans, Irish, English, Japanese, Hungarians, as well as Americans, Black and White."

"The majority of patrons, however, were Jewish," Williams says. But the actual results don't seem all that extraordinary. "The total number of bathers in 1898 was 21,656, or an average of 88 per day, although the capacity of the bath was over 900 per day; only 256 persons patronized the laundry. As in other cities, the patronage also varied greatly between winter and summer; in July 1898 there were 4,945 bathers and in November the total was 787."

In 1903, though, the PBA set up another bath—for women only—across the street at 413–15 Gaskill. Eventually, the PBA constructed six public bath sites in the city.

However, starting in 1929, around the time of the Great Depression, patronage and surpluses declined, and repair costs and deficits mounted. In 1942, the PBA closed the Gaskill baths and dissolved the entire organization in 1950.

But in its time, the PBA filled a serious civic need and left behind a sustained record of public service. Not a bad legacy.

Fast Facts

First Gaskill Bath Opened: April 20, 1898, at 410–12 Gaskill Street, serving men and women on different floors

Second Gaskill Bath Opened: 1903, at 413–15 Gaskill Street, serving women only. This property still exists and was purchased by Congregation Kesher Israel in 2015.

Fee: 5 cents for a shower bath, towel, and soap, 365 days a year; no charge for children under ten years of age with parents

Claim to Fame: First public baths in the United States with a public laundry

Promotional Slogan: Baths for everybody: For comfort, for health, for cleanliness

Gaskill Baths Closed: 1942

Nearby Attractions: South Street, Hill-Physick House, and Philadelphia's Magic Gardens

This updated story first ran in the Spring/Summer 2012 issue of the *Society Hill Reporter* and is reprinted with permission.

10 The Grand Battery (or the Association Battery)

This fort was designed to protect the city against naval enemies.
In the summer of 1747, many Philadelphians were afraid.

Why? The city's enviable prosperity and extensive sea trade made it a tempting target for marauding privateers. Yet the anti-war, nonviolent Quakers who ran Philadelphia were decidedly uninterested in defending the unfortified city.

That became a major problem for Philadelphia during King George's War (1744–48)—another of England's many wars with France. During this conflict, both Spanish and French privateers boldly cruised the Delaware Capes, searching for easy booty. Some even traveled upriver to raid plantations in New Castle County.

A highly publicized violent incident took place on July 12, 1747. Some fifteen or twenty armed men from a French privateer went ashore in New Castle, plundered one house, carried off most of the property and slaves, and then attacked another plantation nearby, shooting the owner's wife in the process.

On their way out of Delaware Bay, the crew captured a valuable ship headed for Philadelphia from Antigua and wounded the captain. Philadelphia was thought to be the next target.

Tired of waiting years for their do-little government to protect them, Philadelphians, led by Ben Franklin, finally took action in late 1747.

In a famous pamphlet titled "Plain Truth," Franklin proposed forming a volunteer citizen defense association. He signed it: "A Tradesman of Philadelphia." Within days, more than one thousand people had joined.

At that, Pennsylvania's colonial government agreed to supply arms and ammunition—if Philadelphia could provide the fort. It did, with the help of a Franklin-organized lottery that quickly raised £3,000.

Work began almost immediately. A small thirteen-gun battery on William Atwood's wharf in Society Hill near Lombard Street was operational in just days.

The larger, more formidable Grand Battery (or Association Battery) was built on a hill about three hundred yards downstream

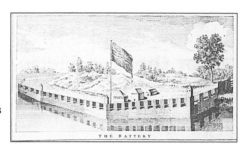

The Grand Battery was funded by a Ben Franklin lottery to help defend Philadelphia. This view is part of Scull and Heap's *East Prospect of Philadelphia*, 1768. (Prints and Photographs Division, Library of Congress.)

from the current Gloria Dei (or Old Swedes') Church. It was ready by the spring of 1748. Later, the site became the location of the first Philadelphia Navy Yard.

The new fort included three buildings surrounded by a brick or stone wall about fifteen feet high. The Grand Battery started with twenty-seven cannons; later, the number rose to fifty.

Interesting Oddities

- Philadelphia's efforts to borrow cannons for its battery were not warmly received by New York's Governor George Clinton. The reason: Defense cost New York £45,000 each year, while Pennsylvania spent little or nothing. After an initial curt refusal, lots of Madeira wine and some friendly socializing made the city's request more palatable. Franklin recalls that the governor "soften'd by degrees, and said he would lend us Six. After a few more Bumpers he advanc'd to Ten. And at length he very good-naturedly conceded Eighteen."
- Franklin's lottery was designed to raise £3,000 to erect the battery. He later boasted that the Philadelphia lottery came as close to selling out in seven weeks as New York's and New England's did in seven months.
- The war ended soon after the battery was established, and the guns never were fired in defense of the city. When the British captured Philadelphia, however, they mounted guns there and used them against American ships on the Delaware River.

Forming the Association was Ben Franklin's first foray into politics. Fortunately for Philadelphia and the United States, it was not his last.

Fast Facts

Name: Grand Battery (or Association Battery)

Historical Marker Location: East side of Columbus Boulevard, just south of Washington Avenue, at the U.S. Coast Guard Station

Marker Copy: "Known also as the Association Battery, this was Pennsylvania's largest early fortification. Originally built in 1748, shortly after formation of a volunteer military force called the Association, it mounted twenty-seven guns; within a few years it held some fifty guns. Later the first Philadelphia Navy Yard was here, 1800–1875. A short distance to the north, the smaller Society Hill Battery was built in April 1748; it mounted thirteen guns."

Year Built: 1747–48

Claim to Fame: First fortification on the Delaware River built to defend Philadelphia. This spot later became the site of the first Philadelphia Navy Yard.

Nearby Attractions: Gloria Dei Church, Immigration Station historical marker, and *Land Buoy* sculpture at Washington Avenue Pier

This updated story first ran in the November 2017 issue of *QVNA Magazine* and is reprinted with permission.

11 Washington Avenue Immigration Station

Here's where almost one million immigrants entered the United States.

While walking south on Columbus Boulevard one Sunday afternoon, I suddenly noticed a blue and gold Pennsylvania historical marker identifying the site of the Washington Avenue Immigration Station.

The marker—at the foot of Washington Avenue—reads, "Since the 1870s, the station was an entry point and processing center for immigrants, primarily from Southern and Eastern Europe. From here, newcomers moved into the city or other parts of the state. It was demolished in 1915."

Even though I've lived my entire life within ten miles of this spot, I had never realized that Philadelphia had an immigration station. I had assumed, incorrectly, that our ancestors all came through Ellis Island.

I was equally surprised to learn that almost one million immigrants first set foot on U.S. soil at Washington Avenue.

Philadelphia is actually one of eight cities that at different times were runners-up to New York as a top entry point for immigrants. The others were Boston, Baltimore, Miami, New Orleans, Los Angeles, San Francisco, and later Honolulu.

The Washington Avenue Immigration Center "was like a big warehouse," says Bob Skiba, a past president and a founding member of the Association of Philadelphia Tour Guides.

Built by the Pennsylvania Railroad near the docks of the American Line—which it also owned—the two-story station included a restaurant, ticket office, money exchange, and comfort stations on the ground floor, plus a large lobby. Passengers disembarked onto the second floor, where they were examined and questioned by customs inspectors.

After a $10,000 expansion in 1896, which also included the addition of electric lights and steam heating, eight inspectors were able to handle 300 English-speaking or 150 non-English-speaking immigrants per hour, or up to 1,500 per day. Before the improvements, the maximum was three hundred per day.

The Washington Avenue wharves were a busy, bustling place, says Fredric M. Miller in "Philadelphia: Immigrant City," a Balch online resource. Nearby were factories, warehouses, sugar refineries, and grain elevators, "all connected to the vast yards of the Pennsylvania Railroad."

Outside the station, a crowd of entrepreneurs usually gathered, ready and willing to charge newcomers exorbitant rates for their many services.

Inside, "the station naturally became one of the most colorful places in Philadelphia," Miller says. For example, a part of the examination room was called the "Altar." Why? "Since under some conditions single women were prevented from landing, many hurried unions were celebrated on the spot."

The American Line, the only one offering weekly sailings, brought 17,342 passengers to Philadelphia from Liverpool in 1882 alone. Even after it began serving New York in the 1890s, the line

The Pennsylvania Railroad built this immigration station, which operated from 1873 until it was demolished in 1915. Washington Avenue Immigration Station photograph, Philadelphia Record Photograph Morgue. (Historical Society of Pennsylvania.)

added "ships with such local names as the *Kensington, Southwark, Haverford* and *Merion* to the Philadelphia run around the turn of the century."

In 1898, the Hamburg-American Line began service to Philadelphia, bringing many Polish and Jewish immigrants here. In all, transatlantic steamers brought more than sixty thousand immigrants to the city in 1913, the peak. From 1910 to 1914, at the height of immigration from Southern and Eastern Europe, Philadelphia was the third-largest immigrant portal in the country.

World War I and restrictive immigration quotas quickly changed that. The annual average of arrivals in Philadelphia plummeted from 49,644 in 1910–14 to 5,598 in 1915–24 and just 408 from 1925–30.

Even though the city is no longer a major immigration portal, its Washington Avenue corridor still attracts foreign-born residents.

A cursory glance at the Southeast Asian temples, shops, and restaurants along Washington Avenue, plus the Mexican taquerias, cantinas, and stores that have sprung up nearby, shows that this area is again an immigrant gateway—with all the energy and excitement that comes with it.

Fast Facts

Name: Washington Avenue Immigration Station

Location: Washington Avenue Pier, Formerly Pier 53, Washington Avenue and Columbus Boulevard (near current U.S. Coast Guard Station)

Years in Service: 1873–1915

Number of Immigrants Processed Here: Almost one million

Original Name: International Navigation Company Immigration Station

Built By: The Pennsylvania Railroad, which wanted to expand its freight and passenger service into the transatlantic market and bypass New York

Nearby Attractions: *Land Buoy* sculpture at Washington Avenue Pier, Gloria Dei Church, and the Grand Battery

This updated story first ran in the January/February 2013 issue of the *Society Hill Reporter* and is reprinted with permission.

Part IV

Heroes, Sung and Unsung

⑫ Charles Willson Peale

He was a true Renaissance man.

As a young man in Maryland, Charles Willson Peale believed that he could do just about anything. Evidently, he was correct.

Today, he's known mostly for more than 1,100 paintings of Revolutionary War colleagues and notables he created. More than one hundred of them are in the Second Bank of the United States, at 420 Chestnut Street.

But Peale, who never saw a painting before he was twenty-one years old, was far more than a painter. He was also an inventor, silversmith, watchmaker, soldier, and leader in just about everything he touched.

The artist outlived three wives (with whom he had seventeen children, eleven reaching maturity). At least nine were named after painters. Late in life, he began naming his children after scientists.

Along the way, he helped found the Pennsylvania Academy of the Fine Arts, the first and oldest museum and art school in the United States.

In addition, he set up the Philadelphia Museum, the country's first museum of natural history. After outgrowing space in his home, Peale moved the museum to Philosophical Hall, and in 1802, it was moved to the second floor of what is now Independence Hall.

One of its most popular attractions was Peale's display of a mastodon skeleton found in New York State. After his death, much of his museum's collection was sold to P. T. Barnum.

Interesting Oddities

- Charles was named after a rich uncle, Wilson Peale, whose fortune and land he was expected to inherit. When that didn't happen, Peale added an "L" to his middle name to distance himself from the Wilson family. Then, he moved on with his life.
- His artistic talent may have come from his father, Charles Peale, a noted forger exiled from England to Maryland for embezzling money from London's General Post Office. The prosecutor expressed wonder at the elder Peale's "artfulness" and "close resemblance of his forgeries to the genuine hands."

Charles Willson Peale, *The Artist in His Museum*, appears here in a self-portrait created at age eighty-one. (Courtesy of the Pennsylvania Academy of the Fine Arts, Philadelphia. Gift of Mrs. Sarah Harrison [The Joseph Harrison, Jr. Collection].)

- Peale evidently liked the work of the painter Titian. He named two of his children Titian Ramsay Peale, the second one in 1799, after his eighteen-year-old son, and reportedly a favorite, died.
- Peale's full-length battlefield portrait of *George Washington at Princeton*, one of eight of Washington he painted between 1779 and 1781, was sold for $21.3 million in January 2006. That price set a world record at the time for the sale of an American portrait.

• Peale was probably Philly's first nude model, says James Thomas Flexner in his book *America's Old Masters*. Believing that artists should "draw from the living figure," Peale searched the city for someone willing to pose nude for an academy art class. When an impoverished but bashful baker agreed—and then begged off at the last minute—Peale stepped into the breach and posed himself. The prolific artist lived his final years at Belfield, his estate that's now part of the campus at LaSalle University.

While not as well known as Ben Franklin (whom he painted), Peale was a universal genius and Renaissance man. And he's given us the best visual record of our country's Founding Fathers. If you haven't yet seen his portraits at the Second Bank of the United States, I heartily recommend a visit. They really make history come alive.

Fast Facts

Name: Charles Willson Peale
Born: April 15, 1741
Died: February 22, 1827
Buried: St. Peter's Churchyard, 313 Pine Street
Claim to Fame: Painter, soldier, saddle-maker, museologist, inventor, and impresario
Historical Marker Dedicated: 1991
Marker Status: Missing. Listed as SW corner of Third and Lombard Streets
Nearby Attractions: Second Bank of the United States (where many of Peale's paintings are), Old Pine Street Church, and the Powel House

This updated story first ran in the January 2017 issue of *QVNA Magazine* and is reprinted with permission.

⑬ Francis Daniel Pastorius

His bronze historical marker is missing from his Philly home.
When I began writing a story about the eleven Pennsylvania historical markers in Queen Village, it seemed like a pretty simple assignment: Go to the various sites, research the subjects, and then plot the spots on a map so readers of the *QVNA Magazine* could find them.

But it didn't turn out to be that easy. Why? The very first place I went to—502 South Front Street, **the original home of Francis Daniel Pastorius**—was missing its historic plaque.

And I have no idea where it is.

The location, though, is important. It's the first home of the man who eventually founded Germantown. He drafted the first antislavery document in America in 1688. And the first thirteen German settlers he represented drew straws here for their Germantown lots on October 25, 1683.

His temporary "home" on Front Street was actually a cave, fifteen feet wide and thirty feet long, "half under and half above ground." It furnished shelter for him and some twenty people while their houses were being built in Germantown.

Over the door, Pastorius wrote an inscription that translates as "A little house, but a friend to the good, keep away, ye profane!" When William Penn saw it, Pastorius says, he "burst into laughter, and encouraged me to keep on building."

The now-missing twenty-eight-by-forty-eight-inch bronze plaque was placed on Pastorius's house on October 25, 1924. Like twenty-five others, the plaque was designed

Francis Daniel Pastorius, head-and-shoulders portrait, left profile, bas-relief, founder of Germantown, Pennsylvania. (Library of Congress.)

by famous architect Paul Philippe Cret. Later, the Pennsylvania Museum and Historical Commission developed the blue and gold historical markers you see today.

Penn agreed to let Pastorius purchase three lots in the city behind each other at Front, Second, and Third Streets. The first two were "a hundred feet broad and four hundred long." Lot #1 was carved out of William Penn Jr.'s land at the northwest corner of Front and Cedar Streets (now South Street). He was three years old at the time.

Interesting Oddities

- Pastorius described early Philadelphia variously as "several small houses set in the midst of a howling wilderness" and "consisting of 3 or 4 little Cottages, all the Residue being only Woods, Underwoods, Timber and Trees." He also said, "It is nothing but forest, and very few cleared places are to be found."
- The Germans diabolically dubbed a June 1942 coordinated sabotage attack against the United States "Operation Pastorius"—an unlikely reference to the peaceful leader of the first German settlement in America. Fortunately all eight spies who landed off Long Island and Florida were captured within days.
- Pastorius—an accomplished leader, lawyer, and educator who wrote in seven languages—was the hero of *The Pennsylvania Pilgrim*, a 546-line narrative poem by John Greenleaf Whittier.
- While laying out Germantown in the fall of 1683, Pastorius said Penn's woods were "a very Eden of beauty, only cursed with a plethora of rattlesnakes."

Fast Facts

Name: Francis Daniel Pastorius
Address: 502 South Front Street
Former Location of Plaque: It appears to have been at the northwest corner of Naudain and Front Streets.
Nearby Attractions: Mason-Dixon Survey historical marker, Stephen Decatur's historical marker, and Gloria Dei (Old Swedes') Church

This updated story first ran in the September 2016 issue of *QVNA Magazine* and is reprinted with permission.

14 Isaiah Zagar

This mosaic artist makes Philadelphia glitter.

After moving to Philadelphia from the suburbs in 2008, I was fascinated by the colorful, shimmering mosaics I found on Gaskill, Leithgow, and South Streets. But I didn't know who had created them.

So, I looked online. Surprisingly, one of the first stories I found on artist Isaiah Zagar, the man responsible for more than two hundred mosaic murals in the city, was from the *Seattle Times*'s Sally and John Macdonald.

Digging deeper, I learned about **Zagar's opus, Philadelphia's Magic Gardens, a unique, labyrinthian sculpture garden on South Street**. I read about the documentary *In a Dream* that his son Jeremiah had filmed about him. And finally, I sat down one morning with the artist himself, a friendly, polite, soft-spoken man, for breakfast at the Fitzwater Café.

Zagar told me he was born in the city at the former Osteopathic Hospital—then at Forty-Eighth and Spruce Streets—grew up in Brooklyn, and received a B.A. in painting and graphics from Pratt Institute in New York City.

After serving three years in rural Peru (with no electricity or heat) for the Peace Corps, Zagar and his wife, Julia, moved to the Germantown section of Philadelphia. In short order, he suffered "reverse culture shock" and found himself in a mental institution.

He felt like a failure and even attempted suicide. Then, he started to live again. His recovery period took nine months, "the gestation period of his son Ezekiel."

Reinventing himself, Zagar and his family moved to South Street in 1968, then a downtrodden, depressed, crime-ridden area just waiting to be demolished for the Crosstown Expressway.

Zagar regained his confidence by focusing on a successful period in his life at Pratt, where—on a summer scholarship—he had worked with Clarence Schmidt, a noted practitioner of the "outside" or "outsider art" environment. That's work created by self-taught or out-of-the-mainstream artists.

The Zagars then developed a plan: get a piece of real estate cheap

You'll see Isaiah Zagar's colorful murals all over the South Street area.
(Photo by Jim Murphy.)

and open a store, sell Isaiah's art as well as folk art they brought back from Peru, and "make the place our business and our home into an outside environment."

Done, done, and done.

Zagar learned construction techniques and rebuilt the Eyes Gallery space at Fourth and South Streets with materials he found nearby at abandoned warehouses. These included glass, tile, shoe ornaments, and more.

Top Tidbits from Our Conversation

His Biggest Mural: The old firehouse at 1016–18 South Street. When he completed it, he said, "Now I have entered the consciousness of Philadelphia."

His Favorite Mural: *Animal Dreams*, which was on the side of Society Hill Playhouse until the playhouse was torn down for condos in 2016. He says it was "in a beautiful, quiet location with homes and trees."

Where He'll Work: Any blank wall made of unpainted masonry that is open to the public for twenty-four hours and within one-half mile of his workshop at Tenth and South Streets.

Problematic Location: Society Hill, whose Zoning and Historic Preservation Committee believes that his work "is inconsistent with the neighborhood character." Zagar says, "It's off the map for me." If he did a job, "there would be such consternation, anger would erupt."

Society Hill Playhouse (in Its Glory Days): When Zagar saw that a painted mural on the north side of the building in Washington Square West was decaying, he asked Deen Kogan, then owner and operator of the playhouse, whether he could do a mosaic there. She said, "Yes," upsetting two nearby residents, who made quite a fuss. The result: "It's wonderful," said Kogan, who died in 2018. "You have no idea how many people come by and take photos of it. They love it."

When You Visit Philadelphia's Magic Gardens: Expect to be simply overwhelmed by colors, objects, and a dazzling array of tiles in this artistic tour de force. Your eye just doesn't know where to go first . . . or next . . . because the entire place is a feast for the eyes. Wherever you glance—up, down, or sideways—you see something new and different: blues, greens, reds, with discarded figures, bottles, wheel rims, reflecting tiles, and more. There's even a chuppah, a canopy where marriages are performed. Children love the gardens, because they can go down steps and through tunnels and explore on their own. It's a truly unique and enjoyable experience for all ages.

Fast Facts

Artist: Isaiah Zagar
Number of Mosaics in Philadelphia: 120 to 200 or more
Largest Artwork: Magic Gardens, 1020 South Street
Size: Three thousand square feet
Hours: Wednesday through Monday, 11 A.M. to 6 P.M.; closed Tuesday
Admission: Adults, $10; seniors and students, $8; ages six to twelve, $5; ages five and under, free
Phone: 215-733-0390

Website: www.phillymagicgardens.org
Documentary about Zagar: *In a Dream*
Nearby Attractions: William Way LGBT Community Center, Academy of Music, and Union League

This updated story first ran in the May/June 2014 issue of the *Society Hill Reporter* and is reprinted with permission.

 James Forten

A unique skill saved him from a life of servitude.

Like many Philadelphians, I've long known of James Forten's reputation as a successful Black sailmaker and businessman.

But I had no idea how loyal, courageous, and generous he was. After doing more research on him, I'm ready to place him quite high on Philadelphia's list of civic heroes.

Here's why.

After being captured by the British on just his second voyage as a fourteen-year-old crewman on a privateer, Forten gave up a unique opportunity at a life of wealth and privilege.

All he had to do was agree to live in England with the family of Captain John Bazely, commander of the ship that captured him (more on this below). Forten refused to betray his country. As a result, he then spent seven months on the HMS *Jersey*, a British hellhole of a prison ship. An average of eight prisoners a day died on the *Jersey*.

Forten also gave up a chance to escape from that prison ship. Learning that a naval officer was to be exchanged, Forten reportedly asked to stow away in the man's sea chest. At the last minute, Forten let Daniel Brewson, a White Philadelphian two years younger and "his companion in suffering," go in his place. Then, he "assisted in taking down 'the chest of old clothes' . . . from the sides of the prison ship," says Julie Winch in her book, *A Gentleman of Color: The Life of James Forten*. To me, that was an amazing act of charity.

Interesting Oddities

- Forten was not James's real name. A free Black man, he changed it from "Fortune," which was a common name among slaves. In addi-

James Forten portrait, 1818.
(Historical Society of Pennsylvania.
Leon Gardiner Collection of
American Negro Historical Society
Records [0008]. [Reproduced with
permission from the Historical
Society of Pennsylvania].)

tion, nine slaves with that name had fled to the British side. So, Fortune was not a name that would help Forten make his.

- Forten's ability to shoot marbles "helped save him from a life of West Indian servitude." How? His "unerring hand" impressed Henry Bazely, the twelve-year-old son of the ship captain and a youth then training for his own career in the Royal Navy. Excited, he told his father about Forten's skill, who then witnessed it for himself. After that demonstration, Forten received greater freedom than other prisoners. And even though he turned down Captain Bazely's offer to join Henry in England, the officer sent a letter to the commander of the prison ship to commend Forten, a kindness that James never forgot.

- Like many other Black people, Forten and his family could not venture out of their Philadelphia home on July 4. If they did, they risked attacks from White people. Forten wrote, "The poor Black is assailed like the destroying Hyena or the avaricious Wolf," and asked, "Is it not wonderful that the day set apart for the festival of Liberty, should be abused by the advocates of freedom, in endeavoring to sully what they profess to adore?"

Forten effectively used the power of the pen to fight racial injustice. In 1813, he anonymously wrote "Letters from a Man of Colour on a Late Bill before the Senate of Pennsylvania." This pamphlet strongly denounced a bill in the Pennsylvania legislature requiring emigrating Black people to register with the state. The bill failed.

He fought against slavery in many different ways. He spent half of his fortune purchasing the freedom of slaves. He financially supported William Lloyd Garrison's paper, the *Liberator*, and also wrote for it. In addition, Forten's home on Lombard Street served as a station for the Underground Railroad. And the American Antislavery Society was founded in his home.

He also left a powerful legacy: a family of activist children and their spouses, who kept the abolitionist movement going. He was a man who left the world far better than he found it. What more could anyone ask for?

Fast Facts

Born: September 2, 1766
Died: March 4, 1842
Buried: Eden Cemetery, Collingdale, Delaware County
Wrote: "Letters from a Man of Colour on a Late Bill before the Senate of Pennsylvania"
Claim to Fame: Prisoner of war, Black businessman, abolitionist, activist
Lived At: 336 Lombard Street
Historical Marker Dedicated: April 24, 1990
Marker Copy: "A wealthy sailmaker who employed multi-racial craftsmen, Forten was a leader of the African-American community in Philadelphia and a champion of reform causes. The American Antislavery Society was organized in his house here in 1833."
Nearby Attractions: St. Peter's Church, Old Pine Street Church, and Mother Bethel Church

This updated story first ran in the November 2016 issue of *QVNA Magazine* and is reprinted with permission.

16 Lucretia Mott

This tiny woman made a huge difference in nineteenth-century America.

By all accounts, Lucretia Mott was never a pushover.

Under five feet tall and weighing fewer than one hundred pounds, the Nantucket native who moved to Philadelphia in 1809 was described by her young schoolmates as a "spitfire."

Fearless might have been more accurate. **Mott had the courage and tenacity to speak her mind to anyone, anywhere, including to President John Tyler.**

At a time when women's opinions were not sought after or often listened to, Mott served as a Quaker minister, traveled without the obligatory chaperone, preached against slavery, promoted the rights of women, and spoke to "promiscuous" groups that included both men and women.

Surprisingly, Mott did this all without notes. She spoke spontaneously, letting her "inner light" and quick mind guide her. And it appears that her message was clear and effective.

Along the way, Mott also formed the Philadelphia Female Anti-Slave Society, traveled to the first World Anti-Slavery Convention in London, and was part of the first Women's Rights Convention at Seneca Falls, New York, in July 1848.

And despite being called a heretic, infidel, disturber of the peace, and more, she thought for herself. And she gave as good as she got.

Once told by Quaker elders to stop preaching against slavery, she replied, "It is regarded a greater crime to do an innocent thing on the first day of the week [Sunday]—to use the needle for instance—

Portrait of Lucretia Mott by Joseph Kyle. (Smithsonian National Portrait Gallery. Gift of Mrs. Alan Valentine.)

than to put a human being on the auction block on the second day [Monday]."

Fellow activist Elizabeth Cady Stanton described her this way: "I found in this new friend a woman emancipated from all faith in man-made creeds, from all fear of denunciation. Nothing was too sacred for her to question, as to its rightfulness in principle and practice."

Interesting Oddities

* Fervent as she was about promoting the rights of women, even Mott wasn't ready at Seneca Falls to publicly state that women had the right to vote. "Why Lizzie," she reportedly told Stanton—who was strongly pushing for women's suffrage—"thee will make us ridiculous." Later, Mott changed her mind.
* Mott helped famed journalist and abolitionist William Lloyd Garrison become better at spreading his anti-slavery message. After arranging a public meeting for him in Philadelphia, Mott cringed when she saw Garrison read his manuscript word for word. Critics assailed his presentation as "uninviting." Mott counseled him, "William, if thee expects to set forth thy cause by word of mouth thee must lay aside thy paper and trust to the leading of the spirit." He listened, learned, and became an outstanding spokesman for his cause.
* After anti-abolitionists burned down Pennsylvania Hall, a newly opened building (near the present WHYY building at 150 North Sixth Street) that was hosting the second Anti-Slavery Convention of American Women, protestors headed for Mott's home nearby. She sent her younger children out of the house and quietly waited in the parlor with her husband, James, and friends for whatever would happen. Fortunately, a young man friendly to the family yelled to the mob, "On to Mott's"—and then led them up the wrong street.

Always active, Mott participated in the Underground Railroad, enabling slaves to escape, and helped found Swarthmore College and what later became Women's Medical College and Moore College of Design. She even hosted the wife of abolitionist John Brown in her home while Brown awaited execution for his raid at Harpers Ferry.

Later, the integrated town of LaMott just north of Philadelphia was named for her. Mott was an extraordinary woman of courage and integrity who fought for causes she believed in. She proved that one determined individual can make a global difference—a good lesson for all of us.

Fast Facts

Name: Lucretia Mott
Born: January 3, 1793
Died: November 11, 1880
Buried: Fair Hill Burial Ground, 2901 Germantown Avenue (phone: 215-870-8348). This three-hundred-year-old Quaker burial ground is now a history and education center.
Noted For: Her work in support of civil rights, women's rights, and anti-slavery efforts
Mother Of: Six children
Most Famous Relative: Ben Franklin was her cousin.
Washington, D.C., Monument: Mott's bust is one of three represented in the U.S. Capitol Rotunda's *Portrait Monument* of key suffragists.
Historical Marker Location: PA 611 at Latham Parkway, north of Cheltenham Avenue, Elkins Park
Marker Copy: "Nearby stood *Roadside*, the home of the ardent Quakeress, Lucretia C. Mott (1793–1880). Her most notable work was in connection with antislavery, women's rights, temperance and peace."
Nearby Attractions: Historic Germantown is about 5 miles away; Fair Hill Burial Ground is 5.3 miles away. (Map location for this chapter is Pennsylvania Hall. Lucretia Mott spoke at dedication ceremonies there shortly before a mob burned the building down.)

17 Richard Allen

He founded Bethel Church, the oldest African Methodist Episcopal (AME) congregation in the United States.

Go past the intersection of Sixth and Lombard Streets, and you know right away you're in an important spot.

You see an impressive bronze statue of an animated preacher; a huge, Romanesque church made of stone and brick, with spec-

Richard Allen's bronze statue attracts a lot of attention at Sixth and Lombard Streets. (Photo by Jim Murphy.)

tacular stained-glass windows; and two gold-on-blue Pennsylvania historical markers close by.

Then you spot large block letters: "MOTHER BETHEL AFRICAN METHODIST EPISCOPAL (AME) CHURCH." You realize that this place is sacred territory for African Americans.

Richard Allen founded this first AME church. He did this soon after he, his friend the Reverend Absalom Jones, and other Black people were discriminated against by a trustee at St. George's United Methodist Church on Fourth Street, their usual place of worship.

Here's what happened: As the Black worshipers entered St. George's one Sunday, contrary to the normal practice, they were told by the sexton to go up to the gallery. They complied and knelt above what had been their usual seats. Suddenly, Jones was pulled up off his knees by one of the trustees, who said, "You must get up—you must not kneel here." Jones said that he would get up as soon as prayer was over.

That wasn't good enough, and the trustee beckoned to another for help. "By this time prayer was over," Allen writes. "We all went out of the church in a body, and they were no more plagued with us in the church."

Eventually, Allen and Jones started two different churches: Mother Bethel and the African Episcopal Church of St. Thomas. The two also continued working together in the Free African Society, a Black mutual-aid organization.

When a disastrous yellow fever epidemic hit Philadelphia in 1793, they faced an entirely new racial controversy. Responding to a newspaper ad asking for help from "people of colour" to aid yellow fever victims—because Dr. Benjamin Rush, who had placed the ad, mistakenly thought that Black people were immune from the disease—Allen, Jones, and many others responded to help White families.

But newspaper publisher Matthew Carey, who fled the city during the epidemic that killed more than 5,000 people (including 240 Black people), saw things differently. He accused Black people of profiteering and stealing from the sick, making his accusations in a pamphlet so popular it was reprinted at least four times.

Jones and Allen responded with their own long-titled defense piece: "A Narrative of the Proceedings of the Black People during the Late Awful Calamity in Philadelphia in the Year 1793 and a Refutation of Some Censures, Thrown upon Them in Some Late Publications."

Using the initials A. J. and R. A., they copyrighted their pamphlet, which may well be the first copyrighted written work by Black people in the United States. It carried the number 54, District of Pennsylvania, on the copyright page.

Mother Bethel Church itself is also historic and said to be on the oldest parcel of ground continuously owned by African Americans in the United States.

Margaret Jerrido, archivist at Mother Bethel Church, says that "Mother" was added to the name Bethel in 1953, when women were allowed to participate in the corporation. Bethel itself means "Church of God." The stone part is the original section of the church, Jerrido says.

Interesting Oddities

- We don't know why the slave known as "Negro Richard" chose the last name of Allen after purchasing his freedom in 1783. Even his most recent biographer, Richard S. Newman, doesn't seem to. It's a mystery.
- Allen's family was once enslaved by Benjamin Chew, owner of the Cliveden estate in Germantown and chief supreme court justice of Pennsylvania. Allen even begins his biography this way: "I was born in the year of our lord 1760, on February 14th, a slave to Benjamin Chew, of Philadelphia."
- An influential minister, writer, and educator, Allen was also elected the first bishop of the AME Church in 1816.
- Although many refer to Mother Bethel as part of the Underground Railroad that helped slaves escape, Jerrido has no written historical documentation of this claim. Still, she says, it was likely.

According to the church's history, Allen purchased an old blacksmith shop and had it hauled to the Sixth and Lombard Streets site. Carpenters then helped turn it into a historic place of worship, the first of four churches on this site.

You'll find an impressive museum in the basement of Mother Bethel Church. Items include a colorful mural; Allen's pulpit chair; his Bible, believed to have been printed in the 1600s; several long rifles; and a bust of Allen that was found at Wilberforce College. A tomb houses the remains of Allen; his second wife, Sarah; and the second bishop, Morris Brown. The museum is well worth a visit.

Fast Facts

Name: Mother Bethel AME Church
Address: 419 South Sixth Street
Phone: 215-925-0616
Church Tours with Docents: Tuesday to Saturday, 10 A.M. to 3 P.M.

Bethel Burial Ground: Historic cemetery located at Fourth and Queen Streets under part of the Weccacoe Playground
Church Honors: U.S. National Register of Historical Churches, U.S. National Historic Landmark
Nearby Attractions: Octavius Catto historical marker at 812 South Street, W. E. B. Du Bois mural at Sixth and South Streets, and James Forten historical marker at 336 Lombard Street

18 Robert Smith

He was Philly's most important colonial builder/architect.

Whether you call Robert Smith a master builder, an architect, or just a magnificent carpenter, one thing is clear: If you removed his many stunning Philadelphia buildings—including eight churches—this city would be far less beautiful and impressive.

As it is, this Scottish immigrant from a family of masons has been called the most important builder/architect in the colonies. But possibly because his last name is so common, he's simply not that well known today.

Among the fifty-two projects he created in his twenty-nine-year work history, though, are some of Philadelphia's most important buildings.

Smith's masterpieces include the steeple at Christ Church, St. Peter's Church, Old Pine Street Church, St. Paul's Church, and the Walnut Street Prison. Some say that he designed the East Wing of Pennsylvania Hospital too. He also was chosen by his fellow carpenters to build Carpenters' Hall, a huge honor.

Outside the state, he built Nassau Hall and the President's House at Princeton as well as the oddly named Hospital for Idiots and Lunatics at Williamsburg.

In the days leading up to the Revolution, he was Philadelphia's go-to person for large public buildings and religious projects.

Interesting Oddities

* The 196-foot tower and steeple Smith added to Christ Church in 1754 made it the tallest building in the thirteen colonies until 1810, and the tallest structure in Philadelphia until 1856.

St. Peter's Church, with its large Palladian window, is one of many area churches designed by Robert Smith. He also designed Carpenters' Hall. (Photo by Jim Murphy.)

- An inventory of Smith's estate reveals that he owned "Sundrey Books of Architecture and Drawing Instrumts"—and three of his precious books are now part of the Carpenters' Hall Library. One was not signed with his name; one he signed, "Robert Smith." The third simply reads, "Rob Smith His Book 1756." All were important to him.

- Smith was called in to reinforce the beautiful Powel House's famous dance floor. He added iron strappings to weight-supporting trusses so that the improved ballroom "could withstand the rhythmic vibrations of dancing feet." George Washington, an excellent dancer, spent much time on that dance floor.

Defending the Delaware River

But probably Smith's most important work was his role in keeping 250 British ships tied up in the Delaware River for about six weeks in late 1777 after British troops invaded Philadelphia.

To make navigation difficult for the British, the Carpenters' Company says that Smith designed and helped install sixty-five chevaux-de-frise—rows of sharpened spikes hidden in the Delaware River. He placed them near the two forts defending the city: Fort Mifflin, or Mud Island, as the British called it, near today's airport; and Fort Mercer on the New Jersey side.

As big as two-story houses, these deadly devices had diagonal strips tipped with iron spears to pierce the bottom of British ships and impale them. Only ten captains of pilot boats knew their locations. Loaded with ballast stones and connected with a chain to keep them in position, the chevaux-de-frise were towed to crucial locations on the bottom of the Delaware.

Smith's devices helped bottle up the British fleet and keep vital munitions and supplies from reaching its troops in Philadelphia. The delay also gave General Washington just enough time to escape to winter quarters at Valley Forge and fight another day.

Unfortunately, Smith's long hours overseeing the building and placement of these devices in frigid conditions along the river may have weakened him. While rushing to complete the building of barracks in December 1776 at Fort Billingsport (current-day Paulsboro, New Jersey), he became ill. Smith died two months later.

So, he never saw the fruits of his military labors.

Fast Facts

Name: Robert Smith
Born: January 14, 1722
Died: February 11, 1777

Buried: In an unmarked grave at the Friends Arch Street Meeting-house Burial Ground

Claim to Fame: The leading master builder in the city during his time

Historical Marker Location: 606 South Second Street

Marker Dedication: January 14, 1983

Nearby Attractions: Old Pine Church, St. Peter's Church, and Hill-Physick House

This updated story first ran in the March 2017 issue of *QVNA Magazine* and is reprinted with permission.

W. E. B. Du Bois

He did a groundbreaking study of *The Philadelphia Negro.*

I wonder what residents of Philadelphia's Seventh Ward, with its large sections of poverty and crime, thought **in August 1896, when they first saw W. E. B. Du Bois stroll into their neighborhood in a top hat and tails to begin his research study of *The Philadelphia Negro.***

Du Bois (pronounced doo-boyz) must have been a remarkable sight in this formal attire. And his house-to-house study of homes between Spruce and South Streets and Seventh Street to the Schuylkill River is still one of the most important sociological research projects ever done.

Started at the request of Susan P. Wharton, a wealthy White Quaker woman who lived at 910 Clinton Street, the two-year project, commissioned by the University of Pennsylvania, was designed to study the city's "Negro problem" and rising crime and disorder in the area.

Du Bois, hired as an "assistant in sociology" by Penn, moved to the Seventh Ward to stay at the Philadelphia College Settlement House near where Starr Garden Playground is today.

"In a residence of eleven months in the centre of the slums, I never was once accosted or insulted," he says. "The ladies of the College Settlement report similar experience. I have seen, however, some strangers here roughly handled."

A Pennsylvania historical marker for W. E. B. Du Bois stands next to Starr Garden Playground along South Sixth Street between Lombard and South Streets. (Photo by Jim Murphy.)

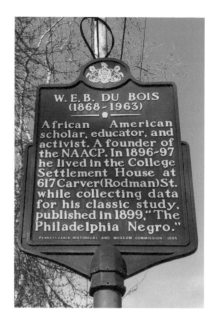

W. E. B. DU BOIS
(1868–1963)

African American scholar, educator, and activist. A founder of the NAACP. In 1896–97 he lived in the College Settlement House at 617 Carver(Rodman)St. while collecting data for his classic study, published in 1899, "The Philadelphia Negro."

PENNSYLVANIA HISTORICAL AND MUSEUM COMMISSION 1995

With the help of Isabel Eaton, an employee of Philadelphia College Settlement, the two researchers interviewed more than five thousand Black inhabitants in a ward where close to ten thousand lived. At the time, Philadelphia's total Black population was about forty thousand.

Du Bois pulled no punches in his questions or his writing, discussing everything from crime to drink, and from family life to the role of Black churches.

In his study and detailed maps, he broke his subjects into four groups: "poor," "working people," "middle class," and the "vicious and criminal class."

Du Bois went door to door with his questions, "prying into private lives," taking ten minutes to an hour at each home, and averaging fifteen to twenty-five minutes per visit. He was only turned down at twelve homes—most of them brothels.

Interesting Oddities

- In a footnote, Du Bois says, "I shall throughout this study use the term 'Negro,' to designate all persons of Negro descent. . . . I shall, moreover, capitalize the word, because I believe that eight million Americans are entitled to a capital letter."
- Amy Hillier, associate professor of social policy and practice at Penn, and her staff have developed a board game, walking tour, curriculum, and video about Du Bois's work. They also were able

to get a colorful mural of Du Bois, the community, and firefighters from the local firehouse placed at Sixth and South Streets. It's worth a visit.

- Du Bois writes about more than twenty qualified "Negroes" (today, we say "Blacks" or "African Americans") unable to get jobs simply because of their color and because White employers believed that "my men will not work with you."

Fortunately, Midvale Steel Works thought otherwise. A manager, identified by Isabel Eaton as "a crank," believed that Black and White people could work together without friction or trouble. He hired 200 Black people in a workforce of 1,200 and spread them through the various work gangs. Black workers did the same grades of work as the White workers, he reported, "and they do it as well as any of the others." The "crank" was later identified in the 1967 edition of the work as Frederick W. Taylor, "the father of scientific management," by famed sociologist E. Digby Baltzell of the University of Pennsylvania.

Despite Du Bois's call for fairness in hiring, too little has changed since he wrote his report. Even with all the construction taking place today in Philadelphia, Black people still are very poorly represented in the building trades unions, says *Philadelphia Magazine*.

Du Bois would be disappointed that color discrimination is still going on—but probably would not be too surprised.

Fast Facts

Name: W. E. B. Du Bois
How He Pronounced It: "Doo-Boyz"
Born: February 23, 1868
Died: August 27, 1963, in Ghana
Claim to Fame: Performed pioneering survey of *The Philadelphia Negro* in 1896–97. He was also a historian, writer, editor, and civil rights activist.
Historical Marker Location: Northwest corner of South Sixth and Rodman Streets
Mural Location: Northwest corner of Sixth and South Streets
Video: https://vimeo.com/22239485: This nineteen-minute documentary discussing Du Bois's research was filmed and edited

by high school and college students at the University of Penn-sylvania and Haverford College.

Nearby Attractions: Mother Bethel Church, Octavius V. Catto his-torical marker at 812 South Street, and Lombard Street Riot historical marker at Sixth and Lombard Streets

This updated story first ran in the May 2018 issue of *QVNA Magazine* and is reprinted with permission.

— Part V —

Mob Rule

20 Bible Riots

Nativist Protestants fought Irish Catholic immigrants here in deadly 1844 clashes.

This is no joke: Some of Philadelphia's **most murderous riots ever were caused by a dispute over a Bible.** How's that for irony?

When the smoke cleared, more than twenty people had been killed, one hundred people injured, two Catholic churches burned to the ground, one church shot at by cannon, businesses and homes destroyed, and many people left homeless.

One church publication said, "Ah! Philadelphia, the city of Brotherly Love, had become in '44 the vestibule of infernal hate."

The controversy began because public schools in Philadelphia routinely began the day with Bible reading. When Roman Catholic Bishop Francis Kenrick asked that Catholic students be allowed to read the Catholic Bible, not the King James Bible, all hell broke loose.

A group of native-born Protestants called nativists (including many fiercely anti-Catholics of Scotch-Irish ancestry—who were also longtime residents of the city) protested that new immigrant Catholics were "Banning the Bible."

Fanning the flames was Lewis C. Levin, a merchant and schoolmaster from South Carolina who owned two nativist newspapers here. Once indicted for attempted murder in Philadelphia, Levin was by many accounts a powerful, brilliant, and unscrupulous orator. Zachary M. Schrag, a professor of history at George Mason University, describes him as a "rabble-rouser, conspiracy theorist, bigot."

In May 1844, Levin, who later became a three-time U.S. Congressman, used his persuasive powers to inflame a gathering near the Nanny Goat Market in Kensington.

Holding a nativist Protestant rally in a heavily Catholic neighborhood seemed like an ideal way to incite a riot—and it worked.

Ken Milano, author of *The Philadelphia Nativist Riots*, told *Hidden City Philadelphia*'s Bradley Maule that it was "akin to the Ku Klux Klan having a rally in the middle of North Philadelphia today."

After one man was killed in the riot, Levin made good use of his newspapers, the Bible, and American flag to promote the cause of "Native Americans" or native-born White people by making the young man a martyr and attacking Philadelphia Catholics.

Here's a sample of his inflammatory rhetoric:

> Armed recruits in aid of the Roman Catholics are pouring in from various neighboring towns! We write at this moment with our garments stained and sprinkled with the blood of victims to Native American rights—the rights of conscience—the rights of persons—the holy safeguards and privileges of freedom. Yes, we write with our garments sprinkled with the precious life-drops of martyrs to freedom. Men murdered with ruthless ferocity, because they dare peacefully to erect that flag, which even foreign Despots have been taught to respect.—*The Sun*

Later, even Levin professed to be distraught by the violence he encouraged. But once you let the genie out of the bottle, it's hard to put it back.

St. Michael's Church in Kensington was burned, along with the rectory, the nunnery, the school, the Nanny Goat Market, Hibernia Hose Company, and sixty Irish Catholic homes and stores, Milano says. St. Augustine's Church and its school at Fourth and Vine Streets were also burned, along with a theological library of three thousand volumes.

In July, nativists attacked St. Philip Neri Church on Queen Street in South Philadelphia with a sixteen-pound cannon. Before that riot ended several days later, twenty were dead and scores more wounded.

Interesting Oddities

- Before the Consolidation Act of 1854 made the boundaries of Philadelphia City and County identical, criminals in William Penn's original city could simply run across South Street or Vine Street and escape. To go after them, first a constable had to call the county sheriff, who then organized a posse in Southwark or Kensington. That wasn't very fast or effective.
- Partly because of the 1844 Bible Riots, Philadelphia consolidated on February 2, 1854, and extended its boundaries from 2 square miles to about 130.

Looking peaceful today, St. Augustine's Church was burned down in 1844 anti-Catholic riots and rebuilt in 1847. More recently, scenes from the movie *The Sixth Sense* were filmed here. (Photo by Jim Murphy.)

- Among the city's goals for consolidation were "an efficient police force" and a "controlled fire department." The first was much easier to achieve than the second, but both eventually occurred.
- Although Levin may have hated Catholics, his wife and child eventually converted to Catholicism.
- Construction on what is now the Cathedral Basilica of Sts. Peter and Paul began just two years after these riots. To prevent broken

windows by anti-Catholic vandals, legend says that the architect and construction workers threw rocks as high as they could. Windows were then placed above that height. Today, though, you will see lower stained-glass windows added during 1955–57 renovations.

After the riots, Philadelphia consolidated its many municipalities into one 130-square-mile territory, with one police force and fire department; Bishop Kenrick, appalled at the hate and destruction, helped the Catholic Church set up its own system of parochial schools.

Fast Facts

Name: Bible Riots
Year Occurred: 1844
Churches Burned Down: St. Michael's in Kensington and St. Augustine's in Old City
Church Fired On by Cannons: St. Philip Neri in Queen Village
Parties Involved: Protestant nativists and Irish Catholic immigrants
Worthwhile Websites: https://exhibits.library.villanova.edu/chaos-in-the-streets-the-philadelphia-riots-of-1844 and https://web.archive.org/web/20070822112107/http://churchofstphilipneri.org/history/NATIVIST%20RIOTS.pdf
Historical Marker Location: St. Augustine's Roman Catholic Church at 235 North Fourth Street
Marker Copy: "First U.S. foundation, Augustinian Order, 1796. In 1844 the original church here was burned during Nativist riots. This and other violence led to a state law requiring police forces, 1845, and to consolidation of the city and county, 1854."
Nearby Attractions: Penn Treaty Park, Ben Franklin Bridge, and Elfreth's Alley

㉑ Lombard Street Riot

This terrible battle showed a deep racial divide in Philadelphia.
Mix two races and cultures competing for the city's lowest-paying jobs. Cram them together in dark living conditions. Add emotional calls to abolish slavery . . . and equally powerful defenders of this horrible practice. Bring to a boil. Then, watch the neighborhood blow.

Those were some of the sources fueling **a three-day riot that erupted on August 1, 1842, between Irish immigrants and African American residents**. A Pennsylvania historical marker on Lombard Street near Sixth Street pinpoints where the fighting began.

This struggle was not the first between the two groups, either. The city experienced riots in 1820, 1829, 1834, 1835, 1838, 1842, and 1849, says the Encyclopedia of American Race Riots.

This time, more than one thousand Black people took part in a temperance parade commemorating the eighth anniversary of slavery's abolition in the West Indies.

At one point, says the newsletter of the Preservation Alliance for Greater Philadelphia, the marchers held up a banner depicting a Black man breaking his chains. It read: "How grand in age, how fair in truth, are holy Friendship, Love, and Truth."

Doesn't seem too provocative. But White Irish bystanders thought the picture represented the 1804 Haiti massacre of three to five thousand White people in Santo Domingo. Suddenly, they began attacking the marchers near the public market at Sixth and Lombard Streets.

The mob beat many of the marchers, looted Black homes in the area, and continued the assault for three days. During it, they burned down the Second African Presbyterian Church as well as Smith's Hall. The latter building had served as the site of abolition lectures after Pennsylvania Hall—a beautiful new abolition meetinghouse—had been burned down by rioters days after it opened in 1838.

The rioters then headed for the home of Robert Purvis at Ninth and Lombard Streets. An outspoken leader of the local Vigilance Committee and known for being a friend of fugitives, Purvis helped 163 Black people flee to freedom in just nine months that year via the Underground Railroad.

On the first day of the riot, Purvis "sat on the staircase of his

This marker by the Pennsylvania Historical and Museum Commission is the first in Philadelphia to have the word "riot" in the title. It's located at Sixth and Lombard Streets. (Photo by Jim Murphy.)

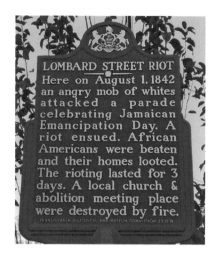

LOMBARD STREET RIOT
Here on August 1, 1842 an angry mob of whites attacked a parade celebrating Jamaican Emancipation Day. A riot ensued. African Americans were beaten and their homes looted. The rioting lasted for 3 days. A local church & abolition meeting place were destroyed by fire.
PENNSYLVANIA HISTORICAL AND MUSEUM COMMISSION 2005 Ⓑ

house, facing the front door, armed with guns and pistols and prepared to shoot the first intruder."

A Catholic priest helped stop the crowd that time. Later, when the local sheriff said he could no longer offer protection, Purvis fled to his home in Bucks County, "shaken to his core."

The riot ended only after the mayor called out seven militia companies with more than one thousand troops.

Interesting Oddity

The Lombard Street Riot historical marker actually arose from a high school homework assignment. Teacher Amy Cohen directed her contemporary issues class at the Julia R. Masterman School to research past city race riots. Why? "They were important, rarely acknowledged events in our city's history."

Cohen wanted her students to petition for a state marker. So she asked them: "Isn't it strange that when you look for historical markers about the Underground Railroad, you can find them? But why no markers about the riots?"

The students prepared nominations for two riots: the Lombard Street Riot and the Kensington Nanny Goat Market Riot in 1844. The first was accepted by the state.

At the marker's dedication in 2005, Cohen told *Philadelphia Weekly*, "It's exciting for the students to see that their work in school really had an impact. This will be here forever."

Cohen's interest in Philadelphia's past continues. She now works for History Making Productions, a documentary film company that explores Philadelphia history.

Fast Facts

Name: Lombard Street Riot

Dates: August 1–3, 1842

Historical Marker Location: Southeast corner of Sixth and Lombard Streets

Dedication Date: November 23, 2005

Marker Text: "Here on August 1, 1842 an angry mob of Whites attacked a parade celebrating Jamaican Emancipation Day. A riot ensued. African Americans were beaten and their homes looted. The rioting lasted for three days. A local church & abolition meeting place were destroyed by fire."

Claim to Fame: Of more than three hundred Philadelphia historical markers erected by the Pennsylvania Historical and Museum Commission, this is the first to have the word "riot" in the title.

Nearby Attractions: Mother Bethel Church, *Mapping Courage* mural at Sixth and South Streets, Octavius V. Catto historical marker at 812 South Street, and Philadelphia's Magic Gardens

This updated story first ran in the January 2018 issue of *QVNA Magazine* and is reprinted with permission.

⊹ Part VI ⊹

In the Neighborhoods

22 Ninth Street Market (aka the Italian Market)

It's still changing after all these years.
Domenick Crimi has been part of Philadelphia's South Ninth Street Italian Market for almost his entire life.

In fact, his earliest market memory is from about age five. His job was to sit on the steps outside his parents' shop and sell shopping bags with his brother. The boys weren't allowed to go past the steps. Before he was ten, though, Crimi says, "Everyone on the street knew me."

Many of them still do. While he completely left the family business for about two years, he's back now at Cappuccio's Meats as general manager, plus as president of the United Merchants of the South Ninth Street Business Association. And he's pleased with his decision.

Crimi's family's shop at 1019 South Ninth Street, where I met to talk with him about the market, is like a meat museum. His grandparents opened a butcher shop here in 1920. Most of the rails used to move the meat overhead, as well as the butcher blocks and floors in the store, are original.

The Ninth Street Market began in the 1880s, soon after Antonio Palumbo, an Italian immigrant, opened a boarding house at 824 Catharine Street. According to street legend, many of the arriving Italian immigrants wore tags addressing them to Palumbo's.

Businesses quickly began serving this fast-growing community. The market looked very much like those in Sicily, Crimi says. Now, it's what the business association claims is **the largest, continuous outdoor market in the country, complete with appetizing aromas, colorful awnings, and distinctive fire barrels.**

Interesting Oddities

- Outsiders call this the Italian Market, Crimi says. Old-timers refer to it as Ninth Street. The name "Italian Market" was a late 1960s and 1970s marketing tool.
- New Yorkers ask him for "chopped beef." Philadelphians want "ground beef."

The distinctive Ninth Street Market, commonly referred to as the Italian Market, is known for wonderful food, great aromas, and fire barrels that provide warmth in the winter. (Photo by Jim Murphy.)

- Sylvester Stallone's turnaround-catch of an orange in the Italian Market during the first *Rocky* film was unplanned, says the Internet Movie Database (IMDb.com). The fruit-stand employee who threw it had no idea the van and the runner were part of a soon-to-be-famous movie.
- The Ninth Street Market always included a variety of nationalities and ethnicities. From its earliest days, Jewish merchants sold clothing and jewelry, and the Italians dealt mostly meat, fruits, and vegetables.

Today, the mix of stores includes Jewish, Italian, Mexican, Korean, and Vietnamese options, and even a French restaurant or two. The merchants work six days a week, from curb spots and indoor shops. Some take Mondays off.

The market changed dramatically in the 1980s. Korean merchants arrived with actual suitcases of cash and began buying up whole corners of the market. Third-generation merchants, with no one to leave their businesses to—and tired of being open in the cold and heat seven days a week—got "palm trees in their eyes," took the money, and went to Florida, Crimi says.

Of the many Mexican merchants in today's market, he says, "They work their asses off, warm in the summer and freezing in the winter. They are like the Italians and the Irish one hundred years ago. They are out there hustling."

The meat business is tough now, he says. "Fifty grocery stores are selling meat for less than I pay for it." The good news: "We are getting millennials to come back. They want to know where their meats are from."

His goal is to keep the market relevant and to bring back any lost business. To help, many of the market's merchants now offer online ordering, local delivery for the same price as in-store purchases, and also free food pickup.

While Crimi ran his own professional photography studio for fifteen years and also was employed by Aramark, he continued working part-time in the butcher shop. He even met his wife, Maria, at the market, marrying her some twenty-eight years after first eyeing her at a local store.

Crimi believes that his grandfather called him back to the Ninth Street Market. "No one was ready to take over, but me," he says. The move back "also served my grandfather, my idol, in many ways."

And Crimi is happy to be back. "I love it. The business and the people."

Fast Facts

Association Name: United Merchants of the South Ninth Street Business Association

Boundaries: Eighth, Ninth, and Tenth Streets, with Fitzwater Street on the north and Wharton Street on the south

Number of Blocks Included: Twenty

Year Market Started: Late 1880s
Year Association Began: 1915
Number of Businesses at the Market: More than two hundred
Hours: Tuesday through Sunday; more than half of the merchants are open Monday
Visitor Center and Gift Shop: 919 South Ninth Street
Phone: 215-278-2903
Website: www.italianmarketphilly.org
Walking Tour Map: www.italianmarketphilly.org/map.html
Movie and TV Fame: The market appears in the movies *Rocky*, *Rocky II*, and *Trading Places* and in the TV shows *Hack* and *It's Always Sunny in Philadelphia*.
Nearby Attractions: St. Mary Magdalen de Pazzi Church and St. Paul's Catholic Church, both helped by the market's "Give Back Wednesday" fundraising programs; Pat's Steaks, and Geno's Steaks, both at Ninth and Wharton Streets; Jim's Steaks at Fourth and South Streets

23 Chinatown

It's small in area but large in impact.

Life in Philly's Chinatown has always been challenging. And it's likely to stay that way.

With Chinatown's population jumping 143 percent from 1990 to 2010, the need for affordable housing grew too. Yet buyers attracted to Callowhill Street are driving up real-estate prices north of traditional Chinatown and gentrifying the neighborhood. And the new, nearby Rail Park is expected to magnify that pressure as well.

Chinatown's big challenge is to remain a hub for its expanding Asian American community and retain its current feel and character; provide reasonable housing for both lower-income immigrants and older residents; and entice millennials moving in near Callowhill Street to become regular customers at its restaurants, shops, and stores.

Not an easy task. But then, life's never been easy in Chinatown.

Sure, neighborhood protests in the 1960s, 1970s, and 1980s delayed and eventually reduced the size of the Vine Street Expressway, saving their Catholic Church and school from the wrecking

The colorful Friendship Gate at Tenth and Arch Streets lets you know you're in Philadelphia's Chinatown. Forty feet high and weighing eighty tons, it was constructed by artisans from Tianjin, China, a sister city of Philadelphia. (Photo by Jim Murphy.)

ball. Residents also founded the Philadelphia Chinatown Development Corporation (PCDC) and, with the help of Asian Americans United, fought off a federal prison near the school, a baseball stadium, a casino near Market Street, and more.

Despite these apparent neighborhood wins, the city still sliced five blocks from Chinatown's tiny footprint, leaving it with about seven.

That's probably why current residents talk about being "hemmed in" and "in a cage." And it's why the PCDC opened a twenty-story Crane Chinatown apartment tower and community center in Chinatown North—an area just above its former commonly accepted boundary of Vine Street.

Chased from the west by White anti-immigrant labor leaders after completing the Transcontinental Railroad in 1869, some Chinese laborers ended up here in Philadelphia. Records say that Lee Fong opened the first laundry in Chinatown in 1870, on the 900 block of Race Street, near where a Pennsylvania historical marker is now located.

But life here still was not easy. Many of these laborers left wives back in China while they tried to profit from the gold rush. And after the Chinese Exclusion Act of 1882—which barred existing Chinese residents from becoming naturalized and kept new ones from entering—these men were doomed to a life of bachelorhood here. Most would never see their wives again . . . or ever marry in the United States.

Interesting Oddities

- The Holy Redeemer Chinese Catholic Church and School, dedicated in 1945, "was the first Catholic Church for Chinese in the Western Hemisphere, and the first school in Chinatown," says Kathryn E. Wilson, author of *Ethnic Renewal in Philadelphia's Chinatown* (published by Temple University Press).
- Philadelphia police made their first gambling raid in Chinatown in August 1882, arresting Fong and his cousin for running an illegal gambling house. It wouldn't be the last. Until the Chinatown community vehemently protested a planned casino at Eighth and Market Streets, I didn't know the Asian American community suffered from a particular gambling problem. But Dr. Timothy Fong, co-director of the UCLA Gambling Studies Program, says the gambling addiction rate ranges from 6 to nearly 60 percent among Asians in the United States, with Southeast Asian refugees at the top. The national rate is 1 to 2 percent.
- Cecilia Moy Yep, a widow and mother of three children, organized Chinatown's first community meeting in 1966. Her goal: Save Holy Redeemer Church and School. Later, when the Phila-

delphia Redevelopment Authority began clearing her block for a Ninth Street ramp to Market East, Yep refused to leave. "I was the only house standing on the whole block from Race to Filbert, from Ninth to Eighth," she says. Even after construction crews piled up mounds of dirt around her house, broke her furnace flue, and almost asphyxiated her family, she stayed. Eventually, Yep, who helped found the PCDC, was forced to move. But she and Chinatown enjoyed some key successes: The Vine Street Expressway was modified, and the Ninth Street ramp was abandoned. Today, Yep is the PCDC's executive director emeritus.

Going forward, one big question remains: How will converting the defunct Reading Railroad viaduct into an elevated rail park affect Chinatown? Will it help or hurt?

The rail park's website says 32 percent of the land around the viaduct remains vacant and undeveloped. If some of that space becomes affordable housing for lower-income Asian Americans, the rail park could be a real boon to Chinatown.

The eventual answer will probably be both interesting and challenging.

Fast Facts

Name: Philadelphia's Chinatown
Year Started: About 1870
Language: Mostly Mandarin or Fujianese today; earlier, Toisanese and Cantonese
Cultures: Hong Kong, Cantonese, Fujianese, Northern Sichuan, Taiwanese, Korean, Thai, Malaysian, Burmese, and Vietnamese influences, says cranechinatown.com
Nearby Attractions: Local Chinese murals: *The History of Chinatown* at 239 North Tenth Street and *House of Dragons Salutes* at 133 North Tenth Street; the rail park entrance on Callowhill between Tenth and Eleventh Streets; and the Reading Terminal Market

24 Philadelphia's LGBT Community

In seventy years, it's gone from "the Furtive Fraternity" to the high-profile "Gayborhood."

Since the 1950s and early 1960s, life has changed greatly for Philadelphia's gay community.

So says Bob Skiba, author of *The Philadelphia Gayborhood Guru* blog and archivist at the William Way LGBT Community Center. *Hidden City Philadelphia* calls William Way the city's largest and oldest lesbian, gay, bisexual, and transgender (LGBT) organization. Skiba is also a past president and a founding member of the Association of Philadelphia Tour Guides.

While Skiba did not arrive in Philly until 1999, he's meticulously researched and written widely about the local LGBT community. And he's seen a lot of changes.

This is a partial view of a huge mural titled *Pride and Progress* that covers the entire west wall of the William Way LGBT Community Center. (Photo by Bob Skiba. Mural, *Pride and Progress*, copyright 2003 by artist Ann Northrup and Mural Arts Philadelphia.)

Today, "the Gayborhood" stretches from Eleventh to Broad Streets and Walnut to Pine Streets and is adorned with seventy-two "rainbow" signs indicating LGBT identity and solidarity. Philadelphia's LGBT community members are highly visible, often outspoken, and politically active. They hold well-publicized gay pride parades, are changing the system, and are even targets for major advertising campaigns.

But it was not always this way. In earlier days, LGBT community members feared arrest and harassment, especially under vehemently anti-gay Frank Rizzo, Philadelphia's mayor from 1972 to 1980.

They became more visible after passage of the Philadelphia 1982 Gay Non-Discrimination Ordinance, also known as Bill 1358. That law showed that gay rights were as important as African American rights, Skiba says. The result of a strong grassroots effort, it "was a big tipping point for us."

In 2008, Philadelphia created the Office of LGBT Affairs to support the community and act as a liaison with it.

Other Major Philly LGBT Milestones

- December 1962: *Greater Philadelphia Magazine* focuses on the gay community in "The Furtive Fraternity." Skiba calls this the first article by a major U.S. publication to highlight a city's gay population.
- April 25, 1965: When what the Janus Society calls "a large number of homosexuals and persons wearing non-conformist clothing" are refused service at a Dewey's restaurant near Rittenhouse Square, the crowd begins protesting; three unidentified teens who refused to leave are arrested. After eight days of picketing and other protests, the restaurant starts serving LGBT customers again. This incident is four full years before the Stonewall riots began at a gay club in New York in June 1969— which history.com calls the "first major protest on behalf of equal rights for homosexuals."
- 1965 to 1969: Protesters from Philadelphia, New York, and Washington, D.C., picket for homosexual rights on July 4 "Reminder Days" outside Independence Hall four years in a row.
- 1972: Ten thousand people take part in Philly's first Gay Pride demonstration. Their march goes from Rittenhouse Square to Independence Mall.

- 1973: Giovanni's Room, reportedly America's oldest gay bookstore, opens at 232 South Street. Named for a James Baldwin gay novel, the store closes for a time in 2014 and reopens four months later as Philly AIDS Thrift @ Giovanni's Room.
- 1976: Mark Segal begins publishing the *Philadelphia Gay News*. That same year, the Gay Community Center of Philadelphia opens at 326 Kater Street. Now called the William Way Community Center, it moves several times and then settles at a building at 1315 Spruce Street in 1997, where it is today. The well-known mural *Pride and Progress* takes up the entire west wall of the William Way Center.
- 1981: Woody's Bar, 202 South Thirteenth Street, named for former owner Bill Wood when it opens, is the first gay bar with windows, Skiba says. Before that, gays didn't want to be seen from the street. One reason: Rizzo, first the police commissioner and then mayor of Philadelphia, routinely raided gay bars and arrested those inside.
- 1995: David Warner, editor of the *City Paper*, writes a headline describing the Outfest—which marks National Coming Out Day—as "a beautiful day in the Gayborhood." The name sticks. And the Gayborhood has become a well-known area of Philadelphia.

Seeing a need to provide low- to moderate-income housing for elderly gays in Philly, *Philadelphia Gay News* publisher Mark Segal accomplished that in 2014. The John C. Anderson Apartments at 251 South Thirteenth Street now provide fifty-six LGBT-friendly units, a community room, and an outdoor courtyard.

What's next for the LGBT community here? Probably a lot. Stay tuned.

Fast Facts

Name: The William Way LGBT Community Center (formerly the Gay Community Center of Philadelphia)
Founded: 1975
Named For: William Way, a city planner, driving force behind the center, and one of the first high-level citizens to disclose that he had AIDS
Address: 1315 Spruce Street

Phone: 215-732-2220

Website: www.waygay.org

Hours: Monday through Friday, noon to 9 P.M.; Saturday and Sunday, noon to 5 P.M.

Services: Confidential and free peer counseling, thirty recovery meetings hosted weekly, library with fourteen thousand LGBT-oriented books and DVDs, John J. Wilcox Jr. Archives

Nearby Attractions: Kimmel Center, Academy of Music, and Avenue of the Arts

Part VII

Hidden in Plain Sight

25 *Ars Medendi*

Mysterious sculptures at Thomas Jefferson University will intrigue and engage you.

If you like word puzzles, riddles, or enigmas, take a walk down Walnut Street near Tenth in Center City. You'll be right in your element.

Just go past the *Winged Ox* sculpture to the western side of Thomas Jefferson University's Scott Memorial Library, and you'll come across an unusual copper cylinder with letters punched out of it.

If you're like me, once you notice the sculpture, you'll be fascinated by it, and by a companion trapezoidal wall on the west side of Tenth Street closer to Locust Street.

The cylinder is interactive, interesting, and enigmatic (maybe to the point of being a little infuriating). But chances are you'll take a little extra time to look at the sculpture and try to understand the artist's purpose.

Titled *Ars Medendi*, Latin for "the Medical Art," both pieces were created by Jim Sanborn and contain historic texts from world medicine.

Sanborn is best known for *Kryptos*, a copper wall at CIA Headquarters in Langley, Virginia. It contains a secret code that has taunted codebreakers for more than twenty years.

In *Ars Medendi*, letters on both the cylinder and the wall represent a variety of alphabets and languages. The cylinder's letters run backward and forward at the seams, and you can look through the cylinder and read them in either direction.

When the cylinder is illuminated at night, the letters are projected both onto the wall of the library building and onto the ground, creating a dramatically different effect from daytime.

The wall's text is easier to understand, and there is a bench nearby for comfortable contemplation. Both sculptures remind me a bit of photos I've seen of the Rosetta Stone or Hammurabi's Code. There's information to be gained there, but it certainly takes some work.

The cylinder includes sections from the human genome code and names of rain-forest plants, plus quotes from Louis Pasteur, Ivan Pavlov, Galen, and more. The wall offers advice from Pliny the

Intriguing and infuriating, the *Ars Medendi* cylinder by Jim Sanborn near Eleventh and Walnut Streets contains historic texts from world medicine. (© Thomas Jefferson University Photography Services.)

Elder, Leonardo da Vinci, Dr. Samuel Gross, Qibo, *Gray's Anatomy*, and the Seneca Nation, among others.

Interestingly, other than a local blog (*Ornamento* by Martha Aleo), two minimal references by Thomas Jefferson University, and some photos on Flickr, there is almost nothing about these sculptures anywhere on the web.

It's almost as if they don't exist.

Sanborn's own website simply lists "Thomas Jefferson University, Philadelphia, PA" among his Selected Public Collections. To quote Winston Churchill—who was, of course, speaking about Russia and not about *Ars Medendi*—the work is "a riddle, wrapped in a mystery, inside an enigma."

A search does show that Thomas Jefferson University commissioned the sculptures in cooperation with the Redevelopment Authority of the City of Philadelphia One Percent for Public Art Program in 2006.

Mysterious as they may be, interacting with these "word" sculptures is a unique experience. You can actually see right through them.

And at the very least, you may want to take a few extra moments to really look at words and the meanings they convey—on something other than a smartphone or computer screen.

There's actual wisdom to be gained here—letter by letter, word by word—in a nondigital medium. What a concept!

Fast Facts

Artwork: *Ars Medendi* (the Medical Art)
Artist: Jim Sanborn
Location: Campus of Thomas Jefferson University
Number of Sculptures: Two
Cylinder: East side of Eleventh Street, on Walnut Street
Screen: West side of Tenth Street, midway between Walnut and Locust Streets
Other Important Work by Artist: *Kryptos*, an encrypted sculpture at CIA Headquarters in Langley, Virginia
Nearby Attractions: Washington Square, PSFS Building, and Reading Terminal Market

This updated story first ran in the January/February 2012 issue of the *Society Hill Reporter* and is reprinted with permission.

26 *The Dream Garden* Tiffany Mosaic

This spectacular glass mosaic is on display in the lobby of a Center City building, not locked away in a museum.
If you're traveling anywhere in Center City near Independence Hall, take a few minutes to treat yourself to something really special.

Walk into the lobby of the Curtis on Sixth Street, between Chestnut and Walnut, and feast your eyes on *The Dream Garden*.

One of the most famous glass mosaics in the world, the shimmering masterpiece is a collaborative effort of two creative geniuses. Noted local artist Maxfield Parrish created the design.

Don't miss this extraordinary mosaic at the Curtis—*The Dream Garden* by Maxfield Parrish and Tiffany Studios. (Courtesy of the Pennsylvania Academy of the Fine Arts, Philadelphia. Partial bequest of John W. Merriam; partial purchase with funds provided by a grant from The Pew Charitable Trusts; partial gift of Bryn Mawr College, The University of the Arts, and The Trustees of the University of Pennsylvania.)

Louis Comfort Tiffany of Tiffany Studios executed it, using special iridescent favrile glass he patented.

As *Inquirer* art critic Edward J. Sozanski said, the scene "more closely resembles a densely vegetated mountain landscape than a garden."

To me, it looks like a beautiful sun-covered mountain scene, with trees, flowers, walkways, a waterfall, and more.

Be sure to notice the theatrical masks in the foreground. The nearby marker says they "evoke Parrish's love of theatre and lend the character of a stage to this ideal landscape."

Reportedly, the painting was inspired by real gardens at the Oaks, Parrish's summer home in Cornish, New Hampshire.

Measuring fifteen by forty-nine feet and weighing nearly four tons, the huge masterpiece includes more than 100,000 pieces of iridescent glass in 260 colors set in 24 panels. Installation alone took more than six months.

Cyrus Curtis, head of Curtis Publishing Company, and Edward W. Bok, then senior editor, commissioned the work to highlight the company's new headquarters. It was unveiled in 1916.

Curtis, owner of *Ladies Home Journal*, the *Saturday Evening Post*, and other enormously popular magazines, was one of the most successful publishers of the early twentieth century. His extraordinary building also includes a two-story marble fountain, terraced waterfall, and twelve-story atrium with faux-Egyptian palm trees.

On a gray January morning, with ice and snow everywhere and no bright colors visible anywhere, I ducked into the Curtis (formerly the Curtis Center) to see *The Dream Garden* for the first time in years.

The dazzling mosaic made me feel like I was at the Philadelphia Flower Show. It also reminded me that the unusually severe winter we were experiencing at the time would actually end some day.

Interesting Oddities

* According to the lobby's informational marker, Parrish, a fabulously successful commercial artist, was the fourth person asked to create the design. The first three died.
* Parrish was generally considered to be America's highest-paid artist in the mid-1920s. According to the *New York Times*, the House of Art, a New York printing company, estimated that a lithograph of Parrish's painting *Daybreak* could be found in one of every four American homes.
* While many people praise the collaboration between Parrish and Tiffany, their interaction evidently was more tumultuous behind the scenes. The website ushistory.org says, "Parrish complained that Tiffany's translation of his design lacked subtlety and 'painterliness.'" Tiffany, on the other hand, believed that Parrish's design sketches were technically vague.

In 1998, Philadelphia almost lost the work when John Merriam, owner of the mural, died. His estate agreed to sell it to casino owner Steve Wynn, who planned to move the piece to one of his casinos in Las Vegas.

Fortunately, the Pew Charitable Trusts, with the help of four local institutions that donated their interests from the estate, purchased *The Dream Garden* for $3.5 million. The Pennsylvania Academy of the Fine Arts is now the permanent owner and custodian, and the mosaic will remain in its original location.

That would please Cyrus Curtis, who wanted art to be accessible to the general public "in their workplace and their everyday lives rather than in museums."

So, see this gorgeous work for yourself—absolutely free. It's got to be the most beautiful bargain in town.

Fast Facts

Name: *The Dream Garden*
Address: The Curtis, 601 Walnut Street; closest entrance is on Sixth Street, between Chestnut and Walnut
Hours: Open daily for mosaic viewing, 7 A.M. to 10 P.M.
Created: 1914–15

Artist: Maxfield Parrish
Mosaic: Executed by Louis Comfort Tiffany
Size: Fifteen by forty-nine feet
Number of Pieces of Glass: One hundred thousand
Number of Colors: 260
Weight: Almost four tons
Nearby Attractions: John Barry Statue, Second Bank of the United
    States, and American Philosophical Society

This updated story first ran in the May/June 2014 issue of the *Society Hill
Reporter* and is reprinted with permission.

Independence National Historical Park

Explore these famous sites where our country really began.
Whether you're a visitor or Philadelphia resident, here are two suggestions:

* If you haven't been to Independence Hall and the Liberty Bell
  recently, spend some quality time there now at Independence
  National Historical Park (INHP). You'll better understand the
  dangers and difficulties involved in starting this new nation.
* Then see all the other interesting things this twenty-block,
  fifty-five-acre, history-packed park has to offer. There's something here for everyone.

    Don't miss the statue of John Barry behind Independence Hall.
He's a naval hero who captured three ships with barges during the
British occupation of Philadelphia, mortifying that country's leaders. Also of interest are Franklin Court, where Ben Franklin, our
inventor extraordinaire, lived; and Congress Hall, where the first
peaceful exchange of power under the new U.S. Constitution took
place on March 4, 1797.
    Plus, see the Second Bank of the United States—its marvel-
ous portraits make our country's founders come to life; the Pres-

Independence Hall, the first UNESCO World Heritage Site in the United States, is where both the Declaration of Independence and the U.S. Constitution were debated and adopted. It's a must-see. (Photo by Jim Murphy.)

ident's House, where one of George Washington's slaves escaped; and Christ Church, which displays William Penn's marvelous six-hundred-year-old octagonal walnut baptismal font.

Why did America start in Philly? In part, because of our two superstars: Penn and Ben. First, William Penn had turned the "howling wilderness" he founded in 1682 into the largest, most cultured, and most important city in the colonies by 1770.

Then, Ben Franklin improved just about everything he touched: helping found America's first subscription library, first public hospital, and Philly's first volunteer fire company; inventing the lightning rod, bifocals, the armonica, and the Franklin stove; and doing so much more. Unfortunately, Penn and Ben missed meeting by about twenty years. But together, they left a huge legacy for us to examine and enjoy.

Interesting Oddities

- Even the Liberty Bell owes its existence to William Penn. The Assembly of Pennsylvania ordered the bell to celebrate the fiftieth anniversary of Penn's Charter of Privileges. This pioneering document laid out the rights and duties of Philadelphia's citizens and provided religious freedom for all—without the heavy religious tax common in many other colonies.

- Independence Hall was not immediately treasured by our young country. Several times in the early 1800s, the Pennsylvania Assembly wanted to sell the former state house or tear it down. Finally, the city stepped in and bought the building from the state for $70,000 in 1818. Fortunately, it was still standing when the Marquis de Lafayette visited the city and referred to the structure as "the Hall of Independence." That's when we really started to treasure it.

- Here's something almost no one knows: The already damaged Liberty Bell received an "additional crack" during its 1893 trip to the World's Columbian Exposition. That info comes from the National Register of Historic Places Nomination Form submitted by INHP on March 3, 1988.

- The Centennial Bell—which replaced the cracked Liberty Bell on July 4, 1876, and rings loudly on the hour in Independence Hall's tower today—itself was recast at least once, and possibly twice. The thirteen-thousand-pound-bell, representing the thirteen original colonies, includes metal from cannons from Revolutionary War and Civil War battles. The INHP Nomination Form says it also includes metal from cannons from the War of 1812, Seminole War, and Mexican War. This bell was donated by Henry Seybert, a Philadelphia scientist and philanthropist.

- Several sites at INHP are privately owned. Among them are Carpenters' Hall, Christ Church, and the American Philosophical Society.

How Big a Gamble Was It for the Thirteen Colonies to Declare Independence from Britain in 1776?

A huge one. We openly defied the most powerful nation on Earth, which had an army that historian David McCullough says was "bigger than the entire population of the largest city in the country"—which was then Philadelphia.

The United States started with virtually no army and no navy, went up against the greatest naval power in the world, and won! It was a gutsy move. Thank goodness, it paid off.

For an online copy of the *Historic Philadelphia Gazette* that lists all the current doings at INHP, go to historicphiladelphia.org and click on the newsletter's image on the right.

For a calendar of special events, go to nps.gov/inde/planyour visit/calendar.htm.

Free daily twilight tours are offered by Independence Historical Trust volunteer guides from Memorial Day through Labor Day. To take one, just stop at the Independence Visitor Center Ranger Desk at 6 P.M. Go to inht.org/events-and-programs/ for information.

Fast Facts

Independence Visitor Center Address: 599 Market Street
Phone: 800-537-7676
National Park: Independence National Historical Park
Formally Established: July 4, 1956
Size: Fifty-five acres, with about twenty open colonial buildings in twenty blocks
Number of Buildings Destroyed to Create Independence Mall: About five hundred, mostly Victorian buildings
Number of Annual Visitors to INHP: 4,576,456 (2018 statistics)
Surprising Fact: Independence Hall was once the site of an old Native American camp, says Charlene Mires in *Independence Hall in American Memory*.
INHP Website: nps.gov/inde/siteindex.htm
Claim to Fame: Independence Hall became a UNESCO World Heritage Site in 1979; Philadelphia became the country's first World Heritage City in 2015.
Nearby Attractions: *The Dream Garden*, Pennsylvania Hospital, and Old St. Joseph's Church

28 *Irish Memorial*

The city's largest bronze work is still unknown to many residents.
It's early morning at Front and Chestnut Streets in Old City. And if you're not looking for it, you could easily pass right by Philadelphia's powerful and poignant tribute to the millions of Irish

The Irish Memorial, the largest bronze work in Philadelphia, commemorates the Great Hunger of 1845. It will be moved for several years while the city places a cap over I-95 between Chestnut and Walnut Streets. Work on the cap project is expected to start in late 2021. (Photo by Jim Murphy. Printed with permission of the Irish Memorial Board of Directors.)

immigrants who fled in "coffin ships" to the United States between 1845 and 1850—and to the million others who died in Ireland.

But look east toward the Delaware River and suddenly, out of the morning mist, you see them: **thirty-five larger-than-life figures making up the monumental *Irish Memorial* sculpted by Glenna Goodacre.**

The *Association of Philadelphia Tour Guides Handbook* says the massive memorial, which commemorates "An Gorta Mor," or the Great Hunger of 1845–50, is the largest bronze work in Philadelphia.

Walk closer and move around the "wedge" that's about twelve feet high, thirty feet long, and twelve feet wide, and you'll see the story of the Irish migration in a nutshell: the famine, sickness, and starvation; the immigrants leaving Ireland; and finally, the weary but hopeful travelers stepping onto American soil in Philadelphia.

Creator Glenna Goodacre, who beat out more than one hundred other artists to win the sculpture commission for the *Irish Memorial*, is also known for two other important works: the *Vietnam*

Women's Memorial on the Mall in Washington, D.C., and the bas-relief of Sacagawea, the Shoshone woman who interpreted for Lewis and Clark, on the U.S. dollar.

A native of Lubbock, Texas, who died in 2020, Goodacre said on LubbockOnline: "I wanted the monument to invite people to walk around it. So many people have picked out a face here or one there and told me it looks like their Uncle Jack or Aunt Sue."

(To me, the figure welcoming the immigrants to Philadelphia looks like a younger version of former U.S. Senator Teddy Kennedy.)

After Goodacre created the "impressionistic" characters in a "mock monument" with six-inch-tall figures, a California company enlarged it sixteen times and set the figures in Styrofoam. Using seven tons of clay, Glenna and assistants in Santa Fe then sculpted the original.

Art Castings of Colorado cast it in four hundred interlocking chunks of bronze, welded them together, and then patinaed and transported the sculpture to Philadelphia in one huge thirty-foot piece. Two satellite figures were attached to the base at installation.

The resilient silicon bronze is easy to maintain and repair, according to the *Irish Memorial*'s website. The dark patina added to the bronze, along with a touch of green, will grow deeper over the years.

Placed near the memorial are eight "information stations" or kiosks. While they provide a great deal of useful history, the engraved stations are hard to read (depending on the light) and appear to be placed in a rather random order.

The kiosks note that many of the Irish who came here were rural, uneducated people thrust into an unwelcoming city. Yet they continued to come in great numbers.

By 1850, 18 percent of Philadelphia's population were Irish. These new immigrants did the dirtiest jobs: digging canals and tunnels, building railroads and bridges, tending furnaces, and more.

Interesting Oddities

- The potato blight that decimated the Irish crop originated in North America and traveled to Europe, not the other way around.
- While five hundred thousand Irish people were dying of starvation and disease, Queen Victoria's troops in 1847 took millions

of pounds worth of food at gunpoint from Ireland and shipped it to England.

- Some 263 natives of Ireland would go on to win the Congressional Medal of Honor, more than from any other foreign country.

Unfortunately, even though the *Irish Memorial* is just blocks away from two other important local sites—the *Korean War Memorial* and the *Philadelphia Vietnam Veterans Memorial*—many area residents I spoke to don't even know it exists.

Yet the lessons the memorial teaches us are meaningful: Immigrants can come here, triumph over tragedy, and use their innate talents in a free country.

As the last information panel puts it so well: "We must be mindful that prejudice still exists, especially toward newly arrived immigrants. Let this memorial serve as a beacon of hope to all who come here. To them we say in greeting: 'Céad míle fáilte!' One hundred thousand welcomes!"

Fast Facts

Name: *Irish Memorial*
Location: Southeast corner of Front and Chestnut Streets
Cost: About $3 million
Park Size: 1.75 acres
Sculptor: Glenna Goodacre, who died in 2020
Opened to Public: October 25, 2003
Number of Informational Plaques: Eight
Admission: No charge
Open: 365 days a year
Website: www.irishmemorial.org
Nearby Attractions: *Philadelphia Vietnam Veterans Memorial, Korean War Memorial, Beirut Memorial, Scottish Memorial,* and the Seaport Museum

This updated story first ran in the September/October 2011 issue of the *Society Hill Reporter* and is reprinted with permission.

29 Mason-Dixon Survey

Their line eventually marked the boundary between the North and the South.

Imagine how difficult it would be to hack your way through 316 miles of wilderness—233 miles east to west, and 83 miles north to south—to accurately determine a crucial border. Then, think how much harder it would've been to do so in the 1760s, without precise modern equipment and a Global Positioning System.

Now you know how extraordinary a task it was for astronomer Charles Mason and surveyor Jeremiah Dixon to develop the Mason-Dixon Line. **Their work defined the border between Pennsylvania and Maryland.** After the Missouri Compromise, it also became the boundary between the North and the South.

A lot of importance rode on the accuracy of their remarkable work.

Pennsylvania and Maryland had battled over their border since King Charles II gave William Penn the colony in 1681.

The problem was that a twelve-mile circle around the city of New Castle made the stated boundaries and location of the fortieth parallel and Maryland's northern border unclear and inaccurate.

If Lord Baltimore (or Charles Calvert, head of the colony of Maryland) got his way, Philadelphia would become "one of the prettiest towns in Maryland." Pennsylvania's founder, William Penn, simply couldn't accept this.

Efforts to settle the dispute for eighty years were unsuccessful. In part, this was due to deliberate delays by Lord Baltimore, says Walter B. Scaife in the *Pennsylvania Magazine of History and Biography*.

After signing papers in 1732 agreeing that the northern border of Maryland "was 15 miles south of the most southerly part of Philadelphia," Baltimore changed his position.

Disaster resulted during the long stalemate. Neither colony received taxes from businesses or residents in the four thousand square miles of disputed territory, and hostilities along the border were common. In 1734, a local war erupted, with Maryland's militia entering Pennsylvania on at least two occasions.

The British Crown directed the two parties to resolve the dispute and pay for the survey. Englishmen Mason and Dixon arrived

The house where Mason and Dixon started their survey would now be in the middle of I-95, not far from the public art sculpture *Stroll (Stickmen)* by William Dickey King. You'll find it on the South Street pedestrian bridge. (Photo by Jim Murphy.)

in Philadelphia in 1763 and set to work. They packed what was then state-of-the-art equipment: an ingenious tripod-mounted survey tool now at Independence Hall, a telescope, navigation transit, sixty-six-foot measuring chains, and more.

While the initial team was small, the task was huge: to cut a vista some twenty-four- to thirty-feet wide across rugged Pennsylvania woodlands and place a five-hundred-pound stone every mile of the way.

The entourage eventually grew to about 115 people, says surveyor Todd Babcock in *Stargazers, Ax-Men and Milkmaids: The Men Who Surveyed Mason and Dixon's Line.*

At its peak, the cast included cooks, tent keepers, chain carriers, fifty-three axmen, thirty-eight packhorse men, horses, cows, wagons, shepherds, and butchers.

The survey stopped abruptly in October 1767 at 233 miles and 20 chains, when the traveling party crossed "the Catawba War Path," which Babcock calls "one of the most important trails in North America."

The chief of the Native Americans accompanying Mason and Dixon refused to go any farther. The last thirty-one miles of the line to Pennsylvania's western border was completed seventeen years later by a team that included Philadelphia's David Rittenhouse, a self-taught inventor and experienced surveyor.

Interesting Oddities

- The official report on their work never mentioned the names Mason or Dixon, so they themselves never heard of the Mason-Dixon Line.
- Both men are buried in unmarked graves: Dixon in England, Mason in the Christ Church Burial Ground. While no one knows exactly where Mason's body is buried, an authentic 1766 Mason-Dixon Line boundary stone and plaque noting Mason's accomplishments were placed in the burial ground in 2013, the 250th anniversary of the survey's start.
- Mason and Dixon were the first to measure a degree of latitude in North America. Dixon also tested the reliability of chronometers in measuring longitude.
- The house on South Street where Mason and Dixon started their survey would now be in the middle of I-95, near the South Street pedestrian bridge.
- Stones sent from England were placed every mile on the line. Crownstones that had the Penn and Calvert coats of arms on opposite sides were placed every five miles.

How Important Was the Mason-Dixon Line?

Abolitionist Harriet Tubman, who escaped from the slave state of Maryland to Philadelphia in 1849, may have said it best: "When I found I had crossed the [Mason-Dixon] [L]ine, I looked at my hands to see if I were the same person . . . the sun came like gold through the tree and over the field and I felt like I was in heaven."

Fast Facts

Name: Mason-Dixon Survey
Historical Marker Location: Front and South Streets
Number of People in the Survey Entourage: 115
Average Weight of the Limestone Markers: Five hundred pounds
Number of Stones Shipped from England: Four hundred
Number of Miles Surveyed: 233 miles west between Pennsylvania and Maryland and 83 miles south between Maryland and Delaware
Claim to Fame: The survey definitively marked the Pennsylvania–Maryland border as being fifteen miles south of the southernmost building in Philadelphia (on Cedar, now South Street) and ended a long dispute. The Mason-Dixon Line is also widely considered the boundary between the North and the South.
Marker Dedicated: August 30, 2013
Popular Mason-Dixon Line Song: "Sailing to Philadelphia," by Mark Knopfler and James Taylor
Nearby Attractions: Independence Seaport Museum, City Tavern, and Gloria Dei Church

This updated story first ran in the March 2018 issue of *QVNA Magazine* and is reprinted with permission.

30 Old Pine Street Churchyard

It has everything from "Our Charley" to "parfait burials" and war heroes.

Walking through the churchyard at Fourth and Pine Streets one day, I looked down at a small gravestone and felt as if I'd been hit in the stomach.

The flat white stone simply read, "Our Charley."

I wondered, was this a child? A pet? Who was it? And why was it causing me such an emotional reaction? I'd never seen a stone like this before.

A tiny stone marker displaying just the words "Our Charley" sparked this writer's interest in Old Pine's churchyard. (Photo by Jim Murphy.)

Further investigation and a meeting with Ronn Shaffer, the church's longtime historian who has since died, revealed many interesting facts about this beautiful colonial churchyard.

"It has the highest density of any graveyard in the city of Philadelphia," Ronn said, with four thousand or more people buried in less than an acre.

He calls the practice of stacking multiple people in the same plot at levels of nine feet, six feet, and three feet "parfait burials."

Up to four adults or six or seven children are stacked in each grave—thirty inches wide, seven feet long, and nine feet deep. Heads are placed at the west and feet to the east so that believers can see the Angel Gabriel when he announces the Great Awakening.

Known originally as the Third Presbyterian Church, Old Pine Street opened in 1768 on land donated by Thomas and Richard Penn.

A once-friendly relationship with the First Presbyterian Church on the south side of Market Street (High Street) near Second Street deteriorated when Old Pine Street hired a radical minister, George Duffield.

That's when the First Church purchased a large adjoining lot on the west side of Old Pine Street and began burying parishioners there. After selling its Bank Street burial ground in 1823, the First Church reinterred nine hundred bodies (and gravestones) at Old Pine Street.

The First Church also moved one thousand bodies to a mass grave at Laurel Hill on Ridge Avenue in Philadelphia, above the Schuylkill River.

Unable to take the gravestones to Laurel Hill, some First Church members brought their ancestors' gravestones to Old Pine and just leaned them against the south and west brick walls.

With many prominent members in arms, Old Pine became known as the "Church of the Patriots" during the Revolutionary War. This reputation worked against it when the British used the church as a hospital and later a stable for their horses. They left the building with just four windowless walls standing, a cedar shake roof, and a barnyard smell.

More than 285 Revolutionary War soldiers are buried in the churchyard, and special thirteen-star flags mark their graves. More flags were added in 2011 by the Sons of the American Revolution.

Others of note buried at Old Pine include William Hurry, the sexton who reportedly rang the Liberty Bell for one hour on July 8, 1776, to announce the first public reading of the Declaration of Independence. (Some question that this actually happened. The statehouse steeple was under repair at the time.) And Jared Ingersoll is the only signer of the Constitution in the churchyard.

More recent burials include the body of In-Ho Oh, a Korean student killed in West Philadelphia in 1958; Eugene Ormandy, who died in 1985 and whose cremains are here along with those of his wife, Gretel; and Reverend Stephen Gloucester, a former slave and one of the first Black ordained ministers in the United States. His body was discovered during renovation of a vacant 160-year-old house nearby and reinterred in a grave next to the foundation of Old Pine Street in 2008.

And finally, what's the story on "Our Charley"?

Unfortunately, he had a short life, and this "lovely little boy of five years" died on May 20, 1849.

As recounted in the book *The Life of Rev. Thomas Brainerd, D.D.* by Mary Brainerd, the death of his youngest son unnerved Dr. Brainerd so much that he had to sit while preaching for the next three years.

"To see his little boy suffering under brain fevers, as the result of his precocious intellect, completely unmanned him." No wonder.

Fast Facts

Name: Old Pine Street Church Historic Colonial Churchyard
Location: 412 Pine Street
Current Church Name: Third, Scots, and Mariners (Old Pine) Presbyterian Church
Phone: 215-925-8051
E-mail: info@oldpine.org
Websites: www.oldpine.org and http://oldpineconservancy.org
Open: Seven days a week during daylight hours
Closed: National holidays
Admission: No charge; contributions are appreciated; to adopt the grave of a fallen patriot soldier and have a thirteen-star flag placed on its marker, the cost is $100.
Recent Claim to Fame: Appeared in the 2004 movie *National Treasure*
Nearby Attractions: St. Peter's Church, Mother Bethel Church, and Hill-Physick House

This updated story first ran in the March/April 2011 issue of the *Society Hill Reporter* and is reprinted with permission.

⊰ Part VIII ⊱

Marvelous Museums

31 The African American Museum in Philadelphia

Here you'll learn about many remarkable Black Americans who triumphed over injustice.

Growing up in Delaware County, I heard family horror stories about the discrimination Irish Catholic immigrants faced when they landed here. And about ads that read: "No Irish need apply." Of course, I knew that African Americans historically suffered far deeper, longer-term discrimination.

But it wasn't until I visited the African American Museum in Philadelphia (AAMP) that I really began to understand the extraordinary trials that Black people faced here. Even in this city, a home of the abolition movement, the injustices were astonishing.

What I Learned

- Free Black people were kidnapped off the streets in Philadelphia and sent south to become slaves. One man was even snatched from the very street I live on, in a story reminiscent of the movie *12 Years a Slave*.
- Black people were not permitted to ride streetcars in Philadelphia. Even African American soldiers fighting for the North in the Civil War were denied entry.
- Black soldiers in that war were paid less than White ones.
- As late as 1858, the Philadelphia, Wilmington, and Baltimore Railroad said that Black passengers could only travel "with a responsible White person."

After learning all this at the African American Museum—and that Frederick Douglass, an invited guest to Philadelphia's Centennial Exposition, was initially turned away and seated only because of the intervention of others—I did more research.

The comments below by Douglass, a renowned orator, abolitionist, and writer, reveal a great deal about the way African Americans were treated in our city:

Nesaika, a public work of art by John Rhoden, stands outside the African American Museum. (Photo by Jim Murphy.)

There is not perhaps anywhere to be found a city in which prejudice against color is more rampant than in Philadelphia. . . . Colored persons, no matter how well dressed or how well behaved, ladies or gentlemen, rich or poor, are not even permitted to ride on any of the many railways through the Christian city. Halls are rented with the express understanding that no person of color shall be allowed to enter, either to attend a concert or listen to a lecture. The whole aspect of city usage at this point is mean, contemptible and barbarous.

Pretty strong stuff from the book *Philadelphia: A 300-Year History*—and pretty nasty ways to hamper people going about their daily lives.

Audacious Freedom: African Americans in Philadelphia 1776–1876, the permanent main exhibit on the first floor, covers these and many other key events in the lives of Black Philadelphians. This interactive audio/visual display, using photos, timelines, documents, and more, looks at people, White and Black, who made a difference in the city.

You'll learn how George Washington rotated his slaves out of Pennsylvania before they were here six months—to avoid their becoming free under Pennsylvania's Gradual Abolition Law. How his slave Ona Judge escaped from the President's House in Philadelphia to New Hampshire, and how a desperate Washington tried to get her back.

At *Philadelphia Conversations* on floor two, you'll interact with African American trailblazers on ten video screens. They include clergymen and abolitionists Richard Allen and Absalom Jones; educator, athlete, and civil rights leader Octavius Catto; and others. You can click on four preselected questions at each display to get a video reply. *Children's Corner* is also on this floor.

Fast Facts

Name: The African American Museum in Philadelphia
Address: 701 Arch Street
Year Opened: 1976
Claim to Fame: It is the first institution funded and built by a major municipality to preserve, interpret, and exhibit the heritage of African Americans.
Affiliation: Smithsonian Institution Affiliations Program
Hours: Wednesday through Saturday, 10 A.M. to 5 P.M.; Sunday, noon to 5 P.M.
Admission: Adults, $14; senior citizens, $10; students w/ID and youths ages four to twelve, $10; AAMP Members, free
Phone: 215-574-0380

Website: www.aampmuseum.org

Exhibits: Permanent displays are on floors one and two, and temporary ones are on three and four.

Public Art: *13 Whispering Bells* by Reginald Beauchamp represents the original thirteen colonies. The bells, without clappers or hammers, are rung by the wind. *Nesaika* by John Rhoden merges aspects of African and American culture into one sculpture.

Nearby Attractions: The Federal Reserve Bank, the National Constitution Center, and the U.S. Mint

This updated story first ran in the September/October 2015 edition of the *Society Hill Reporter* and is reprinted with permission.

32 National Museum of American Jewish History

This is the view from a non-Jew.*

After watching the National Museum of American Jewish History's glass and terra cotta building rising along Fifth Street below Market for what seemed like ages in 2009 and 2010, I was anxious to see what was inside.

And I was not disappointed.

This one-hundred-thousand-square-foot museum tells a powerful story about Jews in America.

Even the heavy security in the lobby—which is like airport security—reminds you that Jews were not always welcomed here earlier and must remain "eternally vigilant" today.

When you enter, your small items go into a basket for X-ray inspection as you pass through a metal detector. Even though the pens I had with me were carefully inspected and returned to me, I didn't realize until I entered the exhibit area that I couldn't use them in the museum. Only pencils are permitted, which means that most of this review is from memory.

My then-editor at the *Society Hill Reporter* asked me to review the museum from the point of view of a non-Jew, and I can fulfill only part of that mission. More on that later.

A trunk from the German transatlantic liner the *St. Louis*. In 1939, many Jewish passengers aboard this ship—who were awaiting visas from the United States—were denied entry into both Cuba and the United States. The ship and more than nine hundred passengers sailed back to Europe. More than 250 of them were reportedly killed in the Holocaust. Steamer trunk used by Josef Joseph on the MS St. Louis, Europe, 1939. Metal, leather, wood, and paper. (Photo by Will Brown. National Museum of American Jewish History, 1995.69.1. Gift of Barry S. and Joann C. Slosberg.)

The quick view: This is an important museum that should interest people of all races and religions, and I highly recommend it. You can easily spend several hours here and not see everything.

In three main floors of exhibit area and a photo gallery/hall of fame, the museum clearly portrays the tremendous impact that Jewish people have had on our culture—from science to entertainment to politics and civil rights protests.

As you enter the exhibit area, you are encouraged to go up to the fourth floor and work down chronologically—from 1654 until today. (Special exhibitions began on the fifth-floor gallery in 2012. Ask about them at the front desk when you enter.)

The view from the top of the airy eighty-five-foot atrium is impressive, with wood-and-glass stairways dramatically crisscrossing the open area and carrying you to the rest of the museum below.

The exhibits are imaginative, instructive, graphically pleasing, and adult- and child-friendly, including some of the bells and whistles of modern interactivity.

Some highlights for me: A spinning ceiling globe light recreating the atmosphere of balls held during the Jewish holiday of Purim; an electronic "map table" illustrating how Jews moved westward; the opportunity to examine a covered wagon, try on pieces of pioneer clothing, visit a trading post, and decide what travelers would pack on a journey westward; a visit to a turn-of-the-twentieth-century tenement apartment; school desks and an exhibit on early-twentieth-century Jewish education; exhibits depicting the lives of garment workers; and timelines showing what has happened among Jews in America in context with world events. Of course, content changes all the time.

The museum presents the differing beliefs of Reform, Conservative, and Orthodox sects and the struggles of Jewish immigrants to pass on their religious traditions to their U.S. children.

I didn't know that the first Jews to arrive in the United States in 1654 were refugees from Recife in Brazil; that there were sizable Jewish settlements in smaller cities, including Charleston and Cincinnati; or that for a short time, Los Angeles had the largest Jewish population in the United States.

Many museum pluses . . . and a few minuses: On the March Sunday afternoon I visited soon after the museum first opened, it was mobbed and difficult to get close to a number of the displays; several guided tours pushed their way through the already clogged rooms, making movement even more difficult; and there was quite a bottleneck on the third floor, where a film about America at war—and the mistreatment of European Jews leading up to the war—attracted a large crowd. But today, many years later, crowds have evened out. So I think you'll be comfortable visiting this interesting museum at any time.

* **Full disclosure:** In early 2011, because my background is Irish, I was asked to review this museum from a non-Jewish perspective. But when my twin brother married a Jewish woman, he underwent routine testing to find out whether he might be a carrier for Tay-Sachs disease. (Anyone can be a carrier, but the disease is much more common among people of eastern European [Ashkenazi] Jewish descent.) Surprisingly to us, my brother was. Upon further testing, we learned that my mother and her five children all are Tay-Sachs carriers. So, I'm not Jewish, but I am a carrier. And I wouldn't be surprised if one of my distant Irish relatives was rather close to a Jewish person at one time. Life is full of unexpected connections.

Fast Facts

Name: National Museum of American Jewish History
Location: 101 South Independence Mall East; enter at Market Street
Phone: 215-923-3811
Hours: Tuesday through Friday, 10 A.M. to 5 P.M.; Saturday and Sunday, 10 A.M. to 5:30 P.M.
Website: www.nmajh.org
Nearby Attractions: The Bourse, the Second Bank of the United States, and the Museum of the American Revolution

This updated story first ran in the Spring/Summer 2011 issue of the *Society Hill Reporter* and is reprinted with permission.

33 Pennsylvania Academy of the Fine Arts

Eclectic, engaging, and exceptional, this Frank Furness masterpiece is my all-time favorite building in Philadelphia.
If you asked me to rank Philadelphia's must-see sights, the unique Pennsylvania Academy of the Fine Arts (PAFA) Historic Landmark Building on North Broad Street would easily top my list of buildings.

To me, **this one-of-a-kind creation, designed by famous Philadelphia architects Frank Furness and George Hewitt, and located just up the street from City Hall, should be number one on every Philadelphian's bucket list**. It's that spectacular.

Interesting Oddities

* Furness's name is really pronounced "furnace." I first learned the correct pronunciation while viewing a Penn website about Furness's superb campus library (now the Fisher Fine Arts Library). Most Philadelphians I know still mispronounce it.
* Furness is the only major architect to receive the Congressional Medal of Honor. He was cited for bravery at the Battle of Trevilian Station, Virginia, on June 12, 1864. Captain Furness

The remarkable Pennsylvania Academy of the Fine Arts Furness-Hewitt building dazzles both inside and out. (Photo by Jim Murphy.)

commanded Company F of the Sixth Pennsylvania Cavalry, also known as Rush's Lancers, during the Civil War.

- The gorgeous Grand Stairhall was not Furness's original design. Instead, says Harry Philbrick, then-director of the museum at PAFA when I interviewed him in 2014, the stunning stairhall sweeping up to the gallery level was the steering committee's idea, and it worked. Furness's design was a more conventional up-and-back stairway.

Innovations to Look For

- A trend-setting truss: Furness installed a massive steel truss, typically used on bridges, along the north side of the building. Why? He wanted to install brick on the outside wall of the gallery above the large windows, and glass can't hold up brick.

Besides supporting the second-floor galleries, the truss allows the lower part of the wall to be a non-load-bearing or "curtain wall." As cultural and architectural historian George Thomas explains, "Curtain walls are integral to virtually every modern skyscraper, pointing out just how revolutionary and future-oriented this building was." (Thomas is the author of two recent books on Furness: *First Modern: Pennsylvania Academy of the Fine Arts*, published in 2017; and *Frank Furness: Architect in the Age of the Great Machines*, published in 2018. The latter won the 2019 Victorian Society Book of the Year award.)

- Furness's futuristic plans: While the building opened five years before the Brush Electric Light Company, a PECO predecessor, went into business, Furness's drawings show that he designed for the new power source.

- A passive ventilation system: Not only did Furness provide abundant lighting with a gallery skylight; his mostly glass roof above it acts like a greenhouse too. Furness "designed a mechanical sash system that opened up large panels of the roof to let out heat," Thomas says.

- A large freight elevator: Controlled with ropes, it opens to the street and the gallery from the back of the building. The elevator transported large equipment—as well as horses—brought in twice a year as subjects for student projects. Horses don't handle steps well.

- Industrial touches: Look carefully and you'll see that Furness placed pistons, gears, cogs, drive shafts, and more as ornaments inside and outside the museum. He also used the four card suits—hearts, clubs, diamonds, and spades—in many places.

Unfortunately, Furness's reputation suffered greatly in his later years, as more "modern" architectural styles became popular. Many of his most notable works were torn down.

But do yourself a favor. Visit this marvelous building soon and look at the outstanding art inside. View paintings by such luminaries as Gilbert Stuart, Thomas Eakins, Charles Willson Peale, Violet Oakley, and more. Experience the beauty, workmanship, and technology that surround you. And enjoy the fact that you are standing inside a truly amazing "factory for fine art."

Fast Facts

Name: Pennsylvania Academy of the Fine Arts

Address: 118 N. Broad Street

Honors: National Register of Historic Places and National Historic Landmark

First: Art school and museum in the United States

Style: Renaissance, Gothic, and Eclectic

Constructed: 1871–76

Hours: Tuesday through Saturday, 10 A.M. to 5 P.M.; Sunday, 11 A.M. to 5 P.M.; closed Monday and legal holidays

Admission: Adults, $15; seniors ages sixty and up and students with ID, $12; youth ages thirteen to eighteen, $8; children ages twelve and under, military personnel (excluding groups), and members, free

Docent Tours (free with admission): Tuesday through Sunday, 1 and 2 P.M.

Phone: 215-972-7600

Website: www.pafa.org

Nearby Attractions: Claes Oldenburg's *Paint Torch* next door, the Masonic Temple, and City Hall

This updated story first ran in the November/December 2014 issue of the *Society Hill Reporter* and is reprinted with permission.

Part IX

Historic Architecture

34 Athenaeum of Philadelphia

This special-collections library and museum welcomes area residents and tourists alike.

In 1814, a group of local learned men—with broad interests in science, literature, politics, and more—announced the opening of two reading rooms run by the Athenaeum of Philadelphia.

Named in honor of Athena, the goddess of wisdom, the member-supported Athenaeum was founded to collect materials "connected with the history and antiquities of America, and the useful arts, and generally to disseminate useful knowledge" for public benefit.

These men also had at least two other goals for the Athenaeum: to offer longer operating hours than both the Library Company of Philadelphia and the American Philosophical Society; and to specialize in periodicals and reference books.

A newspaper notice dated March 7, 1814, the day the museum opened, says that future library plans included U.S. and foreign newspapers and periodicals, pamphlets, scientific journals, maps, charts, "the laws and journals of Congress," and more.

In 1845, when Athenaeum managers decided to construct a new building on Sixth Street, they chose a young architect named John Notman over such superstars as William Strickland, John Haviland, and Thomas Ustick Walter.

It was a magical selection. Notman's building, said to be the first Italian Renaissance Revival–style building in the United States, is a magnificent structure with twenty-four-foot ceilings you must see to appreciate. Part of the National Register of Historic Places, **it's considered one of the most significant American buildings of the nineteenth century**.

Fortunately, you can self-tour the building, including the marvelous reading room. Plus, you can attend many exhibitions and community lectures for free. (For a current list of the Athenaeum's free and paid events, go to the website listed under Fast Facts below.)

Visiting the building? Just sign in with the receptionist and get a Visitor's Tag.

The museum is hidden in plain sight. Despite the Athenaeum's great location on Washington Square next to the Dilworth House,

One of the first brownstone buildings in Philadelphia, the Athenaeum was also one of the first modeled after sixteenth-century Italian palazzos. It often offers free exhibitions on the ground floor. (Photo by Jim Murphy.)

many locals don't know that it is there or that they're welcome inside.

To change that perception, Sandra Tatman, then–executive director when I met with her in 2014, moved her office to the front of the building's ground floor, opened the shutters so people going by could see inside, and, in effect, put out the welcome mat for residents and tourists alike.

She also began offering the building's spaces to other nonprofits for annual meetings and faculty retreats.

Don't miss Joseph Bonaparte's desk, made by cabinetmaker Michael Bouvier; a copy in marble of Pauline Bonaparte Borghese posing as *Venus Vincitrice*; or Frank Hamilton Taylor's watercolor *A Southwestern View of Washington Square*, 1925 (without the brick wall that now surrounds the square).

Interesting Oddities

- To cut expenses, architect John Notman used brownstone instead of marble. His choice influenced many other clubs and residences in the city, including the Union League.
- The Athenaeum's guest book is uniquely titled *The Book of Strangers*. Among its signers are Edgar Allan Poe; Joseph Bonaparte, who registered as the Comte de Survilliers; five U.S. presidents; and the Marquis de Lafayette, who was elected the organization's first honorary member.
- Many people mispronounce "Athenaeum." According to former executive director Peter Conn, the correct way is Ath-a-*nay´*-um (Ath as in "path," a as in "apple," nay as in "bay," and um as in "museum"). You can hear the pronunciation at www.youtube .com/watch?v=reWidenb26s.

In 1851, the Athenaeum of Philadelphia subscribed to sixty-two American newspapers and five foreign ones. Today, it carries no hard-copy newspapers, but the Athenaeum keeps reinventing itself. After two hundred years, it still provides essential information for public benefit—just much of it today in digital form.

In addition, the Athenaeum still houses an international collection of thousands of significant rare books as well as marvelous architecture and design documents, with more than one million library items in all.

Fast Facts

Name: The Athenaeum of Philadelphia—in honor of Athena, the
  goddess of wisdom
Address: 219 South Sixth Street

Distinctions: The building is one of the first brownstone buildings in Philadelphia and the first American building in the Italianate Renaissance Revival palazzo style.

Unique Collections and Services: American Architects & Buildings Project, Greater Philadelphia Geohistory Network, and Regional Digital Imaging Center

Self-Tours: Monday through Friday, 9 A.M. to 5 P.M.; closed major holidays

Admission: Free for self-tours, community lectures, exhibits, and the Socrates Cafe, a discussion group about life's great questions using the Socratic method (second Tuesday of the month); see the event calendar at www.philaathenaeum.org /events.html.

Phone: 215-925-2688

Website: www.philaathenaeum.org

Nearby Attractions: Washington Square, Powel House, and Mother Bethel Church

This updated story first ran in the July/August 2014 issue of the *Society Hill Reporter* and is reprinted with permission.

35 Ben Franklin Bridge

On the day it opened—July 1, 1926—this was the world's longest suspension bridge.

Most of us Philadelphians take the big, blue, beautiful Ben Franklin Bridge for granted.

We hop on, try to get across quickly, and hope its frequent traffic jams don't delay us too long.

But the next time you look at the bridge—or drive, pedal, jog, or walk across it—consider one fact: When it opened in 1926, this was the longest suspension bridge in the world.

Known originally as the Delaware River Bridge, the structure was built by a design dream team: bridge engineer Ralph Modjeski, design engineer Leon Moisseiff, and renowned architect Paul Philippe Cret, who also designed Philadelphia's Rodin Museum, Rittenhouse Square, and more.

Walkers, joggers, and bikers enjoy marvelous views from the bridge's walkway. (Photo by Jim Murphy.)

After opening ceremonies by the Delaware River Joint Bridge Commission, some one hundred thousand people strolled across the bridge.

U.S. President Calvin Coolidge personally dedicated the structure on July 5, the same day he opened the Sesquicentennial Exposition of 1926.

Long desired by people on both the Camden and Philadelphia sides, who wanted fast, easy access across the Delaware River, the new bridge was an instant success.

In his book *Philadelphia's Lost Waterfront*, historian Harry Kyriakodis says the new bridge attracted thirty-five thousand vehicles a day. Initial tolls were 25 cents for a car, 15 cents for a horse and rider, and 30 cents for a horse-drawn carriage.

Today, more than one hundred thousand vehicles and thirty-seven thousand PATCO Speedline passengers travel across it daily.

Before the bridge was built, Kyriakodis says, ferries carried one hundred thousand people a day across the river, departing every three minutes at peak times. But the bridge quickly put most of them out of business.

Interesting Oddities

* During construction, the joint commission rejected the name Franklin Bridge. Its successor, the Delaware River Port Authority (DRPA), had more sense, renaming the span the Ben Franklin Bridge in 1956, the 250th anniversary of Franklin's birth.
* The bridge had no speed limit when it opened, says WHYY.org. Drivers were expected to use common sense.
* The bridge's first traffic accident occurred before it even officially opened. A driver, attempting to get ahead in line on the first day cars could cross, ran into the back of another car. The driver was fined $25.
* Historic St. George's United Methodist Church, America's oldest in continuous use, is now known as "the church that moved the bridge." When it was slated for demolition to accommodate the bridge, church leaders protested in court. They won, and the bridge was shifted slightly southward, missing the church by just fourteen feet.
* St. Augustine's Roman Catholic Church was also affected by the bridge. When Fourth Street was lowered by about fifteen feet to allow for the approach of the bridge, says Kyriakodis, the entrance to the church also was lowered and the rectory removed.
* The huge anchorages on both sides were designed not only to anchor the bridge but also to serve mass transit trolley passengers. Each contains a tiled room with seven beautiful mosaics. But because trolley lines in New Jersey started converting to bus lines before construction was complete, the waiting rooms never opened to the public. And after the terrorist attack on September 11, 2001, they never will, says the DRPA.

Because New Jersey wanted tolls to pay for the bridge and Pennsylvania did not, says Steve Anderson, creator of PhillyRoads

.com, work stopped for a time. "There were even proposals to tear down the bridge," he says. A corruption scandal related to bridge funding ultimately led Pennsylvania to relent and agree to construct tollbooths. Work resumed on the bridge soon after.

A great way to enjoy the bridge's spectacular vistas is to use the South Walkway, which starts near Fifth and Race Streets. It's open for bikes, pedestrians, and joggers.

But if you are walking, be careful and "hug" to the right to avoid speeding bikers and joggers. Some will let you know they are close by. Some won't.

Fast Facts

Length Tower-to-Tower: 1,750 feet
Length End-to-End: 8,300 feet
Number of Lanes: Seven
Height: 135 feet above the river
Towers: 382 feet
Years to Build: Four and one-half
Cost: $37,103,765.42
Fatalities during Construction: Fifteen
Website: http://drpa.org
Pedestrian Walkway Entrances: Philadelphia side, Fifth and Race Streets; Camden side, Fourth and Pearl Streets
Nearby Attractions: Betsy Ross House, Fireman's Hall Museum, and Elfreth's Alley

This updated story first ran in the September/October 2013 issue of the *Society Hill Reporter* and is reprinted with permission.

36 Carpenters' Hall

This site is where America took its first step toward independence. "One of the greatest beginnings in all of history began in this little room." So says historian and two-time Pulitzer Prize winner David McCullough about Carpenters' Hall—the small fifty-foot square middle Georgian structure with ten-foot cutouts at the corners tucked in off the 300 block of Chestnut Street.

Carpenters' Hall is where the First Continental Congress, secret meetings with a French emissary, and the nation's first bank robbery all took place. Check out the wonderful scale model of the building inside. (Photo by Jim Murphy.)

Often overlooked by tourists and Philadelphians alike, Carpenters' Hall is a marvelous example of extraordinary architecture, as you can see in the scale model inside constructed over a two-year period by the Hagley Museum in Delaware.

Nicholas A. Gianopulos, a structural engineer and Carpenters' Company member since 1976, simply says that the building's "squareness and accuracy of construction is equal to that of contemporary structures." He calls the result "a gem of Georgian-style architecture."

Robert Smith, the colonies' most important master builder/architect, designed the building. He also built the steeple at Christ Church and Ben Franklin's house.

Here in late 1774, the First Continental Congress—with delegates from twelve of the thirteen colonies (Georgia was missing)—met for fifty-two days to respond to the Intolerable Acts passed by Britain.

Rather than meet at what is now Independence Hall (which at the time was the seat of Pennsylvania's colonial government), the delegates reportedly chose a spot less public. It's also where they were less likely to be coerced by Joseph Galloway, Pennsylvania's speaker of the Colonial Assembly. His views toward England were too conservative for many of the more radical representatives.

Today's building is far more finished than it was in 1774. At that time, funds were low. The interior was "very plain," says an insurance survey. And both the building's frontispiece and arch for the fanlight would not be completed for about eighteen years.

The members of the Carpenters' Company were not necessarily carpenters as we know them today. In fact, some combined the talents of architect, contractor, and engineer.

Interesting Oddities

- The Carpenters' Company published a secret Price Book or Rule Book for various kinds of construction. Members could be expelled for showing it to outsiders. Even Thomas Jefferson was refused a copy. When a member died, the company called on the widow to retrieve the book.
- The company also provided pensions for widows, educated children of deceased members, and even helped some find positions as apprentices.
- Ben Franklin and John Jay met secretly in Carpenters' Hall with a French emissary on three nights in December 1775. Their talks later led to critical French support of the colonists' war efforts.
- The Continental Congress returned here briefly on June 21, 1783, says member and noted preservationist Charles E. Peterson, "when their usual meeting place—the State House—was besieged by mutinous veterans of the Continental Army" who wanted to be paid. Its members then fled to Princeton.
- The nation's first bank robbery took place right here in 1798— from the vaults of the Bank of Pennsylvania. The loot: $162,821. Although Pat Lyon, the blacksmith who had just changed the locks on the vault's doors, was imprisoned for three months, he was later released and awarded $12,000. The actual culprit was Isaac Davis, a member of the Carpenters' Company. Stupidly, he

began depositing large sums of money into the very bank he had just robbed. Under questioning, he confessed, returned the money, and never served a day in prison.

- Many companies rented space in the building, including the Library Company of Philadelphia, the Franklin Institute, Philadelphia Custom House, and others. C. J. Wolbert & Co., an auction house, was the last tenant. The Carpenters' Company terminated its lease and opened the building to the public as a historic monument in 1857.

Visit Carpenters' Hall soon. Inside, you'll see an impressive detailed model of the building and much more. It's free, a key part of our city's and country's history, and well worth a trip. McCullough says, "To me, it's one of the most eloquent buildings in all of America."

Fast Facts

Name: Carpenters' Hall
Address: 320 Chestnut Street
Phone: 215-925-0167
Hours: Tuesday through Sunday, 10 A.M. to 4 P.M.; closed Monday; closed Tuesdays in January and February
Cost: Free
Website: www.carpentershall.org
Built: 1770–74
Owned By: The Carpenters' Company of the City and County of Philadelphia, founded in 1724, which met for the first time that year; Carpenter's Hall was built fifty years later.
Style: Georgian
Claim to Fame: This remarkable building was home of the First Continental Congress, September 5 to October 26, 1774.
Awards: Named a National Historic Landmark in 1970
Famous Guests: Queen Elizabeth II and Prince Philip of England visited in 1976; King Carl XVI Gustaf and Queen Silvia of Sweden visited in 1994.
Nearby Attractions: First Bank of the United States, Merchants' Exchange, and the Museum of the American Revolution

This updated story first ran in the November/December 2018 issue of *QVNA Magazine* and is reprinted with permission.

37 Christ Church

This magnificent house of worship was the tallest building in the United States for fifty-six years.

With a soaring 196-foot steeple that towers over newer structures nearby, Christ Church is a spectacular historic building and living history at its best.

No musty old buildings or artifacts untouched by human hands are found here. Instead, **this is a flourishing, active modern parish** where members still worship under a brass chandelier (with real candles) that has hung since 1744.

Christ Church's majestic steeple made it the tallest building in the United States until 1810. Famed Carpenters' Company member Robert Smith designed the steeple. (Photo by Jim Murphy.)

Parishioners continue to be baptized at a fifteenth-century octagonal walnut font used by William Penn in 1644. And, says senior guide and historian Neil Ronk, "The bells we rang for the Revolution will ring for a wedding tonight."

Ronk, an engaging, enthusiastic storyteller who has published his own blog, *History Made Fresh*, said he was going to tell the best man at that evening's nuptials, "Thomas Jefferson was best man at a wedding here."

Started as a small log and brick building in 1695, the original church structure was not all that impressive. Alice of Dunk's Ferry, one of Philly's first oral historians (who reportedly lived 116 years) and Christ Church's oldest known parishioner, told people that "she could place the palm of her hand on the ceiling of the center aisle and walk the entire length without removing it."

Little did she realize that this church, whose brick tower resembles one at St. James's Church, Piccadilly, London, would become known as "the nation's church" because of the Revolutionary leaders who worshipped here.

Besides being the first parish of the Church of England in Pennsylvania, it was also the birthplace of the American Episcopal Church.

George Washington, Benjamin Franklin, Robert Morris, Benjamin Rush, and Betsy Ross all rented pews here. (Washington's pew was number fifty-six; Franklin's was number seventy.) You can even sit in their pews and imagine what it was like to be in this church during the Revolutionary War. (To get to those pews, you actually walk over some twenty graves installed inside the church from 1699 to 1796.)

Interesting Oddities

- The tower, added in 1754, made the seven-story church the tallest building in the United States until 1810, and in Philadelphia until 1856. The addition was financed by at least two lotteries that Ben Franklin organized.
- Christ Church contains the largest Palladian window built in America in the eighteenth century.
- From 1747 to 1767, about 25 to 33 percent of Philadelphia's free and enslaved Black residents were baptized here.

- The church's famous two-acre burial ground, which is three blocks away at Fifth and Arch Streets, includes five signers of the Declaration of Independence and 1,400 markers in all.
- Christ Church is thought to be the only place in the original thirteen colonies depicting English royalty on the outside of a public building. A bas-relief of George II appears above the Palladian window on Second Street.

Unlike much of Philadelphia's history, Christ Church is as modern as today's breaking news. As historian Ronk puts it, "What is a place like this for if you can't use the items?"

Fast Facts

Address: 20 North American Street, at Second Street above Market
Founded: 1695
Current Building Opened: 1744
Architectural Style: Georgian
Number of Annual Visitors: 220,000
Tours: Monday through Saturday, 10 A.M. to 5 P.M.; Sunday, 12:30 to 5 P.M. Expected donation: $3. *Note:* The church is closed Monday and Tuesday in January and February. Burial ground tours end at 4 P.M. Admission: Adults, $3; children, $1; with guided tours, adults, $8, children, $3. Burial grounds are closed in December, January, and February.
Phone: 215-922-1695
Website: www.christchurchphila.org
Nearby Attractions: Elfreth's Alley, Fireman's Hall Museum, and Chief Tamanend Statue

This updated story first ran in the January/February 2014 issue of the *Society Hill Reporter* and is reprinted with permission.

38 City Hall

Some critics wanted this extraordinary structure—once the tallest occupied building in the world—to be demolished before it was even completed in 1901.

Whether you love it or hate it, Philadelphia's remarkable City Hall is unique, impressive, and a world leader in several categories.

Built over a thirty-year period at a cost of $24.5 million, **the French Second Empire structure is the largest all-masonry load-bearing building in the world.**

Without the benefit of a steel frame, this mammoth structure of some seven hundred rooms has a floor space of 630,000 square feet and may be the largest municipal building anywhere!

Atop it sits a thirty-seven-foot, twenty-seven-ton sculpture of William Penn, also thought to be the largest statue on top of a building any place in the world.

City Hall itself, at 548 feet in height, was initially designed by architect John McArthur Jr. to be the world's tallest building. But because construction took more than thirty years, the Eiffel Tower and the Washington Monument, both taller, were completed first. Neither of them, however, is an occupied building.

Interesting Oddities

- The clock faces in City Hall Tower, visible for miles along Broad Street, are three-feet larger in diameter than Big Ben, the legendary clock in London's Palace of Westminster. They look smaller, though, because City Hall's clocks are 362 feet above ground, compared to Big Ben at just 180 feet.
- Architect McArthur placed a likeness of himself across from the goddess of architecture at the east portal.
- While many people think the City Hall Tower has a ringing bell, it doesn't. The bell you hear in Center City is the seventeen-ton Founder's Bell. It's located at the top of the tower of the former PNB Building, 1 South Broad Street, across from City Hall.
- Thanks to a long-standing gentleman's agreement, at one time no building in the city could rise higher than William Penn's hat. One Liberty Place broke that agreement in 1987, however, when it soared past Pennsylvania's founder by almost four hundred feet.

Philadelphia's City Hall is thought to be the world's largest all-masonry building. Its clock face is also larger than that of Big Ben at London's Palace of Westminster. (Photo by Jim Murphy.)

• Independence Square, where Independence Hall, Old City Hall, and Congress Hall are located, was once a potential site for the new City Hall too. After that location was wisely taken off the table, citizens voted to place the new building at Centre Square rather than Washington Square. (Centre Square, the geographic center of Philadelphia's original city, was the largest of the five squares that founder William Penn designated as public areas.)

By the time City Hall was completed, it was covered in soot, had homeless people living in its portals, and had bats flying in the hallways.

Possibly the only thing that kept City Hall from being demolished in both the 1920s and 1950 was the fact that it would cost as much to demolish the building as it did to construct it.

Fortunately, wiser heads prevailed. And while urban critics, such as Lewis Mumford, savaged the building, calling it "an architectural nightmare," others took a longer view. The American Institute of Architects says that Philadelphia's City Hall is "perhaps the greatest single effort of late-nineteenth-century American architecture."

But go see for yourself. Take a tour, view the 250 sculptures, and visit the sumptuous rooms. Then peer down from the observation deck just below Penn's statue and enjoy a spectacular view of the city he planned. It just doesn't get much better than this.

Fast Facts

Address: City Hall Visitor Center, Room 121, Broad and Market Streets (close to the Thirteenth Street entrance)

Phone: 267-514-4757

Time to Build: More than thirty years

Cost to Build: $24.5 million

Claim to Fame: Tallest occupied building in the United States until 1909

Number of Bricks: Eighty-eight million (equal to 14,700 typical row houses)

Number of Sculptures: More than 250, by Alexander Milne Calder

Big Numbers: Some of the walls are twenty-two-feet thick; one granite slab weighs close to forty tons; thirty-seven tons of pigeon guano were removed in 1993, when the building was pigeon-proofed.

Height: 548 feet

Style: French Second Empire, influenced by the Louvre in Paris

Chief Architect: John McArthur Jr.

Website: www.phlvisitorcenter.com

Tower-Only Tours: Monday through Friday, 9:30 A.M. to 4:15 P.M.; select Saturdays, 11 A.M. to 4 P.M. Elevator leaves every fifteen minutes. Limit: Four adults. Tickets: Adults, $8; seniors and military, $6; students, $4; children under three, free. There is no handicapped access to the tower.

Interior Tours (including the tower): Monday through Friday, 12:30 P.M. Length: Ninety minutes to two hours. Tickets: Adults, $15; seniors and military, $10; students, $8; children under 3, free.

Nearby Attractions: PSFS Building, Masonic Temple, and Pennsylvania Academy of the Fine Arts

This updated story first ran in the March/April 2014 issue of the *Society Hill Reporter* and is reprinted with permission.

39 Gloria Dei Church (Old Swedes')

It may be the only surviving city building that William Penn set foot in.

The first time I ever saw ship models suspended over a church aisle was at Gloria Dei.

I thought placing models there was unusual. But it made sense. The *Fogel Grip* and *Kalmar Nyckel* safely brought Swedes some 3,700 nautical miles across the ocean to America on four-month voyages. If my ancestors had been on those ships, I would honor them too.

Donated to the church in 1938, the models commemorated the Swedes' first visit in 1638.

Gloria Dei (or Old Swedes') Church, the oldest in Pennsylvania, was consecrated in 1700. Its predecessor, a modified blockhouse (or stand-alone structure used for defense), was completed in 1677 at Wicaco, a tract of land of about eight hundred acres fronting the Delaware River. Sven Svenson and his brothers sold the northern part of Wicaco to William Penn for his city of Philadelphia.

The current building's style mixes gothic and medieval influences and was constructed by Philadelphia builders trained in the English craft guild. The original brick building was thirty feet wide, sixty feet long, and twenty feet high. A tower was completed in 1703. But when the weight of the steep, sloping roof (with eighteen thousand cedar shingles) began to bow the walls in 1704, a sacristy and vestibule were added for support.

The oldest church in Philadelphia (and Pennsylvania), Gloria Dei was consecrated in 1700. It's worth a visit to see the interior of the church and to wander around the historic churchyard. (Photo by Jim Murphy.)

The last major changes came in 1846: the floor was raised, balconies and a center pulpit were added, and a stained-glass window—one of the first in the country—was installed.

Inside, you will find a massive baptismal font created in 1731, wood carvings of two cherubs with wings spreading above the Bible, and a large chandelier donated by Swedish sculptor Carl Miles. Outside is an early lightning rod, possibly courtesy of Ben Franklin, and a historic burial ground.

The Hook & Hastings organ at Gloria Dei is larger than the church needs. Why? The company wanted to showcase its products in the region.

Gloria Dei, the state's oldest church, served as the Swedish Lutheran Church for more than 150 years. It's been a part of the Episcopal Church for 173 years.

Interesting Oddities

* The Swedes preferred water travel over roads and located all their residences near "the freshes of the rivers," says *Historic Tales of Olden Times*. The result: When churchgoers assembled at Gloria Dei on the Lord's Day, you would see "quite a squadron of boats along the river side there." (The river was closer to the church then.)
* Some parishioners with a long commute wanted the church to be at Passyunk rather than at Wicaco. When names were placed in a hat, Wicaco won.
* Only a few parishioners could come to church in winter, wrote Pastor Andreas Rudman. Those in New Jersey could "not come without being in gravest peril from floating ice," which "sometimes breaks large boats right in two. The ice lies piled up on capes and islands in mountainous heaps. Who in Sweden would believe this!"

The church was designated a National Historic Site in 1942. To protect it, the National Park Service purchased land around the property and began demolishing nearby buildings.

On July 1, 1944, a leased warehouse, temporarily storing varnish, oil, and other flammable materials for the war effort, caught fire. Even though wooden trim on the church was scorched and blistered, and a foot of debris covered the churchyard, *The Living Church*, a national weekly newsletter, says that Gloria Dei "was miraculously saved" by favorable winds and skilled firefighters.

Sound advice is inscribed on Gloria Dei's bell, which was moved here from the first settlement at Tinicum: "I to the living call, and to the grave do summon all."

Fast Facts

Name: Gloria Dei (Old Swedes') Church
Address: 916 S. Swanson Street
Built: 1698–1703

Website: www.old-swedes.org

Phone: 215-389-1513

Historical Marker Location: North facade of building, near Christian Street and Christopher Columbus Boulevard

Marker Copy: "Oldest church in Philadelphia. Founded, 1677, by Swedish settlers. This edifice of Swedish architectural design was erected, 1698–1703. The earlier place of worship was a blockhouse." (A blockhouse was a small building easily protected from enemy fire.)

Nearby Attractions: Immigration Station historical marker, Grand Battery historical marker, and Washington Avenue Pier

This updated story first ran in the May 2018 issue of *QVNA Magazine* and is reprinted with permission.

 # Masonic Temple

Inside are truly spectacular halls representing different cultures and architecture.

Some years ago, a Philadelphia tour guide who saw me near the Reading Terminal Market asked whether I had ever been inside the Masonic Temple. When I replied "No," he said, **"You don't have to go to Europe. You can see everything you want right there."** He wasn't far wrong.

This stunning building just north of City Hall on Broad Street is like a fantasyland. Impressive on the outside, it is absolutely mind-blowing inside.

Built between 1868 and 1873 at a cost of $1.6 million (not including decorations and furnishings), it took fifteen to twenty more years and countless dollars to design the inside. And the end result is breathtaking. (Today, the space is also available for receptions and catered affairs.)

"The robust Norman style of the exterior," says a coffee-table book published by the Masonic Temple in 2013, gives "way to a fantasy of Renaissance-inspired neoclassicism in the corridors and stairs and to nineteenth-century 'eclectic revivalism' in the lodge rooms."

Touring this stunning building's seven ornate meeting rooms is like taking a quick trip through some of the world's most interesting cultures. (Photo by Jim Murphy.)

The second you enter the temple, you realize you are in a different, incredibly opulent world. Among the sights are seven magnificent meeting rooms:

Oriental Hall: Decorated in the Moorish style. The colors and decorations were copied from the Alhambra, a thirteenth-century Spanish castle.

Gothic Hall: Also called the Asylum of the Knights Templar. Pointed arches, pinnacles, and spires appear throughout the room.

Ionic Hall: Named for the refined, elegant style of architecture of Ionia, where King Ion reigned in Asia Minor.

Egyptian Hall: Decorated in the style of the Nile Valley. It includes twelve huge columns surrounded by capitals peculiar to the temples of Luxor and Karnak.

Norman Hall: Noted for its round-arch architecture. Contains life-sized figures with the working tools of Freemasonry: the plumb, trowel, square, mallet, and compasses.

Renaissance Hall: Decorated in the Italian Renaissance style. The Seal of Solomon on the ceiling evokes the sun in the midday sky.

Corinthian Hall: Decorated in strict conformity with the principles of classical Grecian architecture. Features mosaics representing fragments from Greek mythology.

Interesting Oddities

- It's amazing to me that three extraordinary buildings—the Masonic Temple, the Pennsylvania Academy of the Fine Arts, and Philadelphia's City Hall—all started construction within about three years of each other . . . and are situated a stone's throw apart on North Broad Street. I don't know of any other city with three such renowned, eclectic structures gathered so close together (by my count, about 287 steps).

- The gavel used to lay the temple's cornerstone in 1868 was the same one used by President George Washington (also a Mason) to lay the cornerstone of the U.S. Capitol in 1793.

- The temple was one of the first buildings in Philadelphia lighted by electricity.

- Its first elevator was installed in 1883, because the temple's long staircase proved troublesome for some members, especially those in ill health or advanced in years.

- The temple's museum is also well worth a visit. It includes more than thirty thousand artifacts, items from George Washington and Ben Franklin, examples of key Masonic symbols, and more.

Do you have questions about Freemasonry, its reputation for secrecy, or associations with *The Da Vinci Code*? Ask your tour guide when you visit.

Fast Facts

Name: Masonic Temple
Home Of: The Grand Lodge of Free and Accepted Masons of Pennsylvania
Address: 1 North Broad Street
Honors: National Historic Landmark, National Register of Historic Places
Architect: James H. Windrim
Interior Design: George Herzog
Cost to Build: $1.6 million
Style: Norman Romanesque
Construction Completed: 1873
Time It Took to Complete the Interior: Fifteen to twenty more years
Tours: Tuesday through Saturday, 10 and 11 A.M. and 1, 2, and 3 P.M. Call ahead to confirm.
Costs: Adults, $15; students with ID, $10; children ages five to twelve, $5; senior citizens ages sixty-five and over, $10; Pennsylvania Masons, active military, and children under age five, free; group rates available. See website for more details.
Phone: 215-988-1917
Website: https://pamasonictemple.org/temple/
Nearby Attractions: City Hall, Reading Terminal Market, and LOVE Park

This updated story first ran in the May/June 2015 issue of the *Society Hill Reporter* and is reprinted with permission.

 # The PSFS Building

There's far more to this deceptively simple skyscraper with the famous PSFS sign than you see right away.
"The PSFS Building is one of the city's most important buildings," claimed Ken Hinde, former director of the Tour Program for the Foundation for Architecture.

Why? I asked myself at one of Hinde's lectures to the Association of Philadelphia Tour Guides in 2016. My untrained eye just couldn't see it.

The Philadelphia Chapter of the American Institute of Architects honored the PSFS Building as the "Building of the Century" in 1969. Pretty high praise. (Photo: © Jeff Goldberg/Esto.)

So, I set up a meeting with Hinde (who died after a brief illness in 2019) and his colleague Arthur J. Petrella (who died in 2018) at 1200 Market Street to better understand what I was missing. I came away a believer.

First, Petrella, a walking encyclopedia of Philadelphia history and architecture, pointed out the building's three distinctive parts, coverings, and colors.

Look carefully and you'll see the following:

- The highly polished gray granite–covered podium base is rounded at the Twelfth and Market Streets side. Inside were retail stores on the ground level, a large banking hall on the second floor, plus several floors of banking offices above—covered by sand-colored limestone. Today, they are part of a beautiful banquet area complete with the bank's preserved safe, Cartier clocks, and original marble.
- The office tower, which includes exposed vertical piers, is covered in the same sand-colored limestone. The tower rises some thirty stories.
- And finally the rear wall of the service core, covering stairwells, elevators, and utilities, is clad in glazed and unglazed black brick.

Not visible—but essential to the design—is a massive truss that is sixteen and one-half feet deep and spans the entire sixty-three-foot width of the banking area. It carries the weight of the office tower.

At night, Petrella said, the tower "looks like it is floating on a delicate glass box."

The PSFS Building was designed by architects George Howe and William Lescaze, with significant input from PSFS president James M. Willcox.

The building, Petrella said, was both the first air-conditioned multistory building in the world and the first international-style skyscraper anywhere. Others call it the first in the United States. Why international style? Because of its sleek modern look, glass facades, steel for exterior support, reinforced concrete inside, plus simplicity, openness, and straight lines, with no applied ornamentation.

Want to see the difference between this and other styles? Compare the U.S. Custom House at Second and Chestnut Streets with the PSFS Building, says Roger W. Moss, executive director emeritus of the Athenaeum of Philadelphia, in the beautiful photography book *Historic Landmarks of Philadelphia*. Completed just two years after the PSFS Building, the U.S. Custom House is massive, immense, and ornate, as opposed to the simple, sleek, and functional PSFS Building.

For banks, the PSFS Building was revolutionary. The name was too, being an acronym for Philadelphia Savings Fund Society. The savings bank exchanged earlier industry emphases on fortresslike security and safety for newfound customer desires for comfort and convenience.

Interesting Oddities

- The safe deposit vault contained more than eighteen thousand boxes, more than any other bank in Pennsylvania.
- Because the Depression drastically lowered prices for materials and labor, the PSFS Building actually cost $5 million less than originally estimated.
- Even so, the building, branded in its sales brochures as "Nothing More Modern," included the very best materials. Among them were stainless steel, luxurious varieties of marble, rare woods, leather, and more.
- Air-conditioning contributed greatly to the building's success. Some 90 percent of prospective tenants listed it as the most appealing feature. However, because some people were convinced that air-conditioning was harmful to their health, the building's engineer spent twenty-four hours a day inside for one full week to prove that it wasn't.
- The iconic PSFS sign, with twenty-seven-foot-high letters that are visible for some twenty miles, actually covers up cooling equipment on the roof. The sign—one of the first to use the Futura Light font—was also one of the first branding elements designed right into a building. At the time, some joked darkly that the letters meant Philadelphia Slowly Facing Starvation.
- After the Philadelphia Savings Fund Society was shut down by federal regulators in 1992, the building reopened as Loews Philadelphia Hotel in 2000. The hotel chain agreed to keep the PSFS sign in place. In 2016, Loews replaced the former neon sign with a light-emitting diode (LED) system said to be less costly and easier to maintain.

Fast Facts

Name: PSFS Building
Address: 1200 Market Street
Style: International
Architects: George Howe and William Lescaze

Constructed By: George A. Fuller Co.

Opened: August 1, 1932

Amenities: Cartier clocks in lobby and elevator lobbies; air-conditioning; sound-absorbing acoustic tile; custom-built tubular steel furniture for the banking floor; "radio outlets" in every office

Honors: National Register of Historic Places, National Historic Landmark; called the first truly modern skyscraper in the United States by *Architectural Review* in 1957

Cost: $7,420,942.37

Number of Stories: Thirty-six

Height: 491 feet high

Office Space: 375,000 square feet

Nearby Attractions: Reading Terminal Market, Chinatown, and City Hall

This updated story first ran in the January/February 2016 issue of the *Society Hill Reporter* and is reprinted with permission.

42 Reading Terminal Market

Near death in the 1970s, this unique food market has bounced back with a flourish.

If the 129-year-old Reading Terminal Market (RTM) were a boxer, it would have been knocked out in the 1970s.

By 1979, eight years after the Reading Company declared bankruptcy, Philadelphia's once-proud central market was stumbling badly. The building was a mess. It was only 20 percent occupied. And the future looked bleak.

For Bassetts Ice Cream, today's only remaining original vendor, sales barely totaled $25 some days.

Fortunately, during the 1970s, Philadelphia preservationists staved off efforts by Market East developers to demolish the building. In 1980, after emerging from bankruptcy, the Reading Company began investing in the market again.

Slowly, the RTM gained strength, especially with the addition of Amish (aka Pennsylvania Dutch) farmers. By 1983, it was 60 percent occupied.

In 1990, the Pennsylvania Convention Center bought the market, and the nonprofit Reading Terminal Market Corporation was appointed to manage it. Then, the old fighter began winning again.

Competition and sales are both way up.

At our 2014 interview, then–general manager Paul Steinke told me that the RTM was 100 percent occupied. (Days after the interview, Steinke resigned to run for a city council seat. Today, he is executive director of Preservation Alliance for Greater Philadelphia.)

Despite great pressure from Trader Joe's, Whole Foods, and a slew of outdoor neighborhood markets, sales were up 20 to 30 percent over a ten-year period, Steinke said.

A reported 7.3 million people now visit the market's eighty-six full-time and ten part-time vendors annually—spending $60 million in the process.

Steinke credited much of the turnaround to millennials, children of baby boomers who were born between about 1981 and 1996. They love cities, he says, and are interested in local and unique foods and business. "Many cities have no local entrepreneurial class. We do."

Steinke was most surprised that the RTM is here at all, noting that Philadelphia is one of very few major U.S. cities to still have a central market. It's also one of the oldest and largest markets.

"We descended from Philadelphia's first market," he says. "No one has what we have here."

Today, the RTM attracts 140,000 people weekly, or enough to fill up Lincoln Financial Field twice. The biggest complaint Steinke has heard: "We're not open late enough. We close at 6 P.M." The market is open seven days a week. Amish merchants are there Tuesday through Saturday. None of the Amish vendors are open on Sunday, and about 30 percent of them close on Monday too.

Interesting Oddities

- By written charter, the market does not want or permit "national chains" inside its doors, Steinke says. The RTM leases space to local food entrepreneurs only and gets about 140 requests a year to fill 2 or 3 openings.
- Children love to put money into the mouth of Philbert the Pig, the market's 225-pound, cast-bronze mascot located near the

This view of Reading Terminal Market shows the single-span arched train shed that was the largest in the world when built in 1893. Beneath it now at this end are meeting rooms of the Pennsylvania Convention Center. Closer to the Market Street end is the Grand Hall area. (Photo by Jim Murphy.)

central seating area. Funds go to the Food Trust, which began in 1992 at the RTM as the Reading Terminal Farmers' Market Trust.

• Opened in 1892, the RTM was first named "One of 10 Great Public Spaces in America" for 2014 by the American Planning Association.

The RTM employs modern technology to keep the momentum going and growing. It uses Facebook, Instagram, and Twitter; provides free Wi-Fi; and has a partnership with Mercato for same-day delivery to area residents from about thirty-five market vendors.

It's no wonder that years ago, even *New York Times* food journalist and blogger Mark Bittman looked lovingly eighty miles south toward the RTM, "the grandest market 'we' have."

Bemoaning the lack of a Big Apple central market, he wrote in March 2013, "We can find groovy retail just about anywhere, but to find a really fantastic indoor food market, we have to go to Philly."

Not bad praise for a venerable institution that almost went out of business some thirty to thirty-five years ago but is still fighting the good fight today.

Fast Facts

Name: Reading Terminal Market
Address: 51 North Twelfth Street
Year Opened: 1892
Retail Space: Seventy-eight thousand square feet
Films Shot Here: *Blow Out*, *Twelve Monkeys*, and *National Treasure*
Hours: Daily, 8 A.M. to 6 P.M.; Amish (aka Pennsylvania Dutch) vendors are closed on Sunday. About 30 percent of them close on Monday too.
Phone: 215-922–2317
Website: https://readingterminalmarket.org
Nearby Attractions: Friendship Gate in Chinatown, African American Museum, and Federal Reserve Bank

This updated story first ran in the January/February 2015 issue of the *Society Hill Reporter* and is reprinted with permission.

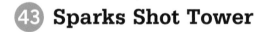 Sparks Shot Tower

It made ammunition for both the War of 1812 and the Civil War.
The giant brick Shot Tower at Carpenter and Front Streets that soars above Queen Village homes is unique in several ways:

- Founded to make shot just for hunting, it later produced small-diameter shot balls for the United States in the War of 1812 and the Civil War. That decision caused Quaker co-owner John Bishop, whose religion was against war and violence, to sell his part of the business to partner John Sparks, for whom the tower is named.
- Originally about 150-feet high, it's the first "smokestack" type of shot tower in the country . . . and a highly visible reminder of U.S. clashes with Great Britain.

Sparks Shot Tower, the first of its type in the United States, provided ammunition for both the War of 1812 and the Civil War. (Photo by Rosemary Noce-Murphy.)

• Ironically, after supplying deadly ammunition for two wars, Shot Tower is now a peaceful playground run by Philadelphia Parks and Recreation. Instead of workers producing musket balls or bullets, youngsters today play beneath the tower, making only childhood memories.

The brick Shot Tower, thirty feet in diameter at the bottom and thirteen feet at the top, was built at Carpenter and Front Streets in 1808, because the cost of imported shot was rising and becoming much harder to get.

Why? Britain, our major supplier of shot—and owner of a marvelous new technology for producing shot without "dimples, scratches and imperfections"—was embroiled in "the Napoleonic Wars" with France.

To try to keep us neutral and help prevent our ships and sailors from being seized by both combatants, the U.S. Embargo Act of 1807 prohibited trade with both nations.

Fortunately, the three partners at Sparks Shot Tower, who were all experienced at working with lead but not with the new shot technology, found someone who had worked at a British shot tower to help them.

The new technology included dropping molten lead from great heights into water—thus, the need for a tower. As the lead dropped through a sieve into the water, it formed perfect spheres.

Larger shot required a drop of 150 feet, about the original height of Sparks Shot Tower.

Interesting Oddities

- About ten feet of the tower was cut off in the nineteenth century. I still don't know why.
- A number of short support buildings, including a barrel shop, storehouses, office building, and more, surrounded the Shot Tower, which employed six men and one boy.
- The raw stock for the shot was pig lead and arsenic, which helped the molten lead flow more smoothly.
- For safety, the Shot Tower had thirteen wooden and two iron fire buckets that were kept in the tower and engine room.
- In 1822, a New York architect wrote, "The Storms drive through the Brick work—It is a slight Building—and rocks very much in a gale of wind." But *PlanPhilly* says, "The brick design, built to withstand gale force winds, served as a model for early lighthouses in the region."
- The Philadelphia Department of Recreation modified the building. It removed the spiral staircase, changed the roof and its pitch, added windows to the first story, and bricked up four vertical sets of windows.
- The Shot Tower's first ad in the *Aurora* on October 20, 1808, boasted: "AMERICAN PATENT SHOT, OF ALL SIZES, EQUALLY AS PERFECT AS ANY IMPORTED."

The one question I have is this: Did anyone then see the danger of naming the Shot Tower after Mr. Sparks? To me, that was tempting fate. Fortunately, the building has remained safe and fire-free for many years.

Fast Facts

Name: Sparks Shot Tower
Address: 101–31 Carpenter Street
Original Dimensions: 150 feet high, 30 feet in diameter at the bottom, 13 feet at the top
Claim to Fame: It was the first "smokestack" shot tower in the United States.

Historical Marker Dedication Date: April 19, 1997
Nearby Attractions: Gloria Dei Church, the Grand Battery historical marker, and the Washington Avenue Immigration Station historical marker

This updated story first ran in the May 2017 issue of *QVNA Magazine* and is reprinted with permission.

Water Works

In the mid-nineteenth century, the Fairmount Water Works was America's second-most-visited destination by foreign and U.S. tourists; Niagara Falls was first.
If you haven't yet been to the Fairmount Water Works Interpretive Center, it's worth a trip. You'll get a fascinating look at a water works that

* set the standard for more than thirty other U.S. cities,
* was praised by such writers as Charles Dickens and Mark Twain, and
* was the second-most-popular tourist destination in the country in the mid-nineteenth century.

Philadelphia's search for clean water was spurred by a deadly yellow fever epidemic in 1793 that killed nearly five thousand residents.

The city responded with a bold, state-of-the-art solution—although it was somewhat off the mark. (Not until about 1900 did scientists learn that mosquitoes, not dirty water, spread the disease.)

Today, more than two hundred years later, **the Fairmount Water Works offers visitors breathtaking views, innovative architecture, and a unique look at municipal problem solving.**

Before Fairmount, Philadelphia's Watering Committee opened the city's first water works in 1801 at Centre Square, where City Hall is now located. Because of maintenance problems, unresolved technical problems, and the need for a more reliable water supply, that site was abandoned in 1815.

Designed by architects skilled at hiding industrial equipment inside beautiful classical revival buildings, the Water Works became a top tourist attraction in the first half of the nineteenth century—especially after it replaced steam engines with water wheels. The site is still well worth a visit today. (Photo by Jim Murphy.)

But the Centre Square site was important for two reasons: its distribution system through pipes laid out in alignment with the street grid and Benjamin Latrobe's beautiful neoclassical building.

At Fairmount, Frederick Graff, a Latrobe disciple and newly named superintendent, continued the tradition of designing elegant classical revival buildings that disguised industrial machinery inside.

As a result, Fairmount was renowned for its marvelous architecture, stunning gardens and promenades, and wonderful water wheels.

Like fictional fighter Rocky Balboa in the *Rocky* movies, the Fairmount Water Works had its ups and downs. At first, it was a national pacesetter and technological marvel.

In 1822, after Superintendent Graff replaced two steam engines with large water wheels, people flocked to Fairmount to see them in action. Later, even-more-efficient turbines replaced the water wheels.

Unfortunately, during the Industrial Revolution, companies north of Philadelphia relentlessly dumped pollution and waste into the Schuylkill River. By 1883, the water was so bad that a physician offered $50 to anyone who could drink a quart of it ten nights in a row without vomiting or dying.

To combat the pollution, the city added new pumping and filtration stations near the Schuylkill and Delaware Rivers. Then, in 1909, after ninety-four years of operation, the water works was closed.

Today, the Philadelphia Art Museum—just up the steps from the nearby *Rocky* statue—sits atop what was once the 3,264,126-gallon water works reservoir.

Inside the old facilities is the Fairmount Water Works Interpretive Center. Opened in 2003, it now educates residents about water in our world.

The staff is warm, welcoming, and helpful. Admission is free. And a twenty-minute movie, interesting exhibits, and interactive displays make it a fun learning experience for young and old alike.

Interesting Oddities

- While the Fairmount Water Works became the nation's "most depicted piece of architecture" in the nineteenth century, says Arthur S. Marks (professor emeritus, department of art, University of North Carolina), Frederick Graff, the superintendent and chief engineer at Fairmount, was unappreciated for his architectural skills. He was not even listed in a biographical dictionary of Philadelphia architects of the period. Yet, Marks says, the water works "was wholly the product of Frederick Graff." Graff designed the buildings, most of the machinery, the distribution system, and the gardens.
- To prevent nearby industries from locating too close to the water supply, Philadelphia purchased the Lemon Hill property of Robert Morris in 1844. That strategy—"to protect and improve the purity of the Schuylkill water supply"—eventually resulted in the creation of Fairmount Park.
- The water works is a National Historic Civil Engineering Landmark, a National Historic Landmark, and a National Historic Mechanical Engineering Landmark.

Fast Facts

Place: Fairmount Water Works Interpretive Center
Address: 640 Waterworks Drive
Admission: Free
Hours: Tuesday through Saturday, 10 A.M. to 5 P.M.; Sunday, 1 to 5 P.M.; closed Monday and city holidays
Nearby Attractions: Philadelphia Museum of Art, Rodin Museum, and Benjamin Franklin Parkway

This updated story first ran in the July/August 2013 issue of the *Society Hill Reporter* and is reprinted with permission.

U.S. Custom House

This large art deco building is visible from many areas of Center City.

Long before our Philadelphia Eagles became Super Bowl champs in 2018, limestone eagles began guarding the U.S. Custom House on Chestnut Street in Old City.

Interestingly, there's even a connection between the limestone and football birds. More on that later.

Look skyward, and you'll see the limestone eagles perched on the upper reaches of the seventeen-story art deco building. And what a remarkable building it is.

Constructed as part of a huge government stimulus project after the Great Depression of 1929 (and just before the Works Project Administration), **the U.S. Custom House contains extraordinary details you won't see in modern buildings today**. I was fortunate to get a tour from Tom Rufo, the operations manager at the General Services Administration (GSA), and Mark Falter Jr., the onsite manager. They pointed out marvelous touches I simply would have missed.

Walk around the front of the building and look up, and you'll see statues, bas-reliefs, ornamental doors, and more. And that's just to prepare you for the amazing extravaganza to come.

Inside, you'll see a spectacular three-story rotunda, seventy-

You can spot the seventeen-story art deco U.S. Custom House from all over the Society Hill, Queen Village, and Old City areas. (Photo by Jim Murphy.)

five feet of murals almost four feet high, two magnificent staircases, and much more. There's even a Federal-style courtroom on the third floor used for tax court.

You may also see travelers with suitcases in the lobby, says Falter. The passport office in the building provides expedited service for U.S. citizens and can process even some same-day applications in emergency situations.

Be aware, though, that this is a U.S. government building with security procedures similar to an airport's.

Interesting Oddities

- While the beautiful three-story, thirty-two-foot-diameter rotunda appears to be in the center of the building, it actually is in the front part, disguising loading docks that take up nearly half of the first floor.
- A large cooling tower, added to the roof for air-conditioning in 1969, once was visible from New Jersey and I-95. Managers fixed that, Rufo says, by cutting the ceiling below and dropping the unit down twelve feet. Now, you can't see it.
- Construction of the building employed more than four thousand workers for two years. That helped spur the Philadelphia economy after the disastrous stock market crash of 1929.
- Some of the beautiful murals on the first floor "have darkened with age," says the National Register of Historic Places Registration Form. The cause: "application of an inappropriate superficial art conservation treatment that cannot be removed." Too bad—they were done by noted Brandywine School artist George Harding.
- Ritter & Shay, the building's architects, had to respond to fast-changing government demands. First, the building went from a planned eight stories to seventeen. Then, the Economy Act of June 30, 1932, reduced the budget by 10 percent. As a result, marble trim, which would have been more compatible with the historic neighborhood's architecture, was replaced by limestone.

Working inside a historic building brings extra challenges, Rufo says. To repaint the rotunda ceiling, for example, colors of forty paint chips had to be tested and verified before work could begin.

Now, back to the Birds for a minute: In 1933, new Philadelphia football team owners, led by Bert Bell, drew inspiration from the National Recovery Act's (NRA's) symbolic blue eagle. While searching for a new name for the football franchise, Bell saw the NRA logo, liked it, and renamed his team the Philadelphia Eagles—while this building was being erected.

Fast Facts

Name: U.S. Custom House
Address: 200 Chestnut Street
Built: 1932–34
Architects: Ritter & Shay
Cost: $3,500,000
Style: Art deco
Amount of Space: 565,000 square feet
Green Roof on Fourth Floor: 22,000 square feet
Number of Employees Housed: 670
Honors: Listed on the National Register of Historic Places in 2011, first U.S. building to receive the Energy Star label (in 1999)
Tenant Agencies: Homeland Security, Justice, Health and Human Services, Interior, State, Agriculture, Tax Court, and more
Claim to Fame: The illuminated terra cotta lantern atop the building tower resembles the famous lighthouse at Rhodes, Greece.
Nearby Attractions: Museum of the American Revolution, National Liberty Museum, and Science History Institute

This updated story first ran in the September/October 2018 issue of *QVNA Magazine* and is reprinted with permission.

⇥ Part X ⇤

Where History Comes Alive

46 Historical Society of Pennsylvania

Many of America's most treasured documents are housed at 1300 Locust Street.

Want to see history really come alive? Just stroll over to the Historical Society of Pennsylvania (HSP).

Here, you'll find **an astonishing collection of unique documents, watercolors, genealogical records, letters, diaries, and more**. Together, they provide a rare behind-the-scenes look at our country's triumphs and tragedies.

What's more, they allow once-dim historic figures to become real flesh-and-blood people too.

For example, here you can read a vivid eyewitness account of George Washington's last minutes of life, written by his secretary, Tobias Lear. Or you can learn about the heavy human price of slavery in the pages of abolitionist William Still's *Journal C of the Underground Railroad in Philadelphia*.

"Luckily, no one ever got hold of it," says Lee Arnold, senior director of the library and collections at HSP. Capture of Still's journal by the wrong hands could have put many people in danger. Why? Still carefully listed the old and new names of the runaway slaves, described their appearances, and sometimes revealed who was hiding them. In addition, he meticulously noted what it cost to harbor the runaways, clean their clothes, or buy new ones to disguise them.

The HSP's extraordinary collection also includes

- the first handwritten draft of the U.S. Constitution, July 1787;
- the first map of Philadelphia, 1683;
- a copy of the Emancipation Proclamation signed by Abraham Lincoln, 1864;
- a copy of "The Star-Spangled Banner," handwritten by Francis Scott Key, about 1840; and
- the earliest surviving American photograph, a daguerreotype taken at Chestnut and Juniper Streets in 1839. It shows Central High School and the armory next door.

One of the more interesting treasures is a draft copy of the Constitution written by James Wilson of Carlisle, Pennsylvania.

William Still's *Journal C of the Underground Railroad in Philadelphia*, one of many priceless documents at the Historical Society of Pennsylvania, provides specific details about enslaved people he helped escape to freedom. (Photo courtesy of the Charles L. Blockson Afro-American Collection, Temple University Libraries, Philadelphia, PA.)

One side of the page contains the draft text, with corrections on the other side.

Another draft of the Constitution begins, "We the People of the States of" and lists the full thirteen states (including Rhode-Island and "Providence Plantations"). Later, Wilson refers to the country's new name as "United People and States of America." Obviously, some of that language changed in the final version.

While some of these treasures are only available to the general public during special exhibitions, the HSP is expanding its digital portal—which already has more than one hundred thousand digitized images—to include even more important documents online.

"Preserving American Freedom," an HSP digital history project, provides fifty key documents for teaching about the evolution of the idea of freedom and practice of liberty in U.S. history.

The HSP's physical collection is staggering in both size and value too. It contains more than 20 million manuscripts and graphics (such as 35,000 prints and maps, 20,000 watercolors and drawings, and 250,000 photographs), plus over 600,000 printed items (including 10,000 published family histories), all in nineteen storage areas.

After a merger with the Balch Institute for Ethnic Studies, the HSP became a leading repository for immigrant and ethnic history.

Researchers at the HSP get free access to Ancestry.com, and the society possesses all the collections of the Genealogical Society of Pennsylvania (these cover every state east of the Mississippi) plus FindMyPast, Heritage Quest, NewsBank, and JSTOR. The HSP also has the collections of the Jewish Genealogical Society of Greater Philadelphia.

For military buffs, the HSP also has an extensive Civil War collection.

Some three thousand visitors use the society's resources in person each year. Half are researching family histories. The others are scholars, historians, professors, and writers.

In the Reading Room, you can request three documents at a time, and you'll get them within about forty-five minutes. "That's faster than the Library of Congress," Arnold says.

To preserve its extraordinary collection, the HSP houses these precious documents in a special fireproof building. When built in 1910, there was no wood inside except for the banister—not even for bookcases or furniture. Ingenious glass fire doors close automatically in the event of a fire.

When you visit 1300 Locust Street, think about the fact that you are in the same building as General George Meade's account of the Battle of Gettysburg, a printer's proof of the Declaration of Independence, and Martha Washington's cookbook!

There's something for everyone here.

Fast Facts

Name: Historical Society of Pennsylvania
Location: 1300 Locust Street
Founded: 1824
Hours: Tuesday through Friday; closed Saturday through Monday and major holidays; call or see website for exact hours
Admission: Nonmember adults, $8; undergraduate and graduate students with current student ID and students in grades six through twelve with current ID, free
Note: Pens, markers, highlighters, lipstick, and anything else that can make a permanent mark on documents are prohibited. You can bring a laptop, charger, silent cellphone, and pencil.
Lockers: Provided, because you can only bring in folders and notepads open on three sides. Portfolio cases, briefcases, and computer cases are not permitted inside.

Website: www.portal.hsp.org
Phone: 215-732-6200
Nearby Attractions: Library Company of Philadelphia, *Pride and Progress* mural, and Rittenhouse Square

This updated story first ran in the September/October 2012 issue of the *Society Hill Reporter* and is reprinted with permission.

47 Library Company of Philadelphia

If you're looking for books, prints, periodicals, photos, or ephemera from colonial America through the nineteenth century, this is the place to go.
Like so many things in our city, the Library Company of Philadelphia (LCP) was a Ben Franklin creation.

He started the Junto, a self-improvement club that debated morals, politics, and natural philosophy. When members realized they needed printed matter to prove their points, Franklin and the Junto began the LCP, the first subscription library in the United States.

A typically pragmatic Franklin solution, the LCP allowed members to pool their resources to buy books from London, something they could not afford on their own.

Fifty subscribers agreed in 1731 to put up forty shillings to maintain a shareholder's library, plus 10 shillings a year after that. You can still buy a share today for $200.

The South East Prospect of the City of Philadelphia is the oldest surviving oil painting of a North American city—and one of the most valuable. It was found in the rubbish of a London curiosity shop about 1857. (Courtesy of the Library Company of Philadelphia [https://librarycompany.org].)

Franklin called the LCP "the Mother of all American Subscription Libraries," and **until the Civil War, it was the largest public library in the United States**. Nonmembers could borrow books too, with collateral.

Dr. Richard S. Newman, director of the LCP when I spoke with him in 2015, says that unlike European libraries that served scholars and noblemen, most of the LCP's members were artisans. So, most early LCP purchases were useful books written in English, not in Latin or Greek.

Interesting Oddities

- One of the library's real treasures, a painting titled *The South East Prospect of the City of Philadelphia*, was found by a member of Parliament in the rubbish of a London curiosity shop about 1857. He gave it to George Mifflin Dallas, then a U.S. minister at the Court of St. James, who sent "the antique daub" back to Philadelphia as a curiosity. This circa-1720 oil painting by Peter Cooper is now the oldest-surviving canvas of any American city and among the most valuable of all Philadelphia paintings.
- Shortly before the Cooper painting arrived, the LCP began experiencing some losses. Then, books belonging to the library were discovered at an auction, "with the labels partially erased or concealed." The book thief turned out to be William Linn Brown, the son of noted author Charles Brockden Brown. William was immediately banned from the library.
- A statue of Franklin, the first public art in Philadelphia, was initially placed outside the library at Fifth Street and eventually moved to the LCP's current location. Over time, part of the

statue was damaged. What you don't see now in his right hand is a scepter, pointing downward to indicate Franklin's opposition to the monarchy.

Some Top Holdings

* The Magna Carta—Franklin's personal copy in Latin, an edition printed in London in 1556—is the gold standard of liberty documents.
* An edition of Euclid in Arabic, published in Rome in 1594, was formerly owned by James Logan and includes his handwritten notes in Arabic.
* "A Narrative of the Proceedings of the Black People, during the Late Awful Calamity in Philadelphia, in the Year 1793" by Absalom Jones and Richard Allen was likely the first copyrighted piece by African Americans in the United States.

Pioneering Collections

* **1969—Negro History, 1553–1903.** Now called the Program in African American History, this collection has attracted more scholars from greater distances than any other at the LCP.
* **1974—Women, 1500–1900.** This is one of the library's most active areas of collecting.

Exhibitions

As part of its outreach, LCP produces two exhibitions a year. More than sixty-five are online.

Fast Facts

Name: The Library Company of Philadelphia
Address: 1314 Locust Street
Year Founded: 1731 by Ben Franklin
What's Inside: An extensive, noncirculating collection of more than one million rare books, pamphlets, manuscripts, and graphics, documenting every aspect of American history and culture through the end of the nineteenth century

Nine: Number of signers of the Declaration of Independence who were LCP members. For many years, the LCP was the de facto Library of Congress.

Admission: Free

Hours: Reading Room and Gallery: Monday through Friday, 9 A.M. to 4:45 P.M.; Print Room: By appointment only

Visiting Scholars: Many stay next door at 1320 Locust Street, the LCP's Fellowship Residence in the former Cassatt House.

Phone: 215-546–3181

Website: www.librarycompany.org

Nearby Attractions: Historical Society of Pennsylvania, the Gayborhood, and William Way LGBT Community Center

This updated story first ran in the November/December 2015 issue of the *Society Hill Reporter* and is reprinted with permission.

⊷ Part XI ⊷

Beyond Center City

48 Cliveden (or the Chew House)

It's a historic mansion and a famous battleground.

There's far more to the famous Germantown summer home Cliveden (rhymes with "lived in") than first meets the eye.

Why? Because the visitor entrance on the street that the neighbors call Cliveden (rhymes with "dived in") brings you to a two-story carriage house that looks to me a bit like an old Wawa store. You don't see the mansion right away.

Fortunately, the carriage house and visitor center provide lots of interesting information about this fascinating site. But the real star here is Cliveden, both the scene of a major battle and a monument to conspicuous consumption built for Benjamin Chew.

A very successful lawyer close to the Penn family and also chief justice of the Supreme Court of the Province of Pennsylvania, Chew was one of the largest owners of enslaved African Americans in the area. His family owned more than nine plantations in Pennsylvania, Delaware, and Maryland.

Chew bought the land Cliveden was built on during a yellow fever epidemic in the 1760s. The reason was to get his family out of the city during the "sickly season"—late summer to the first frost in Philadelphia. Travel to Center City took about two hours by coach and forty-five minutes on horseback.

It's likely that he named his historic home Cliveden after the country house of Frederick, Prince of Wales, whom Chew greatly admired. In England, the name reportedly means "valley among cliffs."

Not only is Cliveden well known for its beautiful Georgian architecture and fine interior; it was also the site of a key Revolutionary War battle on October 4, 1777.

General George Washington led an attack on British General William Howe, whose nine thousand troops were camped in Germantown, says Michael Gabriel of the Washington Library at Mount Vernon. Washington had eleven thousand soldiers who moved to Cliveden in four columns from about fifteen miles away.

In a dense fog, one of Washington's columns surprised Howe's advance guard, forcing about one hundred British soldiers to take refuge at Cliveden. Instead of isolating the British troops where

A monument to conspicuous consumption, Cliveden, the Chew Mansion in Germantown, was built by one of the largest owners of enslaved African Americans in the area. A bloody Revolutionary War battle that took place here helped the colonies get aid from the French. (Copyright 1900 by Detroit Photographic Co. Photochrom Print Collection. Library of Congress Prints and Photographs Division.)

they were, Washington took what turned out to be bad advice from General Knox and bombarded Cliveden for two hours. Confusion reigned, and the attack stalled.

Hearing fire to their rear, some American troops thought they were being encircled and retreated. Unable to see clearly, two other American columns fired on each other. Howe counterattacked, and a potential great victory became a colonial defeat.

All was not lost, however. Encouraged by the Americans' valiant effort and an American victory at Saratoga, the French soon agreed to support the American cause. Their aid helped us win the Revolutionary War.

Interesting Oddities

- A unique "blood portrait" still exists in a second-floor bedroom at Cliveden. Said to have been created by a dying British soldier "painting" with his own blood as his life ebbed away during the battle, this profile of a girlfriend or loved one was confirmed by scientists to be made from organic material, not paint. The inside of Cliveden after the battle was said to look "like a slaughterhouse."

- African American leader Richard Allen, of Mother Bethel fame, was initially enslaved by Benjamin Chew. Allen even began his biography this way: "I was born in the year of our lord 1760, on February 14th, a slave to Benjamin Chew, of Philadelphia."

- The historic foliage at Cliveden includes numerous tulip poplars, sycamores, beeches, and ash trees, as well as Kentucky coffee trees. Some trees are one hundred to two hundred years old.

- The Chews kept extensive written records. Now more than 230,000 of the family's documents reside at the Historical Society of Pennsylvania, where they are prized by researchers.

- It's obvious that Chew and his son both considered enslaved people to be simply another cost or another piece of property. An inventory list of Ben Jr.'s includes the cost of sugar, meat, and fabric along with the value of individually named slaves—which varied, depending on their age and physical ability.

Cliveden is a prime example of a beautiful historic house built on the backs of enslaved people. David W. Young, a former executive director at Cliveden, refers to its "deep and sad history." (Young is also the author of *The Battles of Germantown*, published by Temple University Press.)

Fast Facts

Name: Cliveden (Chew House)
Operated By: Cliveden, Inc., on behalf of the National Trust for Historic Preservation
Address: 6401 Germantown Avenue
Phone: 215-848-1777
Website: www.cliveden.org
Size: Five and one-half acres
Opened: To the family in 1767; to the public as a museum in 1973
Claim to Fame: It's a great example of Georgian architecture and was the site of a major battle in the Revolutionary War that helped bring us assistance from the French.

Design: Probably selected from architectural pattern books by Benjamin Chew and built by German craftsmen, master mason John Hesser and master carpenter Jacob Knorr.

Honors: National Register of Historic Places, National Historic Landmark, and Philadelphia Register of Historic Places

Nearby Attractions: The Johnson House, Germantown White House (Deshler Morris House), and Lest We Forget Museum

 Fort Mifflin

On a muddy little island near the airport sits "the Fort That Saved America."

Thanks to the popular Disney TV series *Davy Crockett*, there's probably not a child in the United States who hasn't heard about the Battle of the Alamo. That 1836 siege lasted thirteen days. Some 182 to 257 Texans were killed, along with 400 to 600 Mexicans, and the battle became a rallying cry for Texas's independence.

Contrast that with the lower-profile six-day siege of Fort Mifflin, a wood-and-stone structure located nine miles from Center City Philadelphia on a muddy island in the Delaware River. **What happened here may well have saved the American Revolution**—yet few people know about it.

An Extraordinary Assault

On November 10–15, 1777, two thousand British troops—with a fleet of ships and 228 cannons—bombarded the twenty-two-acre fort with more than ten thousand cannonballs, eventually destroying the structure.

Inside the fort, a cold, wet, and hungry garrison of 400 men held off the British—with just ten cannons—suffering 240 casualties in the effort. So short were the Americans on ammunition that anyone retrieving a cannonball that could be fired back was promised a gill of rum, or about four ounces.

"Conditions were simply unimaginable," says Elizabeth H. Beatty, executive director at Fort Mifflin. Supplies were gone, it

Whether you enjoy Revolutionary War history, military reenactments, paranormal activity, or simply seeing airplanes take off many times per hour from the nearby airport runway, Fort Mifflin is a great place to visit. (Photo by David R. Schwartz.)

was unseasonably cold, and the parade grounds were iced over. Even the mud froze overnight.

The weather hurt the Continental soldiers in another critical way too. With unusually heavy rains flooding the back channel, two British ships were able to sail up the channel and bombard the fort's only unfinished walls at point-blank range. British Marines even climbed up to the crow's nest of the HMS *Vigilant* and threw hand grenades at soldiers inside the fort.

With the fort walls collapsing around them from the incredible shelling, most of the Americans evacuated after nightfall on November 15. With muffled oars, they rowed across the river to nearby Fort Mercer (now part of Redbank Battlefield Park, Gloucester, New Jersey).

The forty men remaining at Fort Mifflin set fire to what was left of the structure and then joined their comrades. But they left the fort's flag flying, and they never surrendered.

What they accomplished: From late September to early November, the troops at Fort Mifflin prevented 250 British ships in Delaware Bay from passing this Delaware River fort and supplying British troops occupying Philadelphia just to the north.

Until an extraordinary barrage by 228 British cannons on November 15, the Continental soldiers destroyed several British ships; kept food, clothing, gunpowder, and munitions from reaching the British Army; and delayed the inevitable.

By holding out "to the last extremity," as General George Washington had ordered, the men at Fort Mifflin gave Washington time to move his exhausted troops to Valley Forge for the winter—and very possibly saved the country.

After the war, Fort Mifflin was rebuilt. It served as a prison during the Civil War and as a naval munitions depot during World Wars I and II. Executive director Beatty views the fort itself as a veteran that has served and sacrificed for the country over an extended period of time.

Visiting Fort Mifflin, with its fifteen buildings, is a truly unique experience. I know of no military facility like it in the Philadelphia area.

This historic fort has something for everyone. Living history. Military reenactments. Even a strong reputation for paranormal activity.

It's time travel made simple—to a place of remarkable valor and supreme sacrifice.

Leatherneck, the magazine of the Marines, perfectly sums up Fort Mifflin's performance in a story published in 1956. It concludes that "at the finish the little river fort hadn't been defeated. It had simply been obliterated."

Fast Facts

Location: Fort Mifflin and Hog Island Roads
Annual Visitors: Sixteen thousand from all over the world
Named For: General Thomas Mifflin, who helped finish the fort after concerns about war with Britain grew in 1775
Number of British Cannons against the Fort: 228
Defending American Cannons: 10
Number of Cannonballs That Hit the Fort: More than ten thousand
Unusual Activity: Fort Mifflin is said to be one of the most haunted sites in America.
Oddity: Captain John Montrésor of the Royal Engineers designed Fort Mifflin and then was sent here by the British to destroy it. He succeeded.

Phone: 215-685-4167

Hours: March 1 through December 15, Wednesday through Sunday, 10 A.M. to 4 P.M.; call at other times

Admission: Adults, $8; seniors, $6; children ages six to twelve and veterans, $4; children ages five and under, free. For special Living History Events, prices are slightly higher. Purchase those in advance online by using the website's Events Calendar.

GPS Users: Use 6400 Hog Island Road, Philadelphia, PA 19153 as Fort Mifflin's address. Or get directions at www.fortmifflin.us.

Nearby Attractions: The Lazaretto, Bartram's Garden, and John Heinz National Wildlife Refuge

This updated story first ran in the July/August 2012 issue of the *Society Hill Reporter* and is reprinted with permission.

Taller Puertorriqueño

Its unique cultural center is a bold, beautiful building that connects the Latino community.

When I first visited Taller (pronounced "ty-yur") Puertorriqueño in the city's Fairhill section, I was amazed by the airy, colorful, and vibrant look of this cultural center that opened in 2016.

I was especially impressed by the unusually spaced wooden ceiling slats in the lobby that clearly say, "This building is very different."

And it is. Carmen Febo-San Miguel, M.D., the executive director of El Corazón Cultural Center (or the Cultural Heart of Latino Philadelphia), says, "That's what happens when you work with a firm with an architect who shares your vision."

The firm was WRT (Wallace Roberts & Todd). And the architect was Antonio Fiol-Silva, chief designer of the cultural center. Before starting SITIO, his own agency, he worked eighteen years for WRT.

The center's award-winning design, honored by the Urban Land Institute and the American Institute of Architects Philadelphia, is work that both WRT and SITIO can boast about—and do, with good reason.

Built on what was an empty lot, **the center offers the community more than twenty-four thousand square feet of spectacu-**

lar space, flexible dance and theater studio rooms, exhibit and rehearsal areas, after-school programs, a secure parking area, and more.

The building's gallery, classrooms, shop, and cafe surround a central interior plaza that *PlanPhilly*'s Ashley Hahn says is "designed to foster interaction and connection between different users." The day I was there, it sure seemed like a community hub, with people of all ages buzzing around.

Taller, which means "workshop," began in 1974 in the local basement of Aspira, Inc., a national grassroots organization helping develop Hispanic leadership.

Even then, the focus was on art. Members learned silk-screen printing and a practical understanding of their culture and history. Today, the focus has expanded to art of all kinds—digital illustration, printmaking, photography, video, and 3D printing—plus Latino culture.

Interesting Oddities

- When Febo-San Miguel, an area medical director and family practice physician, stepped in as executive director of Taller in 1999, she said, "I'm only going to do this until we find someone else." Her medical time went down, her Taller time went up, and she is still on the frontlines in 2019, working every day to keep the place functioning. No easy task.
- The building project, which took more than twelve years to complete and cost about $11.5 million, got a big jump-start from Philadelphia mayor John Street's administration. It provided $1.5 million in funding to hire an architect. Governor Ed Rendell also was very helpful, says Febo-San Miguel.
- "At the ribbon-cutting," she recalls, "I was going to put out twenty candles—one for each miracle that happened. It's unbelievable that we're here. So many things could have gone wrong."

The brightly colored building routinely is open Monday through Saturday from 10 A.M. to 6 P.M., plus other times for additional events. "It seems like 24/7," says Febo-San Miguel. The center's thirteen full-time and four part-time employees wear a lot of hats to keep things running. "Everyone has to chip in," she says.

The marvelous, airy lobby at Taller Puertorriqueño instantly says, "This building is very different." (Photo by Halkin I Mason Photography.)

With an after-school program that doubled in the new building, plus exhibitions, workshops, community events, book readings, and more, the building stays quite busy.

Febo-San Miguel speaks warmly of the wonderful generosity of the Philadelphia Orchestra and Kimmel Center. In four performances of *West Side Story*, lobby donations raised $35,000 to help Puerto Rican victims devastated by Hurricane Maria in September 2017. "It was very touching," she says.

Taller Puertorriqueño's task is not made easier by its neighborhood. With a poverty rate of 61 percent, the city's lowest median-household income, and a reputation for high drug activity in Fairhill, the center is a critical beacon of hope in a distressed area.

Amazingly, the community donated more than $90,000 to the center's funding, says Febo-San Miguel. And she believes that the building will continue to make a positive difference in Fairhill.

She marvels that "an organization of this size" already beat the odds to create a building like Taller Puertorriqueño. How? "A lot of people believed in it and supported it," she says simply.

Fast Facts

Name: Taller Puertorriqueño
First Word Sounds Like: Ty-yur
Name Means: Puerto Rican Workshop
Address: 2600 North Fifth Street
Phone: 215-426-3311
Website: https://tallerpr.org
Year Founded: 1974
Year Present Building Completed: 2016
Hours: Monday through Saturday, 10 A.M. to 6 P.M.
Building Honors: Urban Land Institute's Willard G. "Bill" Rouse III Award, 2018; American Institute of Architects Philadelphia, Merit Award: Built Category, 2017
Rental Space Available: Hourly, daily, weekly, or longer-term basis
Programs: After-school, for seniors, special exhibitions, and community-wide events
Nearby Attractions: Historic Fair Hill Burial Ground, El Centro de Ora, and Free Library of Philadelphia Lillian Marrero Branch

The Lazaretto

America's oldest quarantine station—"Ellis Island's Great Grandfather"—helped protect Philadelphia residents for ninety-four years.

In the summer and fall of 1793, panic reigned in Philadelphia, then the nation's capital. Yellow fever was quickly spreading through the waterfront area of the new world's busiest port, killing more than one out of ten residents. And no one knew how to stop it.

By October, as many as one hundred people a day were dying. Before the four-month epidemic ended, more than four thousand people had succumbed to the disease. In the meantime, seventeen thousand of the city's forty-five to fifty-five thousand residents, including President George Washington, had fled to safer ground.

The deadly disease, which struck many teenagers and heads of families near the docks instead of the very young and very old, turned the skin yellow. Other symptoms included bleeding from just about any orifice and "black vomit."

The graceful Georgian-style main hospital building of the Lazaretto Quarantine Station (or Philadelphia Lazaretto) still overlooks the Delaware River. It now hosts administrative offices for Tinicum Township, Delaware County. (Photo by Jim Murphy.)

Some medical authorities believe that yellow fever was carried here from Saint-Domingue (now Haiti) by French colonial refugees—some with slaves—who were fleeing a slave revolution there. Billy G. Smith, a professor of history at Montana State and author of several books about the city, thinks that a small British ship, the *Hankey*, carried yellow fever from the west coast of Africa to Philadelphia. However the disease began, it devastated the city.

In response to what David S. Barnes, associate professor and director of the Health and Societies Program at the University of Pennsylvania, calls a devastating "9/11-type experience," **Philadelphia erected a large lazaretto, or quarantine station, in 1799 on the banks of the Delaware River about ten miles south of the city to help prevent further calamity**.

Named for St. Lazarus, the patron saint of lepers, the new lazaretto was more isolated than a closer, smaller station built in 1742 on Province Island near Fort Mifflin. (Historically, lazarettos were built as early as the fourteenth and fifteenth centuries near European port cities.)

While doctors of the day did not know that yellow fever was spread by a type of mosquito, lazaretto personnel stopped and inspected all ships, passengers, and cargo from June to October 1, the usual quarantine season. (Late summer until the first frost is sometimes called "the sickly season.")

If there were no problems, the process would take about a day. If signs of illness or contamination were found on board, or if the ship came from a port known for a contagious disease, the ship would be stopped and held, with the passengers quarantined at the lazaretto.

All cargo and possessions would be fumigated or "purified," and the ship would be scoured and whitewashed clean. The process at this stage could take a day to two weeks or more.

Barnes, who has finished a book manuscript about the lazaretto that is in the editorial process, first learned about the station while working with colleagues at Temple University on a history of public health course.

Instead of "the dilapidated corrugated metal shell" he imagined, Barnes was "blown away" by the noteworthy architecture and scale of the buildings and the "wild, undeveloped Little Tinicum Island." He found the station to be "weirdly bucolic" and "intriguing" and considers it "Ellis Island's great grandfather."

The lazaretto closed in 1895, with some of its local duties moved to Marcus Hook or to federal stations near Lewes or Reedy Island, both in Delaware.

Later, it served as a popular country club, flying school, and one of the country's first seaplane bases.

Today, the site still includes the graceful, three-and-a-half-story main hospital building, now used for administrative offices by tiny Tinicum Township, Delaware County. After preservationists filed a lawsuit over plans to make the area into an airport parking lot, the township purchased the land. Now, you will also find a fire station, ballroom, and small parking lot there as well. Occasionally, special events are held at the site to raise funds.

Did the lazaretto work? Barnes says, "Yes, it probably did help disrupt the cycle by which yellow fever spread into and within urban populations."

And consider this: When yellow fever broke out at the lazaretto in 1870, fourteen people died there. Among them were the quarantine master, head physician, and head nurse. But the disease never reached Philadelphia.

In 1853, New Orleans reported 7,849 deaths from yellow fever, and 4,000 in both 1858 and 1878. Memphis recorded more than 5,000 yellow fever deaths in 1878 alone.

So, if you judge the lazaretto by the lack of a Philadelphia epidemic in 1870—or many other years when cases of yellow fever, cholera, or other epidemic diseases did not spread from the quarantine station to the city—you'd probably have to consider it a rousing success.

Fast Facts

Location: 97 Wanamaker Avenue, Essington, PA (for GPS); Mailing address: 629 North Governor Printz Boulevard, Essington, PA 19029

In Operation: 1801–95

Original Size: Ten acres

Significance: Ninety-two years older than Ellis Island, the Philadelphia lazaretto is the oldest-surviving quarantine facility in the Western Hemisphere and the sixth oldest in the world.

Honor: National Register of Historic Places

Websites: http://lazaretto.site; www.lazaretto.org; www.1799laz aretto.com; http://tthsdelco.org/lazaretto; www.sas.upenn .edu/~dbarnes/Lazaretto.html

Visiting: As of January 2020, you could walk around the old restored building and go down to the river for a closer look at Little Tinicum Island. It's also now open for township business on Monday through Friday, 8 A.M. to 4:30 P.M. And there is a space inside designated for an eventual museum.

Directions: From Philadelphia, go south on I-95 to 9A, the Essington Exit. Go south toward Essington for 0.4 mile. Go through the traffic light, merge onto Wanamaker Avenue, and drive about 0.5 mile. Your destination is at Wanamaker Avenue and Second Street.

Nearby Attractions: John Heinz National Wildlife Refuge, Simeone Foundation Automotive Museum, and American Swedish Historical Museum

This updated story first ran in the March/April 2013 issue of the *Society Hill Reporter* and is reprinted with permission.

Bibliography

Part I William Penn's Huge Impact on Philadelphia

1 A City of Churches

Eichel, Larry. "A Report from The Pew Charitable Trusts." *Philadelphia's Historic Sacred Places: Their Past, Present and Future*, Oct. 2017. www.pewtrusts.org/-/media/assets/2017/10/pri_philadelphias_historic_sacred_places_final.pdf.

Hamilton, Alexander. *The Itinerarium of Dr. Alexander Hamilton, 1744*. 2013 ebook. https://archive.org/details/b28979990/page/n6/mode/2up.

Kite, St. Alban. "William Penn and the Catholic Church in America." *The Catholic Historical Review*, vol. 13, no. 3, 1927, pp. 480–496. *JSTOR*, www.jstor.org/stable/25012453.

Schwartz, Sally. "William Penn and Toleration: Foundations of Colonial Pennsylvania." *Pennsylvania History: A Journal of Mid-Atlantic Studies*, vol. 50, no. 4, 1983, pp. 284–312. *JSTOR*, www.jstor.org/stable/27772931.

2 Green from the Get-Go

Albright, Thomas A. "Forests of Pennsylvania, 2016." Resource Update FS-132. *U.S. Department of Agriculture, Forest Service, Northern Research Station*. www.fs.fed.us/nrs/pubs/ru/ru_fs132.pdf.

"City Plan of Philadelphia." *American Society of Civil Engineers*. www.asce.org/project/city-plan-of-philadelphia/.

Finkel, Ken. "Broad and Market Streets: The Intersection of Past and Future." *The PhillyHistory Blog*, 16 Apr. 2015. www.phillyhistory.org/blog/index.php/2015/04/broad-and-market-streets-the-intersection-of-past-and-present/.

Hamilton, Alexander. *The Itinerarium of Dr. Alexander Hamilton, 1744*. 2013 ebook. https://archive.org/details/b28979990/page/n6/mode/2up.

Hubbard, Elbert, and Felix Shay. *The Fra: For Philistines and Roycrofters*, vol. 2. New York: E. Hubbard, 1908.

Kashatus, William C. "William Penn's Legacy: Religious and Spiritual Diversity." *Pennsylvania Heritage*, Spring 2011.

Lingelbach, William E. "William Penn and City Planning." *Pennsylvania Magazine of History and Biography*, vol. 68, no. 4, Oct. 1944, pp. 398–414. https://jour nals.psu.edu/pmhb/article/view/30007/29762.

Penn, William. "William Penn's 1681 Pamphlet." *The Original 13 Settlers of Germantown, Pennsylvania*. RootsWeb, http://freepages.rootsweb.com/~original13/ge nealogy/penns-pamphlet.htm.

Saffron, Inga. "Green Country Town." *The Encyclopedia of Greater Philadelphia*. https://philadelphiaencyclopedia.org/archive/green-country-town/.

Satullo, Chris. "City of Brotherly Love." *The Encyclopedia of Greater Philadelphia*. https://philadelphiaencyclopedia.org/archive/city-of-brotherly-love/.

Watson, John F., and Willis P. Hazard. *Annals of Philadelphia and Pennsylvania in the Older Time*, vol. 3. Philadelphia: E. S. Stuart, 1884. https://archive.org/details /annalsofphiladel03wats/page/n6/mode/2up.

Werner, Emma J. Lapasnasky. "Holy Experiment." *The Encyclopedia of Greater Philadelphia*. https://philadelphiaencyclopedia.org/archive/holy-experiment-2/.

3 Philly's Flag

Acrelius, Israel. *A History of New Sweden*. Philadelphia: The Historical Society of Pennsylvania, 1874.

Axelrod, Alan P. *Profiles in Folly: History's Worst Decisions and Why They Went Wrong*. New York: Sterling Publishing Company, 2008.

Balch, Thomas Willing, "Johan Printz." *Officers, Members, Charter, By-laws, Colonial Governors, Addresses*, vol. 1. Pennsylvania Society of Colonial Governors Society, 1916.

Bridenbaugh, Carl. "The Old and New Societies of the Delaware Valley in the Seventeenth Century." *The Pennsylvania Magazine of History and Biography*, vol. 100, no. 2, 1976, pp. 143–172. JSTOR, www.jstor.org/stable/20091051.

Burlando, Michael. "Let's Fly a Better Flag for Philadelphia." *Hidden City Philadelphia*, 11 Oct. 2013. https://hiddencityphila.org/2013/10/lets-fly-a-better -flag-for-philadelphia/.

Craig, Peter Stebbins. "Chronology of Colonial Swedes on the Delaware 1638–1713." *Swedish Colonial News*, vol. 2, no. 5, Fall 2001. http://colonialswedes.net /History/Chronology.html.

"Fort Christina." A Tour of New Netherlands. *New Netherland Institute*. www.new netherlandinstitute.org/history-and-heritage/digital-exhibitions/a-tour-of -new-netherland/delaware/fort-christina/.

Johnson, Amandus. *The Swedish Settlements on the Delaware 1638–1664*, vol. 2. Philadelphia Swedish Colonial Society, 1911. https://ia800306.us.archive .org/22/items/swedishsettlem02john/swedishsettlem02john_bw.pdf.

"Log Cabins in America: The Finnish Experience." Teaching with Historic Places Lesson Plans. *National Park Service*. www.nps.gov/nr/twhp/wwwlps/lessons/4log cabins/4logcabins.htm.

Robinson, Sam. "Behind Philadelphia Maneto: Dissecting the City Seal." *Hidden City Philadelphia*, 5 Nov. 2013. https://hiddencityphila.org/2013/11/behind-phila delphia-maneto-dissecting-the-city-seal/.

Scharf, J. Thomas, and Thompson Wescott. *History of Philadelphia*. Philadelphia: L. H. Everts and Company, 1884.

Springer, Ruth L., Louise Wallman, And. Rudman, and Andreas Sandell. "Two Swedish Pastors Describe Philadelphia, 1700 and 1702." *The Pennsylvania Mag-*

azine of History and Biography, vol. 84, no. 2, 1960, pp. 194–218. *JSTOR*, www
.jstor.org/stable/20089287.

Weslager, C. A. "Log Houses in Pennsylvania during the Seventeenth Century." *Pennsylvania History: A Journal of Mid-Atlantic Studies*, vol. 22, no. 3, 1955,
pp. 256–266. *JSTOR*, www.jstor.org/stable/27769605.

"What Do the Colors on the Swedish Flag Represent?" *Reference*. www.reference
.com/world-view/colors-swedish-flag-represent-3de66b5b9d8fadfa.

"Where the Phillies Wore Blue and Yellow for Swedish Heritage." *Uni Watch*, 2
Aug. 2013. https://uni-watch.com/2013/08/02/phillies-took-city-flag-colors
-for-a-time-plus-a-full-no-pelicans-review/.

Young, John Russell, ed. *Memorial History of the City of Philadelphia*, vol. 2. New
York: New York History Company, 1898.

4 Welcome Park

Carson, Hampton L. "William Penn as a Law-Giver." *The Pennsylvania Magazine
of History and Biography*, vol. 30, no. 1, 1906, pp. 1–29. *JSTOR*, www.jstor.org
/stable/20085320.

Darrach, Henry. "Annual Meeting of the Welcome Society." *Voyage of William Penn
in Ship Welcome: 1682 with A View of Philadelphia*. 1917. https://ia802905.us.ar
chive.org/34/items/voyageofwilliamp00phil/voyageofwilliamp00phil.pdf.

Dunn, Mary Maples. *William Penn: Politics and Conscience*. Princeton: Princeton University Press, 1967.

Gallery, John Andrew. *The Planning of Center City Philadelphia: From William Penn
to the Present*. Philadelphia: The Center for Architecture, 2007.

Geiger, Mary K. *William Penn*. Harlow, UK: Pearson Education, 2000.

Kenny, Kevin. *Peaceable Kingdom Lost*. New York: Oxford University Press, 2009.

Kyriakodis, Harry. *Philadelphia's Lost Waterfront*. Charleston, SC: The History Press,
2011.

Moretta, John A. *William Penn and the Quaker Legacy*. New York: Pearson Education, Inc., 2007.

Murphy, Andrew R. *William Penn: A Life*. New York: Oxford University Press, 2019.

Peare, Catherine Owens. *William Penn: A Biography*. Ann Arbor: University of Mich-
igan Press, 1966.

Penn, William, "Charter of Privileges for the Province of Pennsylvania, 1701." Treasures of the APS, *American Philosophical Society*. www.amphilsoc.org/exhibits
/treasures/charter.htm.

Powell, Jim. "William Penn: America's First Great Champion for Liberty and
Peace." *The Freeman*. https://quaker.org/legacy/wmpenn.html.

Soderlund, Jean R., ed. *William Penn and the Founding of Pennsylvania: A Documentary History*. Philadelphia: University of Pennsylvania Press, 1983.

Weigley, Russell F., ed. *Philadelphia: A 300-Year History*. New York: W. W. Norton
and Company, 1982.

Part II Military Leaders

5 Captain Gustavus Conyngham

"Captain Gustavus Conyngham, Continental Navy (1747–1819)." *Naval Historical Center*, 2003. www.ibiblio.org/hyperwar/OnlineLibrary/photos/pers-us
/uspers-c/g-conyng.htm.

Clark, R. *Wickes and Conyngham in European Waters.* www.schoonerman.com/na valhistory/wickes_and_conyngham_in_european.htm.

Conyngham, Gustavus. "Narrative of Captain Gustavus Conyngham, U. S. N., While in Command of the 'Surprise' and 'Revenge,' 1777–1779." *The Pennsylvania Magazine of History and Biography,* vol. 22, no. 4, 1898, pp. 479–488. *JSTOR,* www .jstor.org/stable/20085820.

Fredriksen, John C. *Revolutionary War Almanac.* New York: Infobase Publishing, 2006.

Harness, James. "A Sea Story: James Harness's Romance of the Adventures of Capt. Gustavus Conyngham." *New York Times,* 8 Nov. 1902, p. 21. https://timesmachine .nytimes.com/timesmachine/1902/11/08/118484907.html?pageNumber=21.

Hazard, Samuel, ed. "Gustavus Conyngham." *Hazard's Register of Pennsylvania,* vol. 5, no. 26, 26 Jun. 1830, pp. 401–403.

Jones, Charles Henry. *Captain Gustavus Conyngham: A Sketch of the Services He Rendered to the Cause of American Independence.* Pennsylvania Sons of the Revolution, 1903.

McGrath, Tim. *Give Me a Fast Ship.* New York: The Penguin Group, 2014.

Norton, Louis Arthur. "Captain Gustavus Conyngham: America's Successful Naval Captain or Accidental Pirate?" *Journal of the American Revolution,* 15 Apr. 2015. https://allthingsliberty.com/2015/04/captain-gustavus-conyngham-ameri cas-accidental-pirate/.

6 Commodore John Barry

Bakshian, Adam, Jr. "The Revolutionary War's Other Naval Hero." *Wall Street Journal,* 5 Jun. 2010. www.wsj.com/articles/SB10001424052748704717004 575268681479651038.

Boyer, Deborah. "Statues around Philadelphia, Part One." *The PhillyHistory Blog,* 21 Mar. 2009. https://blog.phillyhistory.org/index.php/2009/03/statues -around-philadelphia-part-one/.

McGrath, Tim. "I Passed by Philadelphia with Two Boats." *Naval History Magazine,* vol. 23, no. 3. www.usni.org/magazines/naval-history-magazine/2009 /june/i-passed-philadelphia-two-boats.

———. *John Barry: An American Hero in the Age of Sail.* Yardley: Westholme Publishing, 2010.

Memorial to Commodore John Barry, Father of the Navy of the United States. Philadelphia: Society of the Friendly Sons of St. Patrick of Philadelphia for the Relief of Emigrants from Ireland, 1907.

7 Commodore Stephen Decatur Jr.

Clark, Allen C. "Commodore James Barron, Commodore Stephen Decatur: The Barron-Decatur Duel." *Records of the Columbia Historical Society, Washington, D.C.,* vol. 42/43, 1940, pp. 189–215. *JSTOR,* www.jstor.org/stable/40067579.

Cray, Robert E. "Remembering the USS *Chesapeake*: The Politics of Maritime Death and Impressment." *Journal of the Early Republic,* vol. 25, no. 3, 2005, pp. 445–474. *JSTOR,* www.jstor.org/stable/30043338.

Drake, Ross. "Duel." *The Smithsonian Magazine,* March 2004. www.smithsonian mag.com/history/duel-104161025/.

Hickey, Donald R. *The War of 1812: A Short History.* Urbana: University of Illinois Press, 1995.

Jamlin, Teunis S. "Historic Houses of Washington." *Scribner's Magazine*, vol. 14, no. 1, 1893, pp. 475–491.

Lambert, Frank. *The Barbary Wars: American Independence in the Atlantic World.* New York: Farrar, Straus and Giroux, 2005.

Leiner, Frederick C. "Searching for Nelson's Quote." U.S. Naval Institute. *USNI News*, 22 Jul. 2012. https://news.usni.org/2012/07/22/searching-nelsons-quote.

Long, David F. "William Bainbridge and the Barron-Decatur Duel: Mere Participant or Active Plotter?" *The Pennsylvania Magazine of History and Biography*, vol. 103, 1979, pp. 34–52.

Rolph, Daniel. "The 'Barbary Wars' and Their Philadelphia Connections." *Hidden Histories: Historical Society of Pennsylvania*, 6 May 2009. https://hsp.org/blogs/hidden-histories/the-barbary-wars-and-their-philadelphia-connections.

Spears, John Randolph. *The History of Our Navy: From Its Origin to the End of the War with Spain 1775–1898*, vol. 3. New York: Charles Scribner's Sons, 1902.

Swain, Claudia. "Every Second Counts: The Decatur-Barron Duel of 1820." *Boundary Stones: WETA's Local History Blog.* https://blogs.weta.org/boundarystones/2013/03/22/every-second-counts-decatur-barron-duel-1820.

Tucker, Spencer C. *Stephen Decatur: A Life Most Bold and Daring.* Library of Naval Biography. Annapolis: Naval Institute Press, 2013.

Part III Gone—But Not Forgotten

8 Acadian Connection

Agnew, David Hayes, et al. *History and Reminiscences of the Philadelphia Almshouse and Philadelphia Hospital.* Philadelphia: Detre and Blackburn, 1890.

Griffin, Martin I. J. "Washington Square Philadelphia, the First Burial Ground for Catholics—For Patriots of the American Revolution, and for Martyrs for the Faith, the Exiled Acadians—Their Petition to the King of Great Britain." *The American Catholic Historical Researches*, vol. 18, no. 1, 1901, pp. 38–40. *JSTOR*, www.jstor.org/stable/44374197.

———. "Where Are Evangeline and Gabriel Buried?" *The Magazine of History with Notes and Queries II*, Jun./Dec. 1905, pp. 403–406.

Keels, Thomas H. *Philadelphia Graveyards and Cemeteries.* Charleston, SC: Arcadia Publishing, 2003.

Ledet, Wilton Paul. "Acadian Exiles in Pennsylvania." *Pennsylvania History: A Journal of Mid-Atlantic Studies*, vol. 9, no. 2, Apr. 1942, pp. 118–128. https://journals.psu.edu/phj/article/view/21363/21132.

Longfellow, Henry Wadsworth. "Evangeline: A Tale of Acadie." *Henry Wadsworth Longfellow* [online resource], Maine Historical Society. www.hwlongfellow.org/works_evangeline.shtml.

Scharf, J. Thomas, and Thompson Wescott. *History of Philadelphia, 1609–1884.* Philadelphia: L. H. Everts and Company, 1884.

9 The Gaskill Street Baths

Boonin, Harry D. *The Jewish Quarter of Philadelphia: A History and Guide 1881–1930.* Philadelphia: Jewish Walking Tours of Philadelphia, 1999.

Dinwiddie, Emily W. *Housing Conditions in Philadelphia.* Philadelphia: Octavia Hill Association, 1904.

Glassberg, David. "The Design of Reform: The Public Bath Movement in America." *American Studies*, vol. 20, no. 2, 1979, pp. 5–21. *JSTOR*, www.jstor.org/stable/40641458.

Golab, Caroline. *Immigrant Destinations*. Philadelphia: Temple University Press, 1977.

Grabbe, Hans-Jürgen. "European Immigration to the United States in the Early National Period, 1783–1820." *Proceedings of the American Philosophical Society*, vol. 133, no. 2, 1989, pp. 190–214. *JSTOR*, www.jstor.org/stable/987050.

Klaczynska, Barbara. "Immigration (1870–1930)." *The Encyclopedia of Greater Philadelphia*. https://philadelphiaencyclopedia.org/archive/immigration-1870-1930/.

Major U.S. Immigration Ports. *Ancestry.com*. www.ancestrycdn.com/support/us/2016/11/majorusports.pdf.

Mandell, Melissa M. "Window on the Collections: The Public Baths Association of Philadelphia and the 'Great Unwashed.'" *Historical Society of Pennsylvania*. www.philaplace.org/essay/378/.

Miller, Fredric M. "Philadelphia: Immigrant City." Balch Online Resources, *Historical Society of Pennsylvania*. www2.hsp.org/exhibits/Balch%20resources/phila_ellis_island.html.

Popkin, Nathaniel. "Walking Tour Booklets: The Northern Liberties and South Philadelphia." *PhilaPlace, Historical Society of Pennsylvania*, 2011. www.philaplace.org/pdf/territoryofdreams.pdf.

"Public Baths Association of Philadelphia Records, 1890–1950, Collection 1999." *Historical Society of Pennsylvania*. https://hsp.org/sites/default/files/legacy_files/migrated/findingaid1999publicbaths.pdf.

Sitarski, Stephen M. "From Weccacoe to South Philadelphia: The Changing Face of a Neighborhood." *PhilaPlace, Historical Society of Pennsylvania*. www.philaplace.org/essay/376/.

Szucs, Juliana. "Ports Beyond New York: 5 Things about the Port of Philadelphia." *Ancestry.com*, 3 Jun. 2014. https://blogs.ancestry.com/ancestry/2014/06/03/ports-beyond-new-york-5-things-about-the-port-of-philadelphia/.

"Washington Avenue Steamship Landing and Immigration Station." *PhilaPlace, Historical Society of Pennsylvania*. www.philaplace.org/story/190/.

Williams, Marilyn Thornton. *Washing the Great Unwashed: Public Baths in Urban America, 1840–1920*. Columbus: Ohio State University Press, 1991.

10 The Grand Battery (or the Association Battery)

Boudreau, George W. "'Done by a Tradesman': Franklin's Educational Proposals and the Culture of Eighteenth-Century Pennsylvania." *Pennsylvania History: A Journal of Mid-Atlantic Studies*, vol. 69, no. 4, 2002, pp. 524–557. *JSTOR*, www.jstor.org/stable/27774445.

Dorwart, Jeffrey M. "Forts and Fortifications." *The Encyclopedia of Greater Philadelphia*. https://philadelphiaencyclopedia.org/archive/forts-and-fortifications/.

———. *Invasion and Insurrection: Security, Defense, and War in the Delaware Valley, 1621–1815*. Newark: University of Delaware Press, 2008.

Griffith, Sally F. "Order, Discipline, and a Few Cannon: Benjamin Franklin, the Association, and the Rhetoric and Practice of Boosterism." *The Pennsylvania Magazine of History and Biography*, vol. 116, no. 2, 1992, pp. 131–155. *JSTOR*, www.jstor.org/stable/20092699.

Hayburn, Tim. "Pirates." *The Encyclopedia of Greater Philadelphia*. https://philadelphiaencyclopedia.org/archive/pirates/.

Isaacson, Walter. *Benjamin Franklin: An American Life.* New York: Simon and Schuster, 2003.

Kyriakodis, Harry. "Shaping Up and Shipping Out at Philadelphia's First Navy Yard." *Hidden City Philadelphia*, 18 Jul. 2017. https://hiddencityphila.org/2017/07/shaping-up-and-shipping-out-at-philadelphias-first-navy-yard/.

Lamay, J. A. Leo. *The Life of Benjamin Franklin, Volume 3: Soldier, Scientist and Politician, 1748–1757.* Philadelphia: University of Pennsylvania Press, 2009.

"Plain Truth, 17 November 1747." *Founders Online*, National Archives. https://founders.archives.gov/documents/Franklin/01-03-02-0091. [Original source: *The Papers of Benjamin Franklin, vol. 3, January 1, 1745, through June 30, 1750.* Edited by Leonard W. Labaree. New Haven: Yale University Press, 1961, pp. 180–204.]

Scharf, J. Thomas, and Thompson Wescott. *History of Philadelphia, 1609–1884.* Philadelphia: L. H. Everts and Co., 1884.

"Scheme of the First Philadelphia Lottery, 5 December 1747." *National Archives, Founders Online.* https://founders.archives.gov/documents/Franklin/01-03-02-0097.

Wainwright, Nicholas B. "Scull and Heap's East Prospect of Philadelphia." *The Pennsylvania Magazine of History and Biography*, vol. 73, no. 1, 1949, pp. 16–25. *JSTOR*, www.jstor.org/stable/20088054.

Watson, John Fanning. *Annals of Philadelphia and Pennsylvania in Olden Time.* Philadelphia: John F. Watson, 1830.

———. *Annals of Philadelphia: Being a Collection of Memoirs, Anecdotes and Incidents of the City and Its Inhabitants from the Days of the Pilgrim Founders.* Philadelphia: E. O. Carey and A. Hart, 1830.

Wayman, Matthew J. "Privateering." *The Encyclopedia of Greater Philadelphia.* https://philadelphiaencyclopedia.org/archive/privateering/.

Zipfel, Nathan. "History of Delaware—Scharf." *Delaware Roots*, Chapter 10, "Pirates and Privateers." www.delawareroots.org/index.php/history-of-delaware-j-thomas-scharf/118-chapter-10-pirates-and-privateers.

11 Washington Avenue Immigration Station

Berquist, James. "Immigration (1790–1860)." *The Encyclopedia of Greater Philadelphia.* https://philadelphiaencyclopedia.org/archive/immigration-1790-1860/.

Boyer, Deborah. "Entering America: The Washington Avenue Immigration Station." *The PhillyHistory Blog*, 21 Jan. 2009. www.phillyhistory.org/blog/index.php/2009/01/entering-america-the-washington-avenue-immigration-station/.

Golab, Caroline. *Immigrant Destinations.* Philadelphia: Temple University Press, 1977.

Grabbe, Hans-Jürgen. "European Immigration to the United States in the Early National Period, 1783–1820." *Proceedings of the American Philosophical Society*, vol. 133, no. 2, 1989, pp. 190–214. *JSTOR*, www.jstor.org/stable/987050.

Klaczynska, Barbara. "Immigration (1870–1930)." *The Encyclopedia of Greater Philadelphia.* https://philadelphiaencyclopedia.org/archive/immigration-1870-1930/.

"Major U.S. Immigration Ports." *Ancestry.com.* www.ancestrycdn.com/support/us/2016/11/majorusports.pdf.

McDaniel, Marie Basile. "Immigration and Migration (Colonial Era)." *The Encyclopedia of Greater Philadelphia.* https://philadelphiaencyclopedia.org/archive/immigration-and-migration-colonial-era/.

Miller, Fredric M. "Philadelphia: Immigrant City." Balch Online Resources, *Historical Society of Pennsylvania*. www2.hsp.org/exhibits/Balch%20resources/phi la_ellis_island.html.

"Ship List." *Norway-Heritage: Hands across the Sea.* www.norwayheritage.com/p _shiplist.asp?co=amlin.

Sitarski, Stephen M. "From Weccacoe to South Philadelphia: The Changing Face of a Neighborhood." *PhilaPlace, Historical Society of Pennsylvania.* www.philaplace .org/essay/376/.

Szucs, Juliana. "Ports beyond New York: 5 Things about the Port of Philadelphia." *Ancestry.com*, 3 Jun. 2014. https://blogs.ancestry.com/ancestry/2014/06/03 /ports-beyond-new-york-5-things-about-the-port-of-philadelphia/.

Ujifus, Steven, "A Philadelphia Quaker and Fabric Row." *The PhillyHistory Blog*, 13 Mar. 2013. www.phillyhistory.org/blog/index.php/2013/03/a-philadelphia -quaker-and-fabric-row/.

"Washington Avenue Green." *Pier 53 Project.* http://washingtonavenuegreen .com/02history/02history2.html.

"Washington Avenue Steamship Landing and Immigration Station." *PhilaPlace, Historical Society of Pennsylvania.* www.philaplace.org/story/190/.

Part IV Heroes, Sung and Unsung

12 Charles Willson Peale

"The Artist in His Museum." *Pennsylvania Academy of the Fine Arts.* www.pafa.org /museum/collection/item/artist-his-museum/.

Diethorn, Karie. "Peale's Philadelphia Museum." *The Encyclopedia of Greater Philadelphia.* https://philadelphiaencyclopedia.org/archive/peales-philadelphia-mu seum/.

Flexner, James Thomas. "America's Old Masters." *The Ingenious Mr. Peale.* New York: Dover Publications, Inc., 1964.

———. "The Scope of Painting in the 1790's." *Pennsylvania Magazine of History and Biography*, 1950. PDF file.

"George Washington at Princeton." *United States Senate.* www.senate.gov/artand history/art/artifact/Painting_31_00002.htm.

"George Washington Portrait Sells for $21.3M." *NBC News*, 21 Jan. 2006. www .nbcnews.com/id/10964032/ns/us_news-life/t/george-washington-portrait -sells-m/#.Xe7WSi2ZOMK.

Moulton, Gary E., ed. "The Journals of the Lewis and Clark Expedition." *Discovering Lewis and Clark.* www.lewis-clark.org.article/2822#Sub1/.

Ogden, Kate Nearpass. "Peale Family of Painters." *The Encyclopedia of Greater Philadelphia.* www.philadelphiaencyclopedia.org/archive/peale-family-of-painters/.

"Peale: Pennsylvania Center for the Book." *The Penn State University Libraries.* https://pabook.libraries.psu.edu/peale__charles_willson/.

"Portraits in Revolution." *Encyclopedia Britannica*, 1901 ed., the JDN Group. www .americanrevolution.com/biographies/artists/charles_willson_peale.

Scharf, J. Thomas, and Thompson Westcott. *History of Philadelphia, 1609–1884.* Philadelphia: L. H. Everts and Co., 1884.

Ward, David C., and Charles Willson Peale. *Charles Willson Peale: Art and Selfhood in the Early Republic.* Berkeley: University of California Press, 2004.

13 Francis Daniel Pastorius

First Report of the Historical Commission of Pennsylvania. Lancaster: Press of the New Era Printing Company, 1915.

Hull, William I. *William Penn and the Dutch Quaker Migration to Pennsylvania.* Auckland, New Zealand: Pickle Partners Publishing, 2018. [Originally published in 1935 under same title.]

Kyriakodis, Harry. *Philadelphia's Lost Waterfront.* Charleston, SC: The History Press, 2011.

Learned, Marion Dexter. *The Life of Francis Daniel Pastorius, the Founder of Germantown.* Philadelphia: William J. Campbell, 1908.

Myers, Albert Cook, ed. *Narrative of Early Pennsylvania, West New Jersey and Delaware, 1630–1707.* New York: Charles Scribner's Sons, 1912.

"Nazi Saboteurs and George Dasch." *FBI Famous Cases and Criminals.* www.fbi.gov /history/famous-cases/nazi-saboteurs-and-george-dasch.

Putnam, Christopher S. "Operation Pastorius." *Damn Interesting,* 20 Apr. 2008. www.damninteresting.com/operation-pastorius/.

Taylor, David A. "The Inside Story of How a Nazi Plot to Sabotage the U.S. War Effort Was Foiled." *Smithsonian Magazine,* 28 Jun. 2016. www.smithsonian mag.com/history/inside-story-how-nazi-plot-sabotage-us-war-effort-was -foiled-180959594/.

Turner, Beatrice Pastorius. "William Penn and Pastorius." *The Pennsylvania Magazine of History and Biography,* vol. 57, no. 1, 1933, pp. 66–90. *JSTOR,* www.jstor .org/stable/20086823.

14 Isaiah Zagar

Gleeson, Bridget. "Trash to Treasure: The Mosaics of Isaiah Zagar." *BBC,* published in partnership with Lonely Planet, 27 Dec. 2011. www.bbc.com/travel/story /20111222-trash-to-treasure-the-mosaics-of-isaiah-zagar.

Lidz, Frank. "Studying Dad's Favorite Topic: Himself." *New York Times,* 13 Aug. 2009. www.nytimes.com/2009/08/16/arts/television/16lidz.html.

Wojcik, Daniel. "Outsider Art, Vernacular Traditions, Trauma, and Creativity." *Western Folklore,* vol. 67, no. 2/3, 2008, pp. 179–198. *JSTOR,* www.jstor.org /stable/25474913.

15 James Forten

"James Forten." *Wikipedia,* last modified 24 Feb. 2020. https://en.wikipedia.org/wiki /James_Forten.

Mires, Charlene. *Independence Hall in American Memory.* Philadelphia: University of Pennsylvania Press, 2002.

Newman, Richard. *Black Founders: The Free Black Community in the Early Republic.* The Library Company of Philadelphia. http://librarycompany.org/paah/black founders.pdf.

———. "Not the Only Story in Amistad: The Fictional Joadson and the Real James Forten." *Pennsylvania History,* vol. 67, no. 2, 2000, pp. 218–239. https://jour nals.psu.edu/phj/article/view/25627/25396.

Vallar, Cindy. "James Forten." *Pirates and Privateers: The History of Maritime Piracy.* www.cindyvallar.com/forten.html.

Winch, Julie. *A Gentleman of Color: The Life of James Forten.* Oxford: Oxford University Press, 2002.

———. "The Making and Meaning of James Forten's Letters from a Man of Colour." *The William and Mary Quarterly*, Third Series, vol. 64, no. 1, 2007, pp.
129–138. *JSTOR*, www.jstor.org/stable/4491602.

———. "The Making and Meaning of James Forten's Letters from a Man of Colour
(Web Supplement)." *The William and Mary Quarterly*, Third Series, vol. 64, no. 1,
2007, pp. 129–138. *Omohundro Institute of Early American History and Culture*,
https://oieahc-cf.wm.edu/wmq/Jan07/winch.pdf.

16 Lucretia Mott

"An Abstract of the Life of Lucretia Mott." *Gywnedd Friends Meeting Historical
Notes.* www.gwyneddmeeting.org/history/mott.html.

Appiah, Krystal. "Abolitionist Women at Pennsylvania Hall." *The Library Company
of Philadelphia*, 17 May 2013. https://librarycompany.org/2013/05/17/abolition
ist-women-at-pennsylvania-hall/.

Bacon, Margaret Hope. *Valiant Friend: The Life of Lucretia Mott.* New York: Quaker
Press of Friends General Conference, 1999.

Brown, Ira V. "Racism and Sexism: The Case of Pennsylvania Hall." *Phylon (1960–)*,
vol. 37, no. 2, 1976, pp. 126–136. doi:10.2307/274764.

"Camp William Penn." *The PA Civil War 150 Commemoration.* https://web.archive
.org/web/20190731005154/http://pacivilwar150.com/TheWar/CampWilliam
Penn.html.

Chorley, Richard J., Robert P. Beckinsale, and Antony J. Dunn. *The History of the
Study of Landforms or the Development of Geomorphology, Volume Two: The Life
and Work of William Morris Davis.* New York: Routledge, 1973.

DeAngelis, Gina. *Lucretia Mott.* Broomall: Chelsea House Publishers, 2000.

DeCaro, Louis A., Jr. *John Brown the Abolitionist—A Biographer's Blog*, 29 Nov. 2016.
http://abolitionist-john-brown.blogspot.com/2016/11/john-brown-philadel
phia-and-empty-coffin.html.

Faulkner, Carol. *Lucretia Mott's Heresy: Abolition and Women's Rights in Nineteenth-Century America.* Philadelphia: University of Pennsylvania Press, 2011.

Hallowell, Anne Davis, ed. *James and Lucretia Mott: Life and Letters.* Boston: Hough-
ton Mifflin and Company, 1890.

"Historic LaMott: The Beginnings of Camp William Penn." *The Westbrook-RockHill
Foundation, Inc.* https://historic-lamott-pa.com/the-beginnings-of-camp-wil
liam-penn/.

Hunt, Helen LaKelly. *And the Spirit Moved Them: The Lost Radical History of America's First Feminists.* New York: The Feminist Press at the City University of
New York, 2017.

Karttunen, Frances. "Why Is Lucretia Mott a Famous Daughter of Nantucket?"
Nantucket Historical Association. https://nha.org/research/nantucket-history
/history-topics/why-is-lucretia-mott-a-famous-daughter-of-nantucket/.

"LaMott Historic District, National Register of Historic Places—Nomination
Form." *Pennsylvania Historical and Museum Commission, 1984–85.* www.dot7
.state.pa.us/CRGIS_Attachments/SiteResource/H079657_01H.pdf.

Manseau, Peter. "Abolitionist and Reformer Lucretia Mott." *National Museum of
American History, Behring Center*, 5 Mar. 2018. https://americanhistory.si.edu
/blog/mott.

Marsico, Katie. *Lucretia Mott: Abolitionist and Women's Rights Leader.* Edino, MN:
ABDO Publishing, 2008.

McGready, Blake. "Camp William Penn and the Fight for Historical Memory." *The Journal of the Civil War Era.* https://www.journalofthecivilwarera.org/2016/08/camp-william-penn-fight-historical-memory/.

Mott, Lucretia. *Lucretia Mott Speaks: The Essential Speeches and Sermons.* Edited by Christopher Densmore, Carol Faulkner, Nancy Hewitt, and Beverly Wilson Palmer. Urbana: University of Illinois Press, 2017. *JSTOR,* www.jstor.org/stable/10.5406/j.ctt1n7qktd.

Palmer, Beverly Wilson, ed. "The Lucretia Coffin Mott Papers Project." *Pomona College.* www.mott.pomona.edu/index.htm.

Stanton, Elizabeth Cady, Susan B. Anthony, and Matilda Joslyn Gage, ed. *History of Women's Suffrage, Vol. 1, 1848–1861.* Salem, NH: Ayer Company, 1985. Reprint of 1881 edition.

Unger, Nancy C. "Mott, Lucretia Coffin." *American National Biography.* https://doi.org/10.1093/anb/9780198606697.article.1500494.

Vetter, Lisa Pace. *The Political Thought of America's Founding Feminists.* New York: New York University Press, 2017.

Wert, Jeffry D. "Camp William Penn and the Black Soldier." *Pennsylvania History: A Journal of Mid-Atlantic Studies*, vol. 46, no. 4, 1979, pp. 335–346. *JSTOR,* www.jstor.org/stable/27772625.

Yellin, Jean Fagan, and John C. Van Horne, eds. *The Abolitionist Sisterhood: Women's Political Culture in Antebellum America.* Ithaca, NY: Cornell University Press, 1994. *JSTOR,* www.jstor.org/stable/10.7591/j.ctv1nhkdd.

17 Richard Allen

Allen, Richard. "Eulogy for Washington." *University of Oregon.* https://pages.uoregon.edu/mjdennis/courses/history_456_richard%20allen.htm.

———. *The Life, Experience, and Gospel Labours of the Rt. Rev. Richard Allen.* Excerpted, and images added, by the National Humanities Center for use in a Professional Development Seminar. http://nationalhumanitiescenter.org/pds/livingrev/religion/text7/allen.pdf.

———. *The Life, Experience, and Gospel Labours of the Rt. Rev. Richard Allen. To Which Is Annexed the Rise and Progress of the African Methodist Episcopal Church in the United States of America. Containing a Narrative of the Yellow Fever in the Year of Our Lord 1793: With an Address to the People of Colour in the United States.* Philadelphia: F. Ford and M. A. Ripley, 1880.

Boyer, Deborah. "Richard Allen and the Founding of Mother Bethel A.M.E. Church." *The PhillyHistory Blog*, 30 Jan. 2009. www.phillyhistory.org/blog/index.php/2009/01/richard-allen-and-the-founding-of-mother-bethel-a-m-e-church/.

"Hamilton and Yellow Fever: The Library Where It Happens." *NLM in Focus*, 11 Jan. 2019. https://infocus.nlm.nih.gov/2019/01/11/hamilton-and-yellow-fever-the-library-where-it-happens/.

"Historical Report: Mother Bethel African Methodist Episcopal Church, Philadelphia, Pennsylvania." *National Park Service*, Mar. 1963. http://npshistory.com/publications/proposed-parks/pa-mother-bethel-african-methodist-episcopal-church.pdf.

Hopper, Matthew S. *From Refuge to Strength: The Rise of the African American Church in Philadelphia 1787–1949.* Historic Context Study prepared for the Preservation Alliance for Greater Philadelphia, 1998.

Howell, Ricardo. "Mother Bethel AME Church: Congregation and Community." *The Encyclopedia of Greater Philadelphia*. https://philadelphiaencyclopedia.org /archive/mother-bethel-ame-church-congregation-and-community-2/.

Lapsansky, Phillip. "Black Founders: The Free Black Community in the Early Republic." *Library Company of Philadelphia*. http://librarycompany.org/blackfounders /index.htm#.XmZjLENJmMI.

"Mother Bethel African Methodist Episcopal Church." *PhilaPlace, Historical Society of Pennsylvania*. http://m.philaplace.org/story/59/.

Newman, Richard S. "Black Founders: The Free Black Community in the Early Republic." (This publication accompanied an exhibition of the same title on view at the Library Company from March to October 2008.) http://librarycompany .org/paah/blackfounders.pdf.

———. *Freedom's Prophet: Bishop Richard Allen, the AME Church and the Black Founding Fathers*. New York: New York University Press, 2009.

"The Origins of the African Methodist Episcopal Church." *National Humanities Center Resource Toolbox*, 2007. http://nationalhumanitiescenter.org/pds/maai /community/text3/allenmethodism.pdf.

Persinger, Ryanne. "Richard Allen Statue to Stand Tall, Honor Church's Founder." *The Philadelphia Tribune*, 2 Jul. 2016. www.phillytrib.com/news/richard-allen -statue-to-stand-tall-honor-church-s-founder/article_dc853372-6b9e-5f09 -ba55-5abdd610e2b6.html.

Peterson, Alyssa. "'Water, Earth, and Air Infected': How Movement, Quarantines, and Geographical Limitations Shaped the Movement of Yellow Fever in 1793." *2015 Lavern M. Hamand Graduate Writing Award*. www.eiu.edu/historia/Alys sa%20Peterson%20historia%202016.pdf.

"The Postal Service Celebrates Black History Month Issuing a Forever Stamp Honoring Richard Allen, Founder of the African Methodist Episcopal Church." *USPS.com*, 2 Feb. 2016. https://about.usps.com/news/national-releases/2016 /pr16_003.htm.

"The Yellow Fever Epidemic Online Exhibit." *Historical Society of Pennsylvania*. https://hsp.org/history-online/exhibits/richard-allen-apostle-of-freedom /the-yellow-fever-epidemic.

18 Robert Smith

Beatty, Elizabeth. "Fort Mifflin: The Fort That Saved America." *American Revolution Round Table of Philadelphia*, 26 Sept. 2016. http://arrtop.org/tag/general-thomas -mifflin/.

"Building Architecture." *Old Pine Street Church*. http://oldpine.org/history/building -architecture/.

Cohen, Jeffrey A. "Building a Discipline: Early Institutional Settings for Architectural Education in Philadelphia, 1804–1890." *Journal of the Society of Architectural Historians*, vol. 53, no. 2, 1994, pp. 139–183. doi:10.2307/990890.

Cole, John, Daniel G. Roberts, and Michael Parrington. *The Buried Past: An Archaeological History of Philadelphia*. Philadelphia: University of Pennsylvania Press, 1992.

Harris, Joseph S. "Robert Smith." *The Pennsylvania Magazine of History and Biography*, vol. 4, no. 1, 1880, pp. 79–88. *JSTOR*, www.jstor.org/stable/2008 4444.

Karsch, Carl G. "The Battle for Philadelphia." *Carpenters' Hall*. www.carpentershall .org/battle-for-philadelphia.

———. "A Walk with Robert Smith." *Carpenters' Hall*. www.carpentershall.org/a
-walk-with-robert-smith.

MacDowell, Lillian Ione Rhodes. *The Story of Philadelphia*. New York: American Book Company, 1900.

McDonald, Travis C. *The Public Hospital: An Architectural History and Chronicle of Reconstruction Block 4 Building 11*. Williamsburg: Colonial Williamsburg, 1986. https://research.history.org/DigitalLibrary/View/index.cfm?doc=ResearchRe ports%5CRR0143.xml#p14.

Moss, Roger. "Robert Smith, 1722–1777, Architect Builder." *Philadelphia Architects and Buildings*. www.philadelphiabuildings.org/pab/app/ar_display.cfm/100731.

Olson, Gar. *Blood Spilled for Freedom: America's Struggle for Survival 1776–1815*. Bloomington, IN: AuthorHouse, 2014.

Peterson, Charles Emil, Constance M. Greiff, and Maria M. Thompson. *Robert Smith: Architect, Builder, Patriot, 1722–1777*. Philadelphia: The Athenaeum of Philadelphia, 2000.

"Preservation of a Cheval-de-frise from the Delaware River." *This Week in Pennsylvania Archaeology*, 21 Jun. 2013. http://twipa.blogspot.com/2013/06/preserva tion-of-cheval-de-frise-from.html.

"Robert Erskine 1735–1780." *North Jersey Highlands Historical Society*. www.ring woodmanor.org/robert-erskine.html.

Ruppert, Bob. "Fortifying Philadelphia: A Chain of Redoubts and Floating Bridges." *Journal of the American Revolution*, 15 Feb. 2015. https://allthingsliberty .com/2015/02/philadelphia-chain-of-redoubts-floating-bridges/.

Spencer, Mark G., ed. *The Bloomsday Encyclopedia of the American Enlightenment*, vol. 1. New York: Bloomsday Academic, 2015.

Stedman, David Alonzo. "A History of the Saint Andrew's Society of Philadelphia." http://98.129.112.200/about-us/.

Tatum, George B. *Penn's Great Town: 250 Years of Philadelphia Architecture Illustrated in Prints and Drawings*. Philadelphia: University of Pennsylvania Press, 1961.

19 W. E. B. Du Bois

Baltzell, E. Digby. "Introduction to the 1967 Edition." *The Philadelphia Negro: A Social Study. W. E. B. Du Bois. Together with a Special Report on Domestic Service by Isabel Eaton*. New York: Schocken Books, 1967. https://ia800709.us.archive .org/1/items/philadelphianegr001901mbp/philadelphianegr001901mbp.pdf #page=17&zoom=auto,-335,43.

Burnley, Malcolm. "Parks & Rec Makeover Caught in Clash Over Union Diversity Rules." *Plan Philly*, 23 Mar. 2018. https://whyy.org/articles/parks-rec-make over-caught-in-clash-over-union-diversity-rules/.

"College Settlement House." *PhilaPlace, Historical Society of Pennsylvania*. www .philaplace.org/story/38/.

Davis, Allen F., John F. Sutherland, and Helen Parrish. "Reform and Uplift among Philadelphia Negroes: The Diary of Helen Parrish, 1888." *The Pennsylvania Magazine of History and Biography*, vol. 94, no. 4, 1970, pp. 496–517. JSTOR, www .jstor.org/stable/20090477.

Du Bois, W. E. B., Elijah Anderson, and Isabel Eaton. *The Philadelphia Negro: A Social Study*. Philadelphia: University of Pennsylvania Press, 1996. JSTOR, www.jstor .org/stable/j.ctt3fhpfb.

"First Colored 'Fellow' Appointed." *New York Times*, 30 Sept. 1896. https://timesma chine.nytimes.com/timesmachine/1896/09/30/108251061.html?pageNumber=1.

Hillier, Amy, Samuel Wood, and Mari Christmas. "Walking Tour of the Old Seventh Ward." www.dubois-theward.org/wp-content/uploads/2012/06/New_Walk ing_Tour_2011.pdf.

Johnson, Greg. "The Times and Life of W.E.B. DuBois at Penn." *Penn Today*, 22 Feb. 2019. https://penntoday.upenn.edu/news/times-and-life-web-du-bois-penn.

———. "W.E.B. DuBois at Penn." *Penn Today*, 9 Feb. 2016. https://penntoday.upenn .edu/spotlights/web-dubois-penn.

Jones, Solomon. "Building Trade Unions and Rebuild—A Slippery Slope." *The Philadelphia Inquirer*, 27 Jun. 2017. www.inquirer.com/philly/columnists/solomon _jones/building-trade-unions-and-rebuild-a-slippery-slope-20170627.html.

Mandell, Melissa. "Engine Company No. 11." *PhilaPlace, Historical Society of Pennsylvania*. www.philaplace.org/story/74/.

———. "W.E.B. Du Bois Historic Marker." *PhilaPlace, Historical Society of Pennsylvania*. www.philaplace.org/story/70/.

McGrail, Stephen. "The Philadelphia Negro." *The Encyclopedia of Greater Philadelphia*. https://philadelphiaencyclopedia.org/archive/philadelphia-negro-the/.

Otterbein, Holly. "Can Kenney Help Make White-Dominated Building Trades More Diverse?" *Philadelphia Magazine*, 12 Jan. 2016. www.phillymag.com/citi fied/2016/01/12/jim-kenney-john-dougherty-building-trades/#eGAXWI8x V6uiT4rI.99.

"The Ward: Race and Class in Du Bois' Seventh Ward." *The Ward*. www.dubois-theward .org/resources/mural/.

Part V Mob Rule

20 Bible Riots

"About the Cathedral." *Cathedral Basilica of Saints Peter and Paul*. http://cathedral phila.org/about/about-the-cathedral/#architecture.

"Anti-Catholicism in Jacksonian Philadelphia." *Catholic Historical Research Center of the Archdiocese of Philadelphia*, 26 Mar. 2010. https://chrc-phila.org/anti-catholi cism-in-jacksonian-philadelphia/.

"Chaos in the Streets: The Philadelphia Riots of 1844." *Villanova University, Falvey Memorial Library Online Library Exhibit*. https://exhibits.library.villanova.edu /chaos-in-the-streets-the-philadelphia-riots-of-1844/bible-controversy.

Clark, Dennis. *The Irish in Philadelphia: Ten Generations of Urban Experience*. Philadelphia: Temple University Press, 1982.

Forman, John A. "Lewis Charles Levin: Portrait of an American Demagogue." *American Jewish Archives*, Oct. 1960, pp. 150–194. http://americanjewisharchives .org/publications/journal/PDF/1960_12_02_00_forman.pdf.

Gaydosh, Brenda. "Convents." *The Encyclopedia of Greater Philadelphia*. https://phil adelphiaencyclopedia.org/archive/convents/.

Geffen, Elizabeth M. "Violence in Philadelphia in the 1840s and 1850s." *Pennsylvania History*, vol. 36, Oct. 1969, pp. 381–410. https://journals.psu.edu/phj /article/view/23405/23174.

Kirlin, Joseph L. J. *Catholicity in Philadelphia: From the Earliest Missionaries down to the Present Time*. Philadelphia: John Jos. McVey, 1909.

Kyriakodis, Harry. "A Church, a Riot, a Steeple, and the National Shrine of Santo Nino." *Hidden City Philadelphia*, 23 Dec. 2011. https://hiddencityphila.org/2011/12 /a-church-a-riot-a-steeple-and-the-national-shrine-of-santo-nino/.

Lannie, Vincent P., and Bernard C. Diethorn. "For the Honor and Glory of God: The Philadelphia Bible Riots of 1840." *History of Education Quarterly*, vol. 8, no. 1, 1968, pp. 44–106. doi:10.2307/366986.

"Lewis Charles Levin." *Wikipedia*, last edited 24 Sept. 2019. https://en.wikipedia .org/wiki/Lewis_Charles_Levin.

MacGuill, Dan. "When Fear and Hatred of Irish Catholics Set Fire to an American City." *TheJournal.ie*, Dublin, 3 Jan. 2016. www.thejournal.ie/1844-bible -riots-nativists-philadelphia-irish-catholic-religion-immigration-donald -trump-2434867-Jan2016/.

Mandell, Melissa. "The Kensington Riots of 1844." *PhilaPlace, Historical Society of Philadelphia.* www.philaplace.org/story/316/.

Marie, Sister Blanche. "The Catholic Church in Colonial Pennsylvania." *Pennsylvania History: A Journal of Mid-Atlantic Studies*, vol. 3, no. 4, 1936, pp. 240–258. *JSTOR*, www.jstor.org/stable/27766216.

Maule, Bradley. "Milano's Latest Book Surveys Dark Days of Kensington." *Hidden City Philadelphia*, 20 Jun. 2013. https://hiddencityphila.org/2013/06/milanos -latest-book-surveys-dark-days-of-kensington/.

McCarthy, Michael P. "The Philadelphia Consolidation of 1854: A Reappraisal." *The Pennsylvania Magazine of History and Biography*, vol. 110, no. 4, 1986, pp. 531–548. *JSTOR*, www.jstor.org/stable/20092044.

Morgan, Anne. "The Philadelphia Riots of 1844: Republican Catholicism and Irish Catholic Apologetics." *Pennsylvania History: A Journal of Mid-Atlantic Studies*, vol. 86, no. 1, 2019, pp. 86–102. doi:10.5325/pennhistory.86.1.0086.

"The Nativist Riots, Southwark, 1844." *The Church of St. Philip Neri.* https://web .archive.org/web/20070822112107/http://churchofstphilipneri.org/history /NATIVIST%20RIOTS.pdf.

"Obituary: Lewis C. Levin." *New York Times*, 17 Mar. 1860. https://timesmachine .nytimes.com/timesmachine/1860/03/17/78987393.pdf.

Perry, John B. "A Full and Complete Account of the Late Awful Riots in Philadelphia." *Exploring Diversity in Pennsylvania Ethnic History, Historical Society of Pennsylvania.* https://hsp.org/sites/default/files/legacy_files/migrated/studentread ingriotsinthecityofbrotherlylove.pdf.

"Reader Spotlight: Zachary Schrag on the 'Native Flag.'" *The Library Company of Philadelphia.* https://librarycompany.org/2019/02/24/reader-spotlight-zachary -schrag-on-the-native-flag/.

Robinson, Sam. "In Defense of Consolidation, 160 Years Later." *Hidden City Philadelphia*, 3 Feb. 2014. https://hiddencityphila.org/2014/02/in-defense-of-consolida tion-160-years-later/.

Shrag, Zachary. "Lewis Levin Wasn't Nice." *Tablet Magazine*, 22 Oct. 2018. www .tabletmag.com/jewish-news-and-politics/272885/lewis-levin-wasnt-nice.

———. "Nativist Riots of 1844." *The Encyclopedia of Greater Philadelphia.* https:// philadelphiaencyclopedia.org/archive/nativist-riots-of-1844/.

Wilson, Kathryn, and Jennifer Coval. "City of Unbrotherly Love: Violence in Nineteenth-Century Philadelphia." *Exploring Diversity in Pennsylvania Ethnic History, Historical Society of Pennsylvania.* https://hsp.org/sites/default/files/legacy _files/migrated/thephiladelphiariotsof1844.pdf.

21 Lombard Street Riot

Barrett, Ross. *Rendering Violence: Riots, Strikes, and Upheaval in Nineteenth-Century American Art.* Oakland: University of California Press, 2014. https://books.google.com/books?id=rq8lDQAAQBAJ&printsec=frontcover#v=onepage&q&f=false.

Boromé, Joseph A., Jacob C. White, Robert B. Ayres, and J. M. McKim. "The Vigilant Committee of Philadelphia." *The Pennsylvania Magazine of History and Biography*, vol. 92, no. 3, 1968, pp. 320–351. *JSTOR*, www.jstor.org/stable/20090197.

Buckalew, Terry. *Bethel Burying Ground Project.* https://bethelburyinggroundproject.com/2017/09/.

Caust-Ellenbogen, Celia. "Pennsylvania Hall Association." *Quakers and Slavery.* http://web.tricolib.brynmawr.edu/speccoll/quakersandslavery/commentary/organizations/pennsylvania_hall.php.

DuBois, W. E. B., Elijah Anderson, and Isabel Eaton. *The Philadelphia Negro: A Social Study.* Philadelphia: University of Pennsylvania Press, 1996. *JSTOR*, www.jstor.org/stable/j.ctt3fhpfb.

Geffen, Elizabeth M. "Violence in Philadelphia in the 1840s and 1850s." *Pennsylvania History*, vol. 36, Oct. 1969, pp. 381–410. https://journals.psu.edu/phj/article/view/23405/23174.

Gregory, Kia. "Monumental Achievement: A City History Class Gets the State to Mark the Site of a 19th-Century Race Riot." *Philadelphia Weekly*, 7 Dec. 2005. https://archive.is/20130131131234/http://www.philadelphiaweekly.com/news-and-opinion/monumental_achievement-38403194.html.

Grubbs, Patrick. "Riots (1830s and 1840s)." *The Encyclopedia of Greater Philadelphia.* https://philadelphiaencyclopedia.org/archive/riots-1830s-and-1840s/.

"Historic Markers Commemorate Notable Places and Events." *Preservation Matters*, Winter 2006. www.preservationalliance.com/files/news/Winter2006.pdf.

"Lombard Street Riot." *Wikipedia*, last edited 23 Jan. 2020. https://en.wikipedia.org/wiki/Lombard_Street_riot.

Mandell, Melissa. "Lombard Street Riots Site." *PhilaPlace, Historical Society of Pennsylvania.* www.philaplace.org/story/62/.

Newman, Richard S. "The PAS and American Abolitionism: A Century of Activism from the American Revolutionary Era to the Civil War." *Historical Society of Pennsylvania.* https://hsp.org/history-online/digital-history-projects/pennsylvania-abolition-society-papers/the-pas-and-american-abolitionism-a-century-of-activism-from-the-american-revolutionary-era-to-the-c.

Otter, Samuel. *Philadelphia Stories: America's Literature of Race and Freedom.* New York: Oxford University Press, 2010.

Runcie, John. "'Hunting the Nigs' in Philadelphia: The Race Riot of August 1834." *Pennsylvania History: A Journal of Mid-Atlantic Studies*, vol. 39, no. 2, 1972, pp. 187–218. *JSTOR*, www.jstor.org/stable/27772015.

Silcox, Harry C. "Delay and Neglect: Negro Public Education in Antebellum Philadelphia, 1800–1860." *The Pennsylvania Magazine of History and Biography*, vol. 97, no. 4, 1973, pp. 444–464. *JSTOR*, www.jstor.org/stable/20090789.

Part VI In the Neighborhoods

22 Ninth Street Market (aka the Italian Market)

Astarita, Tommaso. *Between Salt Water and Holy Water: A History of Southern Italy.* New York: W. W. Norton and Company, 2005.

Blumgart, Jake. "The Philadelphia Region's Italian American Legacy Endures." *Keystone Edge*, 11 Dec. 2014. www.keystoneedge.com/2014/12/11/the-philadelphia-regions-italian-american-legacy-endures/.

"The Calabrian Town of Filadelphia, sister of the American Philadelphia?" *Yes, Calabria*. www.yescalabria.com/en/comune-filadelfia-sorella-calabrese-della-philadelphia-americana/.

Dickinson, Joan Younger. "Aspects of Italian Immigration to Philadelphia." *The Pennsylvania Magazine of History and Biography*, vol. 90, no. 4, 1966, pp. 445–465. JSTOR, www.jstor.org/stable/20089965.

"The Earthquake of 1783 and the Rebuilding of Calabria." *Naples: Life, Death and Miracles*. www.naplesldm.com/baracc.php#back2.

"Gaetano Filangieri and Benjamin Franklin: Between the Italian Enlightenment and the U.S. Constitution." http://sedi2.esteri.it/sitiweb/AmbWashington/Pubblicazioni/2_filangieri_interno.pdf.

"Interview: Domenick Crimi (President—South 9th Street Business Men's Association, Philadelphia)." *We the Italians*, 11 May 2015. www.wetheitalians.com/interviews/philly-celebrates-the-100th-anniversary-of-the-9th-street-italian-market.

Luconi, Stefano. "Italians and Italy." *The Encyclopedia of Greater Philadelphia*. https://philadelphiaencyclopedia.org/archive/italians-and-italy/.

Mandell, Melissa. "Palumbo's Restaurant Site." *PhilaPlace, Historical Society of Pennsylvania*. www.philaplace.org/story/107/.

Robbins, William. "About Philadelphia." *New York Times*, 24 May 1984. www.nytimes.com/1984/05/24/us/about-philadelphia.html.

Tangires, Helen. "Italian Market." *The Encyclopedia of Greater Philadelphia*. https://philadelphiaencyclopedia.org/archive/italian-market/.

"Walking Map: The South 9th St. Italian Market." www.italianmarketphilly.org/map.html.

23 Chinatown

Bixler, Michael. "Demolition Proposal for Chinese Landmark Triggers Public Outcry." *Hidden City Philadelphia*, 21 Feb. 2019. https://hiddencityphila.org/2019/02/demolition-proposal-for-chinatown-landmark-triggers-public-outcry/.

Blumgart, Jake. "A New Plan for Chinatown." *PlanPhilly WHYY*, 9 Nov. 2017. https://whyy.org/articles/a-new-plan-for-chinatown/.

———. "On the Ground: The Future of Chinatown." *Flying Kite*, 9 Feb. 2016. www.flyingkitemedia.com/features/futureofchinatown020916.aspx.

Campbell, Alexia Fernández. "Suburbs: The New Chinatowns." *The Atlantic*, 18 May 2016. www.theatlantic.com/business/archive/2016/05/suburbs-the-new-chinatowns/483375/.

Glionna, John M. "Gambling, Addiction, and Asian Culture." *Asian-Nation: The Landscape of Asian America*, 2006. www.asian-nation.org/gambling.shtml.

Greco, JoAnn. "Philadelphia Chinatown Development Corporation at 50." *PlanPhilly*, 2 May 2016. https://whyy.org/articles/philadelphia-chinatown-development-corporation-at-50/.

Hahn, Ashley. "Rail Park Opens, Carrying the Freight of a Changing Neighborhood." *WHYY Eyes on the Street*, 6 Jun. 2018. https://whyy.org/articles/rail-park-opens-carrying-the-freight-of-a-changing-neighborhood/.

Lechner, Zach. "Chinatown at a Glance." *The PhillyHistory Blog*, 18 Aug. 2006. www
.phillyhistory.org/blog/index.php/2006/08/chinatown-at-a-glance/.

Li, Bethany Y., Andrew Leong, Domenic Vitiello, and Arthur Acoca. "Chinatown Then and Now: Gentrification in Boston, New York, and Philadelphia."
Asian American Legal Defense and Education Fund. https://web.archive.org
/web/20150812204205/http://aaldef.org/Chinatown%20Then%20and%20
Now%20AALDEF.pdf.

Li, Jun. "Philadelphia's Chinatown: An Ethnic Enclave Economy in a Changing
Landscape." *University of Pennsylvania Scholarly Commons*, 20 Dec. 2007. https://
repository.upenn.edu/cgi/viewcontent.cgi?article=1094&context=curej.

Louie, Sam. "Asian Gambling Addiction." *Psychology Today*, 10 Jul. 2014. www.psy
chologytoday.com/us/blog/minority-report/201407/asian-gambling-addiction.

Maule, Bradley. "A Cultured Pearl for Chinatown North." *Hidden City Philadelphia*, 22
Apr. 2013. https://hiddencityphila.org/2013/04/a-cultured-pearl-to-identify
-chinatown-north/.

Ostrov, Magda. "The Friendship Arch." *PhilaPlace, Historical Society of Pennsylvania.*
www.philaplace.org/story/1524/.

"Philadelphia, China and Chinatown." *Legacies, Historical Society of Pennsylvania*,
vol. 12, no. 2, May 2012. https://hsp.org/sites/default/files/legacies_china.pdf.

"Philadelphia Chinatown Development Corporation Biennial Report: 2008–2009."
Navigating Crossroads. https://chinatown-pcdc.org/annualreport/annual_re
port0809.pdf.

"Philadelphia Chinatown Development Corporation Biennial Report: 2016–2017."
Celebrating 50 Years of Community Building and Transformation. https://china
town-pcdc.org/wp-content/uploads/2019/04/2016-17-Biennial-Report-com
pressed.pdf.

Roeber, Catharine Dann, and Charlene Mires. "Center City." *The Encyclopedia of Greater Philadelphia.* https://philadelphiaencyclopedia.org/archive/center-city-essay/.

Trindle, Jamila. "Casino Finds Foes in Philly's Chinatown." *NPR*, 3 Mar. 2009. www
.npr.org/templates/story/story.php?storyId=101379378.

Wang, Jianshe, and Kathryn Wilson. "Building the Great Mountain." *Historical Society
of Pennsylvania.* www2.hsp.org/exhibits/Balch%20exhibits/chinatown/ack.html.

Wilson, Kate. "Murals Reclaiming Space in Philadelphia's Chinatown." *Circa*, 27
Aug. 2012. www.thoughtco.com/spanish-accents-and-punctuation-with-a
-mac-3080299.

Wilson, Kathryn. "Chinatown." *The Encyclopedia of Greater Philadelphia.* https://phil
adelphiaencyclopedia.org/archive/chinatown/.

Wilson, Kathryn E. *Ethnic Renewal in Philadelphia's Chinatown: Space, Place, and Struggle.* Philadelphia: Temple University Press, 2015. *JSTOR*, www.jstor.org/stable/j
.ctt14jxv76.

24 Philadelphia's LGBT Community

Baim, Tracy. "Philadelphia's 1965 Protests Remembered." *Windy City Times*, 9 Jul.
2015. www.windycitymediagroup.com/lgbt/Philadelphias-1965-protests-re
membered/52115.html.

"Before Stonewall: The Gay Pride Movement in Philadelphia." *Historical Society of
Pennsylvania*, 22 May 2015. https://hsp.org/news/before-stonewall-the-gay
-pride-movement-in-philadelphia.

Blumgart, Jake. "Philadelphia Was Likely First City to Have a Gayborhood." *Philly Voice*, 1 Apr. 2016. www.phillyvoice.com/philadelphia-was-first-city-have-gay borhood/.

Crimmins, Peter. "Marking 50 Years of Struggle and a Week of Equality, Annual Reminders to March Again in Philly." *WHYY*, 29 Jun. 2015. https://whyy.org /articles/marking-50-years-of-struggle-and-a-week-of-equality-annual-re minders-to-march-again-in-philly/.

———. "Philly Honors History of LGBT Community: Dr. Anonymous, AIDS Library Commemorated." *WHYY*, 3 Oct. 2017. https://whyy.org/articles/philly-hon ors-history-lgbt-community-dr-anonymous-aids-library-commemorated/.

Gillespie, Tyler. "The Last Day at Giovanni's Room, America's Oldest Gay Bookstore." *Rolling Stone*, 21 May 2014. www.rollingstone.com/culture/culture-news/the -last-day-at-giovannis-room-americas-oldest-gay-bookstore-94901/.

Haven-Tietze, Chloe. "Giovanni's Room." *PhilaPlace, Historical Society of Pennsylvania.* www.philaplace.org/story/1358/.

———. "John C. Anderson Apartments." *PhilaPlace, Historical Society of Pennsylvania.* www.philaplace.org/story/1371/.

Hevesi, Dennis. "Frank Rizzo of Philadelphia Dies at 70; A 'Hero' and 'Villain.'" *New York Times*, 17 Jul. 1991. www.nytimes.com/1991/07/17/obituaries/frank-riz zo-of-philadelphia-dies-at-70-a-hero-and-villain.html.

"LGBT History in Philadelphia." *The Constitutional Walking Tour*, 15 Aug. 2018. www .theconstitutional.com/blog/2018/08/15/lgbt-history-philadelphia.

"LGBTQ." *Free Library of Philadelphia.* https://libwww.freelibrary.org/explore/topic /lgbtq.

Noland, Aliana. "Reminder Days." *The Encyclopedia of Greater Philadelphia.* https:// philadelphiaencyclopedia.org/archive/reminder-days/.

Royles, Dan. "Civil Rights (LGBT)." *The Encyclopedia of Greater Philadelphia.* https:// philadelphiaencyclopedia.org/archive/civil-rights-lgbt/.

Skiba, Bob. "Gayborhood." *The Encyclopedia of Greater Philadelphia.* https://philadel phiaencyclopedia.org/archive/category/bob-skiba/.

———. "The Roots of the Gayborhood, The Eve of a Milestone." *Hidden City Philadelphia*, 14 Feb. 2014. https://hiddencityphila.org/2014/02/the-roots-of-the -gayborhood-the-eve-of-a-milestone/.

Winerup, Michael. "Rainbow-Hued Housing for Gays in Golden Years." *New York Times*, 12 Mar. 2014. www.nytimes.com/2014/03/13/business/retirementspe cial/rainbow-hued-housing-for-gays-in-golden-years.html.

Zorrilla, Mónica Marie. "Philly's LGBT History: A Primer on the City's Legacy of Pride." *Billy Penn*, 8 Jun. 2018. https://billypenn.com/2018/06/05/phillys-lgbt -history-a-primer-on-the-citys-legacy-of-pride/.

Part VII Hidden in Plain Sight

25 *Ars Medendi*

Aleo, Martha. "Ars Medendi." *Ornamento.* https://ornamento.blog/2011/03/24 /ars-medendi/.

"Ars Medendi." *Jefferson Digital Commons, Thomas Jefferson University.* https://jdc .jefferson.edu/campus_art_TJU/2/.

Gopnik, Blake. "The Story behind Jim Sanborn's Latest Artwork, 'Terrestrial Physics.'" *Arts and Living, Washington Post*, 25 Aug. 2009. www.washington post.com/wp-dyn/content/article/2009/08/24/AR2009082403317.html.

Zetter, Kim. "Finally, a New Clue to Solve the CIA's Mysterious Kryptos Sculpture." *Wired*, 28 Nov. 2014. www.wired.com/2014/11/second-kryptos-clue/.

26 *The Dream Garden* Tiffany Mosaic

Cotter, Holland. "ART REVIEW; Lush Idylls in Never-Never Land." *New York Times*, 18 Jun. 1999. www.nytimes.com/1999/06/18/arts/art-review-lush-idylls-in -never-never-land.html?pagewanted=all&src=pm.

"Edward Bok Sets Down the Record of His Chief." *New York Times*, 8 Apr. 1923. https:// timesmachine.nytimes.com/timesmachine/1923/04/08/105990482.pdf.

Howels, Derek M. "Cyrus H.K. Curtis." *Pennsylvania Center for the Book*, Spring 2005, updated 2018. https://pabook.libraries.psu.edu/literary-cultural-heritage -map-pa/bios/Curtis__Cyrus.

Sajet, Kim. "Dream Garden." *The Encyclopedia of Greater Philadelphia*. https://phila delphiaencyclopedia.org/archive/dream-garden-the/.

———. "From Grove to Garden: The Making of the Dream Garden Mosaic." *Pennsylvania Academy of the Fine Arts*. www.pafa.org/sites/default/files/documents/press -kits/PAFA_DreamGarden.pdf.

Scott, Susan Hanway. "Dream Garden." *The Hunt*, 5 Nov. 2009. https://thehuntmag azine.com/life-style/dream-garden/#ixzz2tu8XYjaA.

27 Independence National Historical Park

"Benjamin Franklin." *National Park Service*. www.nps.gov/inde/learn/historycul ture/people-franklin.htm.

Biunno, Diane. "Christ Church Archives." *Historical Society of Pennsylvania*, 15 Mar. 2016. https://hsp.org/blogs/archival-adventures-in-small-repositories/christ -church-archives.

Boudreau, George W. *Independence: A Guide to Historic Philadelphia*. Yardley, PA: Westholme Publishing, Inc., 2012.

"Find George Washington's Second-Favorite Horse." *National Park Service*. www.nps .gov/thingstodo/independence-blueskin.htm.

"Franklin Court." *National Park Service*. www.nps.gov/inde/learn/historyculture /places-franklincourt.htm.

"Independence Hall, Independence National Historical Park." *World Heritage Sites*. www.globalmountainsummit.org/independence-hall.html.

Kashatus, William C. "William Penn's Legacy: Religious and Spiritual Diversity." *Pennsylvania Heritage Magazine*, Spring 2011. www.phmc.state.pa.us/portal /communities/pa-heritage/william-penn-legacy-religious-spiritual-diversity .html. (Mistakenly says Penn's grant was for 45,000 acres. It was for 45,000 square miles.)

Maule, Bradley. "Independence Gall." *Hidden City Philadelphia*, 27 Feb. 2012. https:// hiddencityphila.org/2012/02/cloned/.

McGrath, Tim. *John Barry: An American Hero in the Age of Sail*. Yardley, PA: Westholme Publishing, 2010.

Memorial to Commodore John Barry, Father of the Navy of the United States. Philadelphia: Society of the Friendly Sons of St. Patrick of Philadelphia for the Relief of Emigrants from Ireland, 1907.

Mires, Charlene. "Independence Hall." *The Encyclopedia of Greater Philadelphia.* https://philadelphiaencyclopedia.org/archive/independence-hall/.

———. *Independence Hall in American Memory.* Philadelphia: University of Pennsylvania Press, 2002.

———. "Independence National Historical Park." *The Encyclopedia of Greater Philadelphia.* https://philadelphiaencyclopedia.org/archive/independence-national-historical-park/.

"Ona Judge Escapes to Freedom." *National Park Service.* www.nps.gov/articles/independence-oneyjudge.htm.

"The President's House: Freedom and Slavery in the Making of a Nation." *Independence National Historical Park.* https://home.nps.gov/inde/learn/historyculture/upload/pres-hse-brochure.pdf.

Richardson, Harry W., Peter Gordon, and James E. Moore II. *The Economic Costs and Consequences of Terrorism.* Northhampton, MA: Edward Elgar Publishing, Inc., 2007.

Scharf, J. Thomas, and Thompson Wescott. *History of Philadelphia.* Philadelphia: L. H. Everts and Co., 1884.

"Security Fences and Screening Facilities: Environmental Assessment." *Independence National Historical Park,* July 2006. www.nps.gov/inde/upload/environmental_assessment_security.pdf.

Sheridan, Phil. "Backgrounder: The Liberty Bell's Journey." *Independence National Historical Park,* 9 Sept. 2003. www.scribd.com/document/999391/National-Science-Foundation-liberty-bell-backgrounder.

"Ten Reasons Why Benjamin Franklin Was Actually a Superhero." *The Franklin Institute.* www.fi.edu/benjamin-franklin/10-reasons-why-benjamin-franklin-was-actually-a-superhero.

"Tight Security for Independence Hall." *CBS News,* 7 Mar. 2003. www.cbsnews.com/news/tight-security-for-independence-hall/.

Toogood, Anna Coxe. "Independence National Historical Park." *National Register of Historic Places Nomination Form.* Washington, DC: U.S. Department of the Interior, National Park Service, 1984. https://npgallery.nps.gov/GetAsset/64c7c6f0-14ee-4217-992b-cd9d14872a7f.

Urbina, Ian. "City Takes on U.S. in the Battle of Independence Square." *New York Times,* 9 Aug. 2006. www.nytimes.com/2006/08/09/us/09fence.html.

28 *Irish Memorial*

Note: Glenna Goodacre retired in 2016 and closed down her corporation. As a result, many of the links I used to gather information about her in 2011 are no longer available, so I did not include them. She died in 2020.

Boggs, Johnny D. "Glenna Goodacre Leaves a Legacy in Bronze." *HistoryNet,* Dec. 2019. www.historynet.com/glenna-goodacre-leaves-a-legacy-in-bronze.htm.

"Irish Memorial (Leacht Quimhneachain Na Gael) at Penn's Landing in Philadelphia, Pennsylvania." *dcMemorials.com.* http://dcmemorials.com/index_indiv0006521.htm.

"The Irish Memorial Project History." *Galleria Silecchia.* https://galleriasilecchia.com/Goodacre/irish_memorialproject.html.

"The Monument." *The Irish Memorial.* www.irishmemorial.org/about/the-monument/.

Watson, William E. "The Irish and Ireland." *The Encyclopedia of Greater Philadelphia.* https://philadelphiaencyclopedia.org/archive/irish-the-and-ireland/.

29 Mason-Dixon Survey

Babcock, Todd M. "Stargazers, Ax-men and Milkmaids: The Men Who Surveyed Mason and Dixon's Line." *FIG.* www.fig.net/resources/proceedings/fig_proceed ings/fig_2002/HS1/HS1_babcock.pdf.

Black, Janine. "The North Wall of a House: The Start of the Mason and Dixon Survey of 1763." *Kean University.* https://sites.google.com/a/kean.edu/janine-black -ph-d/resources/mason-dixon-survey-1763-2013.

DeVan, Kathryn, "Our Most Famous Border: The Mason-Dixon Line." *The Pennsylvania Center for the Book*, Fall 2008. https://pabook.libraries.psu.edu/literary-cultu ral-heritage-map-pa/feature-articles/our-most-famous-border-mason-dixon-line.

Latrobe, John H. B. "The History of Mason and Dixon's Line." *The Historical Society of Pennsylvania*, 8 Nov. 1854. https://cdn.loc.gov/service/rbc/lcrbmrp/t2205 /t2205.pdf.

"Links to Other Sources and Sites." *The Mason and Dixon Line Preservation Partnership.* www.mdlpp.org/links.

Mitchell, Charles W. "When Maryland Almost Got Philadelphia: The Remarkable Story of the Mason-Dixon Line." *Maryland Historical Society*, 6 Oct. 2015. www .mdhs.org/underbelly/2015/10/06/when-maryland-almost-got-philadelphia -the-remarkable-story-of-the-mason-dixon-line/.

Scaife, Walter B. "The Boundary Dispute between Maryland and Pennsylvania." *The Pennsylvania Magazine of History and Biography*, vol. 9, no. 3, 1885, pp. 241–271. *JSTOR*, www.jstor.org/stable/20084709.

Strang, Cameron B. "Mason-Dixon Line." *The Encyclopedia of Greater Philadelphia.* https://philadelphiaencyclopedia.org/archive/mason-dixon-line/.

Thaler, David S. "Mason and Dixon and Knopfler and Taylor: The BBC Visits the MdHS." *Maryland Historical Society*, 3 Aug. 2017. www.mdhs.org/underbelly /2017/08/03/mason-and-dixon-and-knopfler-and-taylor-the-bbc-visits-the -mdhs/.

———. "The Mystery of the Transit in the Tower." *Backsites, Published by the Surveyors Historical Society*, Spring 2014. www.surveyorshistoricalsociety.com/PDF /BacksightsSpring2014Thaler.pdf.

"Transit and Equal Altitude Instrument." *Smithsonian National Museum of American History.* https://amhistory.si.edu/surveying/type.cfm?typeid=18.

Wainwright, Nicholas B. "Tale of a Runaway Cape: The Penn-Baltimore Agreement of 1732." *The Pennsylvania Magazine of History and Biography*, vol. 87, no. 3, 1963, pp. 251–293. *JSTOR*, www.jstor.org/stable/20089625.

30 Old Pine Street Churchyard

Adams, John. *Letters of John Adams: Addressed to His Wife.* Boston: Charles C. Little and James Brown, 1841.

Brainerd, Mary. *Life of Rev. Thomas Brainerd, D.D.: For Thirty Years, Pastor of Old Pine Church, Philadelphia.* Philadelphia: J. P. Lippincott and Co., 1870.

Contosta, Nicole. "In-Ho Oh Memorial Way Symbolizes How Forgiveness Triumphs over Vengeance." *University City Review*, 3 Aug. 2016. http://ucreview.com /inho-oh-memorial-way-symbolizes-how-forgiveness-triumphs-over-ven geance-p6791-1.htm.

Gibbons, Hughes Oliphant. *A History of Old Pine Street: Being the Record of an Hundred and Forty Years in the Life of a Colonial Church.* Philadelphia: The John C. Winston Company, 1905.

Guillermo, Emil. "'A Very Healing Story': David Oh Believes a 1958 Killing Can Help Bridge Communities." *NBC News*, 29 Jul. 2016. www.nbcnews.com/news/asian-america/very-healing-story-how-1958-killing-can-help-bridge-communities-n619896.

Shaffer, Ronald E. "Eugene Ormandy." *Old Pine Conservancy Blog.* https://oldpineconservancy.org/2019/03/01/eugene-ormandy/.

———. "In-Ho Oh Remembered." *Old Pine Conservancy Blog.* https://oldpineconservancy.org/2019/05/17/in-ho-oh-remembered/.

Part VIII Marvelous Museums

31 The African American Museum in Philadelphia

"Audacious Freedom." *African American Museum in Philadelphia.* Eisterhold and Associates, Inc., 2009. https://eisterhold.com/projects/african-american-museum-in-philadelphia.

Dade, Antoinette. "Copy of African American Museum in Philadelphia." *Prezi*, updated 15 Apr. 2013. https://prezi.com/wzvyanjx7oa9/copy-of-african-american-museum-in-philadelphia.

Grohsmeyer, Janeen. "Frances Harper." *Dictionary of Unitarian and Universalist Biography, Unitarian Universalist History and Heritage Society*, 16 Sept. 2003. http://uudb.org/articles/francesharper.html.

Weigley, Russell F., ed. *Philadelphia: A 300-Year History.* New York: W. W. Norton and Company, 1982.

32 National Museum of American Jewish History

Crimmins, Peter. "Jewish Museum Files for Bankruptcy." *WHYY*, 2 Mar. 2020. https://whyy.org/articles/jewish-museum-files-for-bankruptcy/.

Leichman, Abigail Klein. "Why to Test for Tay-Sachs." *Jewish Standard*, 23 Sept. 2017. https://jewishstandard.timesofisrael.com/why-to-test-for-tay-sachs/.

Polshek, James S. "National Museum of American Jewish History." *Ennead.* www.ennead.com/work/nmajh.

Rothstein, Ed. "Life, Liberty and the Pursuit of Identify. Museum Review." *New York Times*, 11 Nov. 2010. www.nytimes.com/2010/11/12/arts/design/12museum.html.

"Voyage of the St. Louis." *Holocaust Encyclopedia, United States Holocaust Memorial Museum*, last edited 16 Jun. 2016. https://encyclopedia.ushmm.org/content/en/article/voyage-of-the-st-louis.

33 Pennsylvania Academy of the Fine Arts

"Architect Frank Furness; He Did the Unthinkable." *WHYY*, 28 Sept. 2012. https://whyy.org/articles/architect-frank-furness-he-did-the-unthinkable/.

Brin, Joseph. "Stoking the Furnace." *Architecture*, 29 Oct. 2012. www.metropolismag.com/architecture/stoking-the-furnace/.

Dixon, Mark E. "Frank Furness' Legacy of Gilded Age Main Line Architecture." *Main Line Today*, 24 Dec. 2013. https://mainlinetoday.com/life-style/frank-furness-legacy-of-gilded-age-main-line-architecture/?cparticle=2&siarticle=1.

Finkel, Ken. "Why We Love Frank Furness." *The PhillyHistory Blog*, 18 Sept. 2012. www.phillyhistory.org/blog/index.php/2012/09/why-we-love-frank-furness/.

"The Fisher Fine Arts Building: The History." (A guide developed for David Comberg's Spring 2016 Practicum.) *Penn Libraries.* https://guides.library.upenn.edu /comberg/FFAL_History.

Lewis, Michael J. "Building Power: Face and Form: The Art and Caricature of Frank Furness." *Wall Street Journal*, 7 Nov. 2012. www.wsj.com/articles/SB10001424 052970203630604578074961417417452.

———. "This Library Speaks Volumes: Frank Furness Treated Reading as an Active Enterprise." *Wall Street Journal*, 14 Nov. 2009. www.wsj.com/articles/SB10001 424052748704402404574526080260245184.

O'Gorman, James F. *The Architecture of Frank Furness.* Philadelphia: Philadelphia Museum of Art, 1973.

Pitts, Carolyn. "The Pennsylvania Academy of the Fine Arts." *National Register of Historic Places Nomination Form.* Washington, DC: Department of the Interior, National Park Service, 1975. https://npgallery.nps.gov/GetAsset/7b3690b1 -f02f-487a-a66c-f1149a2e7240.

"The Pronunciation of the Furness Name." *Furnesque: The Designs of Frank Furness*, 16 Mar. 2014. https://furnesque.tumblr.com/post/78783054470/i-received -an-anonymous-ask-sharing-more-info-on.

Thomas, George. "Pennsylvania Academy of the Fine Arts." *SAH Archipedia, Society of Architectural Historians.* https://sah-archipedia.org/buildings/PA-02-PH52.

Part IX Historic Architecture

34 Athenaeum of Philadelphia

"The Athenaeum of Philadelphia, National Register of Historic Places Inventory— Nomination Form." *National Park Service*, 29 Jul. 1976. https://npgallery.nps .gov/NRHP/GetAsset/NHLS/72001144_text.

"Bicentennial Video." History Making Productions. *The Athenaeum of Philadelphia.* www.philaathenaeum.org/bicentennialvideo.html.

The Charter, By-Laws, and Seventy-Fifth Annual Report of the Athenaeum of Philadelphia. Philadelphia: Athenaeum of Philadelphia, 1890.

"One Hundred-Ninety-Seventh Annual Report 2011/2012." *The Athenaeum of Philadelphia.* www.philaathenaeum.org/pdf/annualreport.197(webquality).pdf.

Reichhelm, G. C., and W. P. Shipley, eds. "About Chess in 19th Century Philadelphia." *American Chess Monthly*, 1897. *Sarah's Chess Journal.* www.edochess.ca /batgirl/PhilaChess.html.

"Seven Walking Tours through Philadelphia." *U.S. History.org.* www.ushistory.org /districts/washingtonsquare/athen.htm.

Technically Philly. "The Philadelphia Athenaeum: A Historical Treasure with a Seemy Underbelly." *The PhillyHistory Blog*, 2 Jul. 2013. https://blog.phillyhistory .org/index.php/2013/07/the-philadelphia-athenaeum-a-historical-treasure -with-a-seemy-underbelly/.

"This Month in 1814: A Look Back at the Athenaeum's Founding Year." *The Athenaeum of Philadelphia*, Feb. 2014. www.philaathenaeum.org/newsletter/2014-02 /index.html.

Thompson, Maria M. "The Athenaeum of Philadelphia." *Incollect.* https://incollect .com/articles/the-athenaeum-of-philadelphia.

Weigley, Russell F., ed. *Philadelphia: A 300-Year History.* New York: W. W. Norton and Company, 1982.

35 Ben Franklin Bridge

Anderson, Steve. "Benjamin Franklin Bridge: Historical Overview." *PhillyRoads.com.* www.phillyroads.com/crossings/benjamin-franklin/.

Baisden, Cheryl L. *Delaware River Port Authority.* Charleston, SC: Arcadia Publishing Company, 2009.

"Ben Franklin Bridge." *Delaware River Port Authority.* www.drpa.org/bridges/ben -franklin-bridge.asp.

"Ben Franklin Bridge—Abandoned/Never Used Trolley Line." *WHYY.* www.youtube .com/watch?v=eNkPmVIUVow.

Boyer, Deborah. "The Sesquicentennial Exposition of 1926." *The PhillyHistory Blog,* 31 Jul. 2008. www.phillyhistory.org/blog/index.php/2008/07/the-sesquicen tennial-exposition-of-1926/.

"Drive the Bridge. The Electric Ben Franklin." *USHistory.org.* www.ushistory.org /franklin/philadelphia/bridge.htm.

Kyriakodis, Harry. "A Church, a Riot, a Steeple, and the National Shrine of Santo Nino." *Hidden City Philadelphia,* 23 Dec. 2011. https://hiddencityphila.org /2011/12/a-church-a-riot-a-steeple-and-the-national-shrine-of-santo-nino/.

———. *Philadelphia's Lost Waterfront.* Charleston, SC: The History Press, 2011.

Laverty, Bruce. "Experience the Ben Franklin Bridge." *WHYY,* 23 Aug. 2010. https:// video.whyy.org/video/experience-ben-franklin-bridge/.

"Move to End Fight over Bridge Tolls." *New York Times,* 20 Dec. 1925. https://times machine.nytimes.com/timesmachine/1925/12/21/104198494.pdf.

Schenck, Helene, and Michael Parrington. "Benjamin Franklin Bridge." *Workshop of the World.* www.workshopoftheworld.com/center_city/bridge.html.

"Secrets of the Delaware River Bridge." *WriteOnNewJersey.com,* 30 Jul. 2012. www .writeonnewjersey.com/tag/hidden-art-treasures-in-ben-franklin-bridge/.

"St. George's United Methodist Church (Philadelphia)." *Wikipedia,* last edited 22 Nov. 2019. https://en.wikipedia.org/wiki/St._George%27s_United_Methodist _Church_(Philadelphia).

36 Carpenters' Hall

Avery, Ron. "America's First Bank Robbery." *Carpenters' Hall.* www.carpentershall .org/americas-first-bank-robbery.

Bruenig, Elizabeth. "The Battered Aspirations of the American Working Class." *Washington Post,* 16 Jul. 2018. www.washingtonpost.com/opinions/the-bat tered-aspirations-of-the-american-working-class/2018/07/16/51d1ed54-891d -11e8-85ae-511bc1146b0b_story.html.

"Carpenter's Hall." *National Park Service,* reprint from 1962. http://npshistory .com/brochures/inde/1962ch.pdf.

Hazard, Samuel, ed. "Patrick Lyon, the Blacksmith." *Hazard's Register of Pennsylvania,* vol. 5, no. 23, 5 Jun. 1830, p. 356.

Heintzelman, Patricia. "Carpenters' Hall." *National Register of Historic Places Nomination Form.* Washington, DC: U.S. Department of the Interior, National Park Service, 1974. https://npgallery.nps.gov/NRHP/GetAsset/NHLS/70000552 _text.

Karsch, Carl G. "The Battle for Philadelphia." *Carpenters' Hall.* www.carpenters hall.org/battle-for-philadelphia.

———. "The Puzzle Takes Shape." *Carpenters' Hall.* www.carpentershall.org /architectural-history.

Peterson, Charles E. "Carpenters' Hall." *Transactions of the American Philosophical Society*, vol. 43, no. 1, 1953, pp. 96–128. doi:10.2307/1005666.

Printed Price Book, 1805. *Carpenters' Company of the City and County of Philadelphia.* Philadelphia: D. Humphreys, 1805. https://diglib.amphilsoc.org/islandora/object/text:148374#page/11/mode/1up.

Weinsteiger, Brigitte. "*Pat Lyon at the Forge*: Portrait of an American Blacksmith." *Penn State University Center for Medieval Studies.* www.engr.psu.edu/mtah/articles/pat_lyon.htm.

37 Christ Church

"Christ Church." *Philadelphia Guild of Change Ringers.* www.phillyringers.com/christchurch/.

"Christ Church." *USHistory.org.* www.ushistory.org/tour/christ-church.htm.

Hames, Jerry. "Giving Face to a Legend." *Episcopal News Service*, 27 Mar. 2009. http://archive.episcopalchurch.org/81827_106523_ENG_HTM.htm.

Heintzelman, Patricia. "Christ Church." *National Register of Historic Places Nomination Form.* Washington, DC: U.S. Department of the Interior, National Park Service, 1974. https://npgallery.nps.gov/GetAsset/525c8ff9-5dfc-4679-beca-dfcf4490f7ea.

Kyriakodis, Harry. "Skyscraper Page, Circa 1755." *Hidden City Philadelphia*, 3 Dec. 2012. https://hiddencityphila.org/2012/12/skyscraper-page-circa-1755/.

Peterson, Charles E., Nicholas L. Gianopulos, and Bruce Cooper Gill. *The Building and Furnishing of Christ Church Philadelphia.* Philadelphia: Christ Church Philadelphia, 2001.

Watson, John Fanning, and Willis Pope Hazard. *Annals of Philadelphia and Pennsylvania in the Olden Time*, vol. III. Philadelphia: Edwin S. Stuart, 1899.

38 City Hall

Finkel, Ken. "How High Was Up? A History of Philadelphia's 'Gentleman's Agreement.'" *The PhillyHistory Blog*, 25 Jun. 2013. www.phillyhistory.org/blog/index.php/2013/06/how-high-was-up-a-history-of-philadelphias-gentlemans-agreement/.

Gallery, John Andrew. *Philadelphia Architecture: A Guide to the City*, 3rd ed. Philadelphia: Center for Architecture, 2009.

Gillette, Howard. "City Hall (Philadelphia)." *The Encyclopedia of Greater Philadelphia.* https://philadelphiaencyclopedia.org/archive/city-hall-philadelphia/.

———. "Philadelphia's City Hall: Monument to a New Political Machine." *The Pennsylvania Magazine of History and Biography*, vol. 97, no. 2, 1973, pp. 233–249. *JSTOR*, www.jstor.org/stable/20090734.

Hornblum, Allen M., and George J. Holmes. *Philadelphia's City Hall.* Portsmouth, NH: Arcadia Publishing Company, 2003.

Kidder Smith, George E. *Source Book of American Architecture: 500 Notable Buildings from the Tenth Century to the Present.* New York: Princeton Architectural Press, 1996.

Marsh, Bill. "People Stop Fighting City Hall." *New York Times*, 25 Jul. 2006. www.nytimes.com/2006/07/25/arts/design/25hall.html?pagewanted=all.

Moss, Roger W. *Historic Landmarks of Philadelphia.* Philadelphia: University of Pennsylvania Press, 2008.

Nash, Gary B. *First City: Philadelphia and the Forging of Historical Memory.* Philadelphia: University of Pennsylvania Press, 2006. *JSTOR*, www.jstor.org/stable/j.ctt3fj3c5.

Robinson, Sam. "Keeping Time on the City's Watch." *Hidden City Philadelphia*, 11 Apr. 2013. https://hiddencityphila.org/2013/04/keeping-time-on-the-citys-watch/.

39 Gloria Dei Church (Old Swedes')

Bridenbaugh, Carl. "The Old and New Societies of the Delaware Valley in the Seventeenth Century." *The Pennsylvania Magazine of History and Biography*, vol. 100, no. 2, 1976, pp. 143–172. *JSTOR*, www.jstor.org/stable/20091051.

Carson, Hampton L. "Dutch and Swedish Settlements on the Delaware." *The Pennsylvania Magazine of History and Biography*, vol. 33, no. 1, 1909, pp. 1–21. *JSTOR*, www.jstor.org/stable/20085456.

"Hook and Hastings Organ at Gloria Dei." *Gloria Dei (Old Swedes') Episcopal Church*. https://www.old-swedes.org/about/history.

Johnson, Amandus. *The Swedes on the Delaware 1638–1664*. Philadelphia: The Swedish Colonial Society, 1915.

Mandell, Melissa. "Gloria Dei (Old Swedes') Episcopal Church." *PhilaPlace, Historical Society of Pennsylvania*. www.philaplace.org/story/1/.

"Pennsylvania: Gloria Dei (Old Swede's Church) National Historic Site." *National Park Service*, last updated 11 Aug. 2017. www.nps.gov/articles/gloriadei.htm.

Schreiber, Michael. "Plans for a Nature Preserve: The Natural History of Wicaco (Old Swedes' Church)." *Philahistory.org*, 28 Jun. 2017. https://philahistory.org/2017/06/28/plans-for-a-nature-preserve-the-natural-history-of-wicaco-old-swedes-church/.

Sitarski, Stephen M. "From Weccacoe to South Philadelphia: The Changing Face of a Neighborhood." *PhilaPlace, Historical Society of Pennsylvania*. www.philaplace.org/essay/376/.

Springer, Ruth L., Louise Wallman, And. Rudman, and Andreas Sandell. "Two Swedish Pastors Describe Philadelphia, 1700 and 1702." *The Pennsylvania Magazine of History and Biography*, vol. 84, no. 2, 1960, pp. 194–218. *JSTOR*, www.jstor.org/stable/20089287.

Ujifusa, Steven B. "Gloria Dei: A Parish for the Ages." *WHYY*, 22 May 2007. https://whyy.org/articles/1485/.

Watson, John Fanning. *Historic Tales of Olden Time*. Philadelphia: E. Littell and Thomas Holden, 1833.

Williams, Kim-Eric. "Gloria Dei (Old Swedes') Church." *The Swedish Colonial Society*. http://colonialswedes.net/Churches/GloDei.html.

40 Masonic Temple

Gallery, John Andrew. *Philadelphia Architecture: A Guide to the City*, 3rd ed. Philadelphia: Center for Architecture, 2009.

Huhn, Erich M. "Freemansonry." *The Encyclopedia of Greater Philadelphia*. https://philadelphiaencyclopedia.org/archive/freemasonry/.

Liu, Gordon. "The Masonic Temple—Home of the Mysterious Freemasons." *PhilaPlace, Historical Society of Pennsylvania*. www.philaplace.org/story/1743/.

"Masonic Temple (Philadelphia Pennsylvania)," PDF Download. *Wikipedia*, last edited 8 Oct. 2018. https://en.wikipedia.org/w/index.php?title=Special:ElectronPdf&page=Masonic+Temple+%28Philadelphia%2C+Pennsylvania%29&action=show-download-screen.

Moss, Roger W. *Historic Landmarks of Philadelphia*. Philadelphia: University of Pennsylvania Press, 2008.

Pitts, Carolyn. "Masonic Temple." *National Register of Historic Places Nomination Form*. Washington, DC: U.S. Department of the Interior, National Park Service, 1984. https://npgallery.nps.gov/NRHP/GetAsset/NHLS/71000727_text.

Waldman, Glenys A., and Michael R. Harrison. *The Masonic Temple in Philadelphia: A National Historic Landmark*. Philadelphia: The Masonic Library and Museum of Pennsylvania, 2013.

41 The PSFS Building

Drewen, Will. "Philadelphia's PSFS Building in the Hagley Digital Archives." *Hagley Museum and Library*, 7 Apr. 2011. www.hagley.org/librarynews/philadelphias -psfs-building-hagley-digital-archives.

Dunlap, David W. "From Front Office to Front Desk." *New York Times*, 10 Sept. 2000. www.nytimes.com/2000/09/10/realestate/from-front-office-to-front-desk .html?pagewanted=all.

Finkel, Ken. "PSFS: Modernism Remaking the Workaday World." *The PhillyHistory Blog*, 17 Jun. 2013. www.phillyhistory.org/blog/index.php/2013/06/psfs-mod ernism-remaking-the-workaday-world/.

Gallery, John Andrew. *Philadelphia Architecture: A Guide to the City*, 3rd ed. Philadelphia: Center for Architecture, 2009.

"Loews Philadelphia Hotel (Philadelphia Saving Fund Society [PSFS]) Building." *Docomomo US*. www.docomomo-us.org/register/loews-philadelphia-hotel.

"Loews Philadelphia Hotel: The History of Our Building." *NAWIC Philadelphia*. https://nawicphl.org/Resources/Documents/building%20history.pdf.

Maule, Bradley. "Favorite Spot: PSFS Building/Loews Philadelphia Hotel." *Philly Love Notes*, 14 Jan. 2014. www.phillylovenotes.com/psfs-center-city-bradley-maule/.

Moss, Roger W. *Historic Landmarks of Philadelphia*. Philadelphia: University of Pennsylvania Press, 2008.

Pitts, Carolyn. "The Philadelphia Savings Fund Society Building." *National Register of Historic Places Nomination Form*. Washington, DC: U.S. Department of the Interior, National Park Service, 1976. https://npgallery.nps.gov/GetAsset /2861cab5-a55b-4327-80bc-63c926751620.

Poulin, Richard. *Graphic Design and Architecture: A 20th-Century History*. Beverly, MA: Rockport Publishers, 2012.

"PSFS Building." *Wikipedia*, last edited 20 Nov. 2019. https://en.wikipedia.org/wiki /PSFS_Building.

"PSFS Building Historical Building." *ExplorePAHistory.com*. https://explorepahistory .com/hmarker.php?markerId=1-A-354.

"PSFS: Nothing More Modern." *Yale School of Architecture Galleries*, 30 Aug. 2004 to 4 Nov. 2004. www.absolutearts.com/artsnews/2004/08/30/32317.html.

Ribeiro, Alyssa. "PSFS." *The Encyclopedia of Greater Philadelphia*. https://philadelphia encyclopedia.org/archive/psfs/.

Vider, Elise. "PSFS Spells Home by Elise Vider. What Design Elements Make Philadelphia Unique?" *Center for Architecture and Design*, 9 Oct. 2012.

Wilcox, James M. *A History of The Philadelphia Saving Fund Society: 1816–1916*. Philadelphia: J. B. Lippincott Company, 1916.

42 Reading Terminal Market

Bittman, Mark. "A Food Market for New York." *New York Times*, 12 Mar. 2013. https://opinionator.blogs.nytimes.com/2013/03/12/a-food-market-for-new -york/?_r=0.

Hilario, Kenneth. "Reading Terminal Market GM Talks Food, Tourists and Why Chain Restaurants Are Still Banned." *Philadelphia Business Journal*, 9 Sept. 2014. www

.bizjournals.com/philadelphia/news/2014/09/09/reading-terminal-market
-gm-talks-food-touristsand.html?page=all.

Jackson, Joseph. *Market Street, Philadelphia: The Most Historic Highway in America, Its Merchants and Its Story.* Philadelphia: Joseph Jackson, 1918.

Kyriakodis, Harry. "Reading Terminal (Update 2007)." *Workshop of the World—Philadelphia.* www.workshopoftheworld.com/center_city/reading.html.

Nichols, Rick. "Public Markets in Philadelphia." *Reading Terminal Market.* https://readingterminalmarket.org/about-us/history/.

"Reading Terminal and Market." *ExplorePAHistory.com.* http://explorepahistory.com/hmarker.php?markerId=1-A-1D2.

"Reading Terminal Market: Philadelphia Pennsylvania." *Great Places in America: Public Spaces, American Planning Association,* 2014. www.planning.org/greatplaces/spaces/2014/readingterminal.htm.

Reilly, Pamela, "Reading Terminal Market: A Proud Philadelphia Tradition Continues." *Pennsylvania Historic Preservation Office Blog,* 18 Jun. 2014. https://pahistoricpreservation.com/reading-terminal-marketa-proud-philadelphia-tradition-continues/.

Smalarz, Matthew. "Reading Terminal Market." *The Encyclopedia of Greater Philadelphia.* https://philadelphiaencyclopedia.org/archive/reading-terminal-market/.

Zembala, Dennis M. "Philadelphia and Reading Railroad: Terminal Station and Trainshed." *National Register of Historic Places Nomination Form.* Washington, DC: U.S. Department of the Interior, National Park Service, 1976. https://npgallery.nps.gov/GetAsset/4610585f-2c0a-40f2-8419-5971375b3c70/.

43 Sparks Shot Tower

American Chemical Society. *The Journal of Industrial Engineering and Chemistry,* vol. VIII. Easton, PA: Eshenbach Printing Company, 1916.

Avery, Ron. "From Musket Balls to Basketballs—The Sparks Shot Tower." *The PhillyHistory Blog,* 25 Jan. 2008. www.phillyhistory.org/blog/index.php/2008/01/from-musket-balls-to-basketballs-the-sparks-shot-tower/.

Freedley, Edwin T. *Philadelphia and Its Manufactures: A Hand-book of the Great Manufactories and Representative Mercantile Houses of Philadelphia in 1867.* Philadelphia: Edward Young and Co., 1867.

"History of the American Shot Tower." *Pennsylvania Trapshooting Hall of Fame.* www.pssatrap.org/shot-towers-2/shot-towers-page-1.htm.

Jaffe, Alan. "Look Up! 19th-Century Tower Finds Peace in the 21st Century." *PlanPhilly, WHYY,* 14 Aug. 2012. https://whyy.org/articles/look-19th-century-tower-finds-peace-21st-century/.

Kyriakodis, Harry. *Philadelphia's Lost Waterfront.* Charleston, SC: The History Press. 2011.

Minchinton, Walter. "The Shot Tower." *American Heritage's Invention and Technology,* vol. 6, no. 1, Spring/Summer 1990. www.inventionandtech.com/content/shot-tower-1.

The Miscellaneous Documents of the Senate of the United States for the First and Second Sessions of the Thirty-Fourth Congress 1855–'56. Washington, DC: A. O. P. Nicholson, Senate Printer, 1856.

O'Gorman, James F. "A New York Architect Visits Philadelphia in 1822." *The Pennsylvania Magazine of History and Biography,* vol. 117, no. 3, 1993, pp. 153–176. *JSTOR,* www.jstor.org/stable/20092796.

"Philadelphia Shot Tower." *Hexamer General Surveys, vol. 16, GeoHistory Resources*. www.philageohistory.org/rdic-images/view-image.cfm/HGSv16.1491.

"Sparks Shot Tower." *PhilaPlace, Historical Society of Pennsylvania*. www.philaplace .org/story/5/.

Ujifusa, Steven B. "Remnants of Our Industrial Past." *PlanPhilly*, 6 Jul. 2007. https://whyy.org/articles/remnants-our-industrial-past/.

44 Water Works

"Fairmount Water Works 1815–1911: A National Historic Mechanical Engineering Landmark." *Philadelphia Water Department and the American Society of Mechanical Engineers*, 27 Mar. 1977. www.asme.org/wwwasmeorg/media/resourcefiles /aboutasme/who%20we%20are/engineering%20history/landmarks/21-fair mount-water-works.pdf.

Fisher, Christine. "Hidden City Festival Turns Former Water Plant Turned Aquarium Turned Pool into 'Bibotorium.'" *Hidden City Philadelphia*, 29 May 2013. https://whyy.org/articles/hidden-city-festival-turns-former-water-plant -turned-aquarium-turned-pool-into-bibotorium/.

Gallery, John Andrew. *Philadelphia Architecture: A Guide to the City*, 3rd ed. Philadelphia: Center for Architecture, 2009.

Gibson, Jane Mork. "Fairmount Water Works (Update 2007)." *Workshop of the World—Philadelphia*. www.workshopoftheworld.com/fairmount_park/water .html.

Heath, Andrew. "Consolidation Act of 1854." *The Encyclopedia of Greater Philadelphia*. https://philadelphiaencyclopedia.org/archive/consolidation-act-of-1854/.

Kramek, Niva, and Lydia Loh. "The History of Philadelphia's Water Supply and Sanitation System." *Project for the Philadelphia Global Water Initiative*, June 2007. https://pdf4pro.com/view/the-history-of-philadelphia-s-water-supply -and-sanitation-3c8495.html.

Levine, Adam. "Philly H2O: The History of Philadelphia's Watersheds and Sewers." www.phillyh2o.org/.

Lienhard, John H. "The Fairmount Waterworks." *Engines of Our Ingenuity*, no. 310. https://uh.edu/engines/epi310.htm.

Marks, Arthur S. "Palladianism on the Schuylkill: The Work of Frederick Graff at Fairmount." *Proceedings of the American Philosophical Society*, vol. 154, no. 2, 2010, pp. 201–257. *JSTOR*, www.jstor.org/stable/41000099.

Moss, Roger W. *Historic Landmarks of Philadelphia*. Philadelphia: University of Pennsylvania Press, 2008.

Roberts, Christopher. "The Water Works: A Place 'Wondrous to Behold.'" *Delaware River Basin Commission*. www.state.nj.us/drbc/edweb/fairmount-water-works .html.

Sutcliffe, Andrea. *Steam: The Untold Story of America's First Great Invention*. New York: Palgrave Macmillan, 2004.

Wang, Michael. "Cool, Clear Water: The Fairmount Water Works." *The Pennsylvania Center for the Book*. http://pabook2.libraries.psu.edu/palitmap/FairmountWW .html.

Willig, Spencer. "The Life of the Schuylkill: Part 1." *The PhillyHistory Blog*, 30 Mar. 2007. www.phillyhistory.org/blog/index.php/2007/03/the-life-of-the-schuylkill-part -one/.

———. "The Life of the Schuylkill: Part 2." *The PhillyHistory Blog*, 30 Mar. 2007. www
.phillyhistory.org/blog/index.php/2007/04/the-life-of-the-schuylkill-part-two/.

45 U.S. Custom House

Gallery, John Andrew. *Philadelphia Architecture: A Guide to the City*, 3rd ed. Philadelphia: Center for Architecture, 2009.

Horrigan, Joe. "Evolution of Eagles Colors." *NFL Films*. www.nfl.com/videos/phila
delphia-eagles/0ap2000000085803/Evolution-of-the-Eagles-colors.

Kachmarsky, Erica, and Barbara Lamprecht (revised from earlier versions by George
E. Thomas [1992] and Hillier [2004]). "United States Custom House." *National
Register of Historic Places Nomination Form*. Washington, DC: U.S. Department of
the Interior, National Park Service, 2011. www.nps.gov/nr/feature/weekly_fea
tures/2011/USCustomhouse-Philadelphia.pdf.

Moss, Roger W. *Historic Landmarks of Philadelphia*. Philadelphia: University of Pennsylvania Press, 2008.

"U.S. Custom House, Philadelphia, PA." *U.S. General Services Administration*, last
reviewed 13 Aug. 2017. www.gsa.gov/historic-buildings/us-custom-house-phil
adelphia-pa.

Part X Where History Comes Alive

46 Historical Society of Pennsylvania

"Annual Report 2018: Historical Society of Pennsylvania, Philadelphia's Library of
American History." *Historical Society of Pennsylvania*. http://annualreport2018
.hsp.org/.

Arnold, Lee. "What Constitutes a Draft of the U.S. Constitution?" *Historical Society of Pennsylvania*, 5 Feb. 2010. https://processandpreserve.wordpress.com
/2010/02/05/what-constitutes-a-physical-copy-of-the-u-s-constitution/.

Henle, Alea. "Historical Society of Pennsylvania." *The Encyclopedia of Greater Philadelphia*. https://philadelphiaencyclopedia.org/archive/historical-society
-of-pennsylvania/.

"Historical Society of Pennsylvania Marks the 100th Anniversary of Its Landmark
Building." *Historical Society of Pennsylvania*, 16 Mar. 2010. https://hsp.org/news
/historical-society-of-pennsylvania-marks-the-100th-anniversary-of-its-land
mark-building.

Hutto, Carey. "In Late 1839 Philadelphia's Central High School Was Captured with
Which Photographic Process?" *Historical Society of Pennsylvania*, 21 Oct. 2012.
https://hsp.org/blogs/question-of-the-week/in-late-1839-philadelphias-cen
tral-high-school-was-captured-with-which-photographic-process.

"Joseph Saxton's 1839 Photo from the U.S. Mint." *The E-Sylum*, vol. 19, no. 35, 28
Aug. 2016, article 16. www.coinbooks.org/esylum_v19n35a16.html.

Moss, Roger W. *Historic Landmarks of Philadelphia*. Philadelphia: University of Pennsylvania Press, 2008.

"Why Words Matter: Comparing James Wilson's Draft of the Preamble to the United States Constitution to the Final Version." *Historical Society of Pennsylvania*.
https://hsp.org/sites/default/files/attachments/Why%20Words%20Mat
ter%20-%20Preamble.pdf.

47 Library Company of Philadelphia

"About the Library Company of Philadelphia." (Includes a chapter about the Life of Ben Franklin by J. A. Leo Lemay, plus other PDFs, a catalog of books, and more. Invaluable.) *Library Company of Philadelphia.* https://librarycompany.org/about-lcp/.

"At the Instance of Ben Franklin: A Brief History of the Library Company of Philadelphia." *Library Company of Philadelphia.* http://librarycompany.org/about/Instance.pdf.

Finkel, Ken. "Poor Richard in a Roman Toga." *The PhillyHistory Blog*, 24 Apr. 2012. www.phillyhistory.org/blog/index.php/2012/04/poor-richard-in-a-roman-toga/.

"The Library Company." *USHistory.org.* www.ushistory.org/franklin/philadelphia/library.htm.

"Library Company of Philadelphia." *Wikipedia*, last edited 31 Jan. 2020. https://en.wikipedia.org/wiki/Library_Company_of_Philadelphia.

"Library Company of Philadelphia Tour." *C-Span2, Book TV*, 18 Feb. 1999. www.c-span.org/video/?122245-1/library-company-philadelphia-tour.

Nix, Larry T. "The Library Company of Philadelphia." *The Library History Buff.* www.libraryhistorybuff.org/librarycompany.htm.

"Treasures from America's Oldest Subscription Library." *Library Company of Philadelphia.* http://librarycompany.org/treasures/.

Part XI Beyond Center City

48 Cliveden (or the Chew House)

"The Battle of Germantown: A 'Surprise' That Almost Worked." *WHYY*, 5 Oct. 2012. https://whyy.org/articles/the-battle-of-germantown-a-surprise-that-almost-worked/.

Fink, Richard. "How Do You Pronounce 'Cliveden'?" *WHYY*, 28 Dec. 2010. https://whyy.org/articles/how-do-you-pronounce-cliveden/.

Gabriel, Michael P. "Battle of Germantown." *Digital Encyclopedia of George Washington.* www.mountvernon.org/library/digitalhistory/digital-encyclopedia/article/battle-of-germantown/.

Gallery, John Andrew. *Philadelphia Architecture: A Guide to the City*, 3rd ed. Philadelphia: Center for Architecture, 2009.

Greenwood, Richard E. "Chew House, Cliveden." *National Register of Historic Places Nomination Form.* Washington, DC: U.S. Department of the Interior, National Park Service, 1978.

Hanley, Brian. "Slavery, Consumption, and Social Class: A Biography of Chief Justice Benjamin Chew (1722–1810)." *Lehigh Preserve.* https://preserve.lehigh.edu/cgi/viewcontent.cgi?article=1012&context=cas-lehighreview-vol-21.

Kyriakodis, Harry. *Northern Liberties: The Story of a Philadelphia River Ward.* Charlestown, SC: The History Press, 2012.

Lambdin, Alfred C. "Battle of Germantown." *The Pennsylvania Magazine of History and Biography*, vol. 1, no. 4, 1877, pp. 368–403. *JSTOR*, www.jstor.org/stable/20084306.

Leahy, Kristin. "Invisible Hands: Slaves and Servants of the Chew Family." *Cliveden*, 2003. www.cliveden.org/wp-content/uploads/2013/09/Invisible-Hands-Slaves-and-Servants.pdf.

Murphy, Orville T. "The Battle of Germantown and the Franco-American Alliance of 1778." *The Pennsylvania Magazine of History and Biography*, vol. 82, no. 1, 1958, pp. 55–64. *JSTOR*, www.jstor.org/stable/20089039.

Richards, Nancy E. "The City Home of Benjamin Chew, Sr. and His Family: A Case Study of the Textures of Life." *Cliveden of the National Trust, Inc.* www.cliveden .org/wp-content/uploads/2013/09/Benjamin-Chew-townhouse.pdf.

Schenawolf, Harry. "Cliveden House (Chew Mansion) and the Revolutionary War Battle of Germantown." *Revolutionary War Journal*, 15 Jun. 2003. www.revolu tionarywarjournal.com/cliveden/.

Tinkcom, Margaret B. "Cliveden: The Building of a Philadelphia Countryseat, 1763–1767." *The Pennsylvania Magazine of History and Biography*, vol. 88, no. 1, 1964, pp. 2–36. *JSTOR*, www.jstor.org/stable/20089671.

Ujifusa, Steven. "Cliveden: An Historic Germantown Mansion Redefines Its Mission." *The PhillyHistory Blog*, 1 Nov. 2010. www.phillyhistory.org/blog/index .php/2010/11/cliveden-an-historic-germantown-mansion-redefines-its-mis sion/.

Westcott, Thompson. *The Historic Mansions and Buildings of Philadelphia: With Some Notice of Their Owners and Occupants*. Philadelphia: Porter and Coates, 1877.

Young, David W. "Historic Germantown: New Knowledge in a Very Old Neighborhood." *The Encyclopedia of Greater Philadelphia*. https://philadelphiaencyclopedia .org/archive/historic-germantown-new-knowledge-in-a-very-old-neighbor hood-2/.

49 Fort Mifflin

Associated Press. "The British Return to Philadelphia's Ft. Mifflin." *New York Times*, 12 Nov. 1995. www.nytimes.com/1995/11/12/us/the-british-return -to-philadelphia-s-ft-mifflin.html.

Coker, Andrew W. "Mifflin: The Fort That Saved America." *Pennsylvania Center for the Book*. www.pabook.libraries.psu.edu/literary-cultural-heritage-map-pa/fea ture-articles/mifflin-fort-saved-america.

"Fort Mifflin." *Wikipedia*, last edited 6 Mar. 2020. https://en.wikipedia.org/wiki /Fort_Mifflin.

Krick, Lisa, and Jim Graczyk. "Fort Mifflin Investigation." *Ghost Research Society*, 23 Aug. 2010. https://ghostresearch.org/Investigations/mifflin.html.

Moss, Roger W. *Historic Landmarks of Philadelphia*. Philadelphia: University of Pennsylvania Press, 2008.

Nelligan, Murray H. "Fort Mifflin, Pennsylvania: Special Report." *The National Survey of Historic Sites and Buildings, Department of the Interior, National Park Service*, 1969. https://npgallery.nps.gov/NRHP/GetAsset/faad5e6a-b5a6-4385-9d51 -e2aa84e194f0.

Paine, Thomas. *Common Sense and Other Works by Thomas Paine*. Minneapolis: First Avenue Editions, 2019.

"The Siege of Fort Mifflin." *The Pennsylvania Magazine of History and Biography*, vol. 11, no. 1, 1887, pp. 82–88. *JSTOR*, www.jstor.org/stable/20083184.

50 Taller Puertorriqueño

Hahn, Ashley. "Taller Puertorriqueño Closer to Building New Cultural Center on North 5th." *PlanPhilly*, 29 May 2014. https://whyy.org/articles/taller-puertor riqueno-closer-to-building-new-cultural-center-on-north-5th/.

Johnson, Jamila. "The Rise of Taller in North Philadelphia." *Al Día*, 14 Feb. 2017. https://aldianews.com/articles/culture/rise-taller-north-philadelphia/45994.

Levin, Hoag. "Saved from North Philadelphia Street Violence and Jail by Art." *Philadelphia Generocity*, Jan. 2011. www.levins.com/GCAproto/gca_story4.shtml.

Lubrano, Alfred. "Arts Center in City's Poorest Neighborhood Teaches Culture and Salvation." *The Philadelphia Inquirer*, 31 Mar. 2019. www.inquirer.com/news/taller-puertorriqueno-poverty-art-fairhill-painting-20190331.html.

———. "New Census Figures on Philly Neighborhoods Show Inequality, High Numbers of Whites Living in Poverty." *WHYY*, 6 Dec. 2018. https://whyy.org/articles/new-census-figures-on-philly-neighborhoods-show-inequality-high-numbers-of-whites-living-in-poverty/.

"The Philadelphia Orchestra, Kimmel Center, and Taller Puertorriqueño Partner to Raise Funds for Hurricane Relief Efforts in Puerto Rico During West Side Story Concerts." *The Philadelphia Orchestra*, 6 Oct. 2017. www.kimmelcenter.org/globalassets/about-us/pdfs/partnership-to-raise-funds-for-hurricane-relief.pdf.

Ribeiro, Alyssa. "Puerto Rican Migration." *The Encyclopedia of Greater Philadelphia*. https://philadelphiaencyclopedia.org/archive/puerto-rican-migration/.

Schwartz, Chip. "Taller Puertorriqueño's New Facility Heralds the Start of a New Chapter for a North Philly Community." *Knight Foundation*, 3 Apr. 2017. https://knightfoundation.org/articles/taller-puertorriqueno-new-chapter-north-philly/.

51 The Lazaretto

Associated Press. "Tiny Township Saves, Transforms Historic Quarantine Station." *US News.com*, 22 Aug. 2019. www.usnews.com/news/us/articles/2019-08-22/tiny-township-saves-transforms-historic-quarantine-station.

Barnes, David. "Spring 2012: How I Became an Answer on 'Jeopardy.'" *University of Pennsylvania*. www.sas.upenn.edu/~dbarnes/Home.html.

Byrne, Jim. "The Philadelphia Lazaretto: A Most Unloved Institution." *Philadelphia Center for the Book*, Summer 2010. https://pabook.libraries.psu.edu/literary-cultural-heritage-map-pa/feature-articles/philadelphia-lazaretto-most-unloved-institution.

Eisenhower, Lance R. "Lazaretto." *The Encyclopedia of Greater Philadelphia*. https://philadelphiaencyclopedia.org/archive/lazaretto/.

Friends of the 1799 Lazaretto. http://1799lazaretto.blogspot.com/.

Glennon, Patrick. "Lazaretto Ghost Stories." *Historical Society of Pennsylvania*, 5 Mar. 2019. https://hsp.org/blogs/fondly-pennsylvania/lazaretto-ghost-stories.

Horowitz-Behrend, Dona. "The *Ganges* Africans Who Were Held at the Lazaretto Station (Tinicum) in 1800." *USHistory.org*. www.ushistory.org/laz/history/ganges.htm.

"The Jewish Quarter of Philadelphia: Immigration 1891 to 1924." *The Museum of Family History*. www.museumoffamilyhistory.com/jqp-immigration.htm.

"The Lazaretto." *Public Ledger*, 14 Aug. 1879. *University of Pennsylvania*. www.sas.upenn.edu/~dbarnes/1879_description.html.

"Lazaretto Quarantine Station." *USHistory.org*. www.ushistory.org/laz/.

"Lazaretto Quarantine Station Historical Marker." *ExplorePAHistory.com*. http://explorepahistory.com/hmarker.php?markerId=1-A-302.

Leffmann, Henry. *Under the Yellow Flag: An Account of Some Experiences of Henry Leffman as Port Physician of the Port of Philadelphia*. Printed for Presentation Only,

1896. 100 copies printed. https://ia802607.us.archive.org/25/items/underyell owflaga00phil/underyellowflaga00phil.pdf.

Manaugh, Geoff. "On the Other Side of Arrival: An Interview with David Barnes." *BLDGBLOG*, 19 Oct. 2009. www.bldgblog.com/2009/10/on-the-other-side-of -arrival-an-interview-with-david-barnes/.

"The Oldest American Immigration Station—Philadelphia's Lazaretto Built in 1799." *Shtetl Links: Lyakhovichi.* https://kehilalinks.jewishgen.org/lyakhovichi /usportrecords.htm.

Index

Page numbers in italics refer to illustrations.

A longtime resident of Philadelphia, **Jim Murphy** is a certified tour guide who does frequent in-person and online presentations on "The Amazing Success of William Penn." A copywriter and former creative director at Devon Direct Marketing and Advertising, he has owned a marketing communications business since 2004 and was the editor of *Choices*, an award-winning magazine published by the Franklin Mint Federal Credit Union. He has been researching Philadelphia history since 2010 and would love to speak to your group.